1815 The Armies at Waterloo

A MIA MOGLIE

1815
The Armies
at Waterloo

UGO PERICOLI
with additional text by
MICHAEL GLOVER

Introduction by
ELIZABETH LONGFORD

SPHERE BOOKS LIMITED
30/32 Gray's Inn Road, London, WC1 X8JL

First published in Great Britain, 1973 by
SEELEY SERVICE & CO
196 Shaftesbury Avenue, London W C 2

Illustrations copyright © 1973 Ugo Pericoli
Text copyright © 1973 Michael Glover
Introduction copyright © 1973 Elizabeth Longford

Translations from the Italian by A.S.W. Winkworth
Design: Ken Williamson

First SPHERE BOOKS edition, 1973

I would like to thank :
The Dino de Laurentiis film company for allowing me to
use the research material and the drawings which I
prepared for the film 'Waterloo'.
Count Ernesto Vitetti and Signor Enrico Fiorentini for
their valuable collaboration during the making of the
film 'Waterloo'.

UGO PERICOLI

Printed and bound at Les Presses Saint-Augustin, Bruges, Belgium

Contents

Anglo-Netherlands Army

Prussian Army

Introduction
by Elizabeth Longford

Waterloo is one of those monumental landmarks which can never crumble. Its shadow can only grow longer. The compulsion to calculate its effects and to speculate upon its 'ifs' is never ending. If Napoleon had won... No less awesome is the thought of what was actually happening during those few hours on 18 June 1815. Not one of the scores of thousands present knew that Waterloo was to be the last great action of the accepted traditional kind. The typical pitched battle, with its columns, lines and squares all faithfully studied, discussed and well understood for so many decades, met its Waterloo, so to speak, at Waterloo. Nothing like it was ever to be seen again.

Nor, happily, could the participants guess that they were assisting at the turn of a page of history by the bloodiest hand which mankind could so far remember. Whichever side they were on, casualties were devastating. The hand was not that of Napoleon or Wellington or Blücher. It was the hand of destiny, of necessity. A hand which could not do otherwise, when that huge host was gathered together in a small space, almost all carrying weapons which were lethal only at the closest possible range, but then very lethal indeed; protected by armour, if any, which reduced them to so many turtles kicking on their backs (as Wellington observed) when they tumbled off their horses; and with the use of anaesthetics and antiseptics remote from them by distances of twenty-five and fifty years.

There seems to have existed, nonetheless, some instinctive feeling among the soldiers for the elemental nature of their experience. French cavalry hurling themselves upon Allied infantry were described over and over again by diarists and letter-writers in terms of an irresistable tide meeting an immovable rock. A writer of genius, Victor Hugo, visualised this French attack as something almost supernatural; a half-human, half-serpentine mass from another planet:

a prodigy ... undulating and swelling like the rings of a polyp ... smooth and shining as the hydra's scales ...

Today we recognise the portentousness of Waterloo. That, however, is not sufficient. Yes, we say, but what was it really like? After all, those undulating scales were men and horses. Impressions by combatants or even poets are only impressions. They make us see with our imaginations. We want to see with our eyes also. At last we have a unique opportunity to do so. Put briefly, that is the point of this stirring and beautiful book.

I am one of those who wish that the Waterloo film could hover for minutes at a time over its tantalising detail. Instead it must flash at realistic speed from French hussars to English infantrymen, from the orange gleam of the Netherlands to the black streak of a Brunswicker. In this book the fleeting moment is captured. For our visual delight, Ugo Pericoli's wide and sustained researches have produced a large gallery of meticulously accurate pictures. As Professor of Costume Design at the University of Rome, he has had the entrée to the European libraries and museums which possess original watercolours and prints of the Waterloo armies, including the collection of Her Majesty the Queen. The purely visual impact is breath-taking. Not even Solomon in all his glory, we know, was arrayed like a lily of the fields. But as I gaze at the images of cavalry officers, no matter of which army, I cannot help feeling that these astonishing exotics have run the lily pretty close. Yet it is they, believe it or not, who are destined to skid and slither up Wellington's sticky slopes at Waterloo. A recital of the delicate shades of their facings sounds more like a catalogue of garden flowers than the uniforms of regiments at war – pink and primrose, sky blue and scarlet and *aurore;* the last a characteristically French brain-wave for a colour meaning golden yellow, the brilliance of dawn. And the furs and the feathers and the leathers! This curly black lamb or white sheepskin or dyed marmot; this fawn, white or silver fox; this brown or black bearskin; this leopard or panther; this shiny black leather or white buffalo hide; these black ostrich plumes curling over a Scottish bonnet, or this single upright white plume finishing a lancer's czapska that already seems dangerously overloaded with padilion, soutache, turban, peak, hooks and rosettes; – all these are surely the trimmings from a Paris collection of gowns and mantles rather than of saddle-cloths, pistol-holsters, pummel coverings, hussars' pelisses and helmets worn by warriors fighting for their lives.

If grimness was what they needed, uniforms could furnish that too. We see here the immense blue greatcoat unchanged for summer and winter, the towering bearskin, the red epaulettes and cross belts of the Imperial Guard, which together added so much height and breadth to Napoleon's veterans, the terrors of Europe. Not that fierce feathers alone made fierce birds. Candidates for the Guard all had to be men of imposing stature. Indeed, a tremendous military contraption placed upon the head of a puny soldier tended to make him look more pathetic than ever, as the savage cartoonist Gillray took pleasure in showing. His pre-Waterloo caricatures of the British militia or volunteers in high hats and shakos with fuzzy crests were simply figures of fun.

Or if we want an idea of the troops on either side who were famous for their swiftness and agility, we only need to pick out the *greens* from the rainbow assortment of reds, blues and yellows. For a very good reason green was always worn by skirmishers and sharpshooters and riflemen. Since the rifle had a longer range than the musket carried by the vast majority of infantrymen, scouts and skirmishers used rifles; and the longer range made camouflage a practical consideration. Green was to prove in the long run a better colour than scarlet or even *aurore*. And a far better protection in 1815 than the cuirasse. After Waterloo had been lost and won, hundreds of tourists swarmed over the field, buying discarded French cuirasses from Belgian peasants as souvenirs.

All this is visual. But the resolve to understand Waterloo with the mind as well as the eye is splendidly furthered by this book. Michael Glover's stream-lined and gripping narrative of the campaign draws on the knowledge of a distinguished military expert and the freshness of an enthusiast. His story brings us down to earth, but not with a bump. Rather, his method is to explain how and why this amazing fancy dress developed – if indeed there was any rhyme or reason to be found.

Again and again he extracts an essentially wry humour from the evolution of the more bizarre uniforms. The dramatic whiteness of the French carabineers, for instance, was not due to theatricality but to lack of good blue or red dyes. The classical Minerva-type helmets may have aped the goddess in her appearance but definitely not in her fabled wisdom: they heated up a horseman's head as if it were inside a brass cooking-pot, and also upset his equestrian balance. As for wearing a bearskin on horseback, that was near murder; or so the Duke of Wellington found fourteen years after the battle. By that time he was Britain's Prime Minister and George IV on his last legs as king. But the inventive, dress-conscious monarch was not too feeble to design yet another top-heavy piece of head-gear for his long-suffering subjects to wear. Mrs Arbuthnot described in her journal what happened to her friend Wellington when reviewing troops in Hyde Park:

> The Duke fell from his horse the other day at the Review in consequence of having on his head the extravagant Grenadier cap which the King had thought fit to order & with which, in a high wind, it is impossible to balance yourself...

From this ludicrous incident sprang many caricatures and the legend that Wellington was a bad horseman. Michael Glover, I am glad to say, accomplishes the final exposure of the Grenadier cap from the point of view of practicality. He shows that, except psychologically as a horror-object, it was virtually useless. But its mental effect on the enemy could not be ignored. If a man could not add a cubit to his stature, a bearskin could make a brave attempt to do it for him. Paradoxically, however, the Grenadier cap had been originally designed as a utilitarian object. Its shape was thought to be more convenient for a grenade-thrower when swinging his arm than the large three-cornered hat hitherto worn. Hardly was the new cap introduced before the grenade itself went out of use. Like so much else in warfare, it was not clear which the grenade would damage most, the thrower or the thrown at. 'I don't know what the enemy will think of them', as Wellington might have said, 'but my God they frighten me.'

Many other amusing ironies, which the reader will discover for himself, add an astringent touch of lemon to Professor Pericoli's rich feast. My favourite concerns the success of the Prussian forage cap and tunic. Adopted in all their plainness for reasons of economy, these lowly items are almost the only survivors into our own day. Long after all the brass helmets with their furry crests and floating Kubla Khan manes had gone to ground in museums; when the shakos with their fragile embellishments like praliné puddings made by the great Empire chefs had fallen to pieces; when the hussars' jackets with their dizzily braided breasts had disappeared into the family acting-chests; after the ball and the battle were both over, it was the Prussian cap which became the pattern for every army and the Prussian tunic everybody's 'service dress'.

The moral is perhaps an austere one. Nevertheless, it is possible to look back on those vanished military excesses with a modicum of human satisfaction, as well as nostalgia and vivid aesthetic delight. For the psychological magic of ostentatious uniforms worked twice over. Not only did they make one's opponent feel small and trembly but they also gave the wearer a sense of size and invincibility. It is comforting to know that the shining hats and mountainous caps which were of such limited practical good, had their undoubted compensations. The poor fellows inside them, whether or not they were about to receive a ball or a lance in their ribs, felt great. Beneath each Minerva helmet was a little Mars – a god of war. 'About to die, I salute you.' So said the hero of classical times. From a less distant past the armies salute us still, decked out in all the fantastic glory of 1815.

Preface

'Remember,' wrote the Duke of Wellington to a gentleman who proposed to write a history of the campaign of 1815, 'I recommend to you to leave the battle of Waterloo as it is. You may depend upon it you will never make it a satisfactory work.' Some explanation is required for adding to the multitude of authors who have disregarded the Duke's advice over the past hundred and fifty-eight years. It is insufficient that the campaign of Waterloo inspires in the military historian the same kind of ambitions that the role of Hamlet is supposed to raise in the breast of an actor. No military episode is so well rounded, a camapign lasting, for all practical purposes, only four days and culminating in one of the few immediately decisive battles in history. Nevertheless, although the source material about both the camapign and the battle appears to be inexhaust-ible, it has been worked over in the past and it is impossible to put any radical new interpretation on the facts. In so far as this account of the campaign breaks any new ground it is in the interpretation of Wellington's intentions during the hours of darkness on 17/18 June. My reading of the situation at dawn on the day of the battle is derived from two sources, two articles by Lieutenant Colonel J. G. O. Whitehead* and a note unearthed by Lady Longford† in the Raglan MSS. It is now clear that, whatever Wellington said to the Duke of Richmond in the small hours of 16 June, the decision to fight near Waterloo was not taken until dawn on the 18th. The myth that Wellington had planned the whole campaign some time, some have said almost a year, before is further discredited by Lady Longford's disclosure‡ that the Mont St Jean position was not the one that the Duke had provisionally earmarked in advance.

Such a minor point would certainly not justify yet another book about Waterloo and the justification of this work lies entirely in the plates. Professor Pericoli has produced a unique series of paintings which combine the art of Dighton or Drahomet with the minute accuracy of working drawings. In writing the accompanying text, I have had two objects in mind. In Part I, I have tried to show how the battle of Waterloo came about and to give a picture of what the

* J. G. O. Whitehead, *Wellington at Waterloo* and *Waterloo – Wellington's Right Flank* Army Quarterly, October, 1965 and January, 1972.
† Elizabeth Longford, *Wellington – The Years of the Sword* p. 444.
‡ id. p. 441.

battle was like. I have headed my description of the battle with another discouraging quotation from the Duke and, instead of giving a detailed and comprehensive story of the battle, I have tried to build up, using whenever possible the words of the combatants, a picture of what it was like to be engaged in the fighting.

Part II sets out to show why the combatants were dressed in elaborate and expensive uniforms which, to modern eyes, appear to combine a minimum of functionalism with a maximum of inconvenience. To show that few of the seemingly useless elaborations were without some specific purpose, it has been necessary to outline the conditions in which battles were fought at the beginning of the nineteenth century.

In the Notes on the Plates, I have not attempted to give a detailed description of the uniforms. The plates themselves are so clear that to do so would be a work of supererogation. Instead I have tried to give information that the plates cannot show, the way in which the different categories of troops evolved, how this affected their uniform and the distinctions of the various regiments within each category.

Some difficult problems of nomenclature arise which cannot be solved in the Glossary. The term 'heavy infantry' is not one to be found in any military vocabulary but it is impossible to avoid when speaking of the British army where, unlike the French practice, light infantry regiments are numbered in the regiments of the line mixed with those which are not light. Nor is 'Foot Artillery' a wholly satisfactory phrase to distinguish those units which were not Horse Artillery. It is a literal translation of the French *Artillerie à Pied* but the contemporary English equivalent 'Marching Regiments of Artillery' is so cumbersome that it was seldom used outside official documents even at the time.

Translation of some French terms also presents difficulties. *Chasseurs à Pied*, *Tirailleurs*, *Voltigeurs* and *Vélites* are all words which can only be translated into English as 'light infantry'. Nor has *Chasseurs à Cheval* an English equivalent. The nearest would be 'light dragoon' but since British light dragoons were not dragoons in any true sense such a translation would confuse more than it illuminated. On the other hand, I have had no hesitation in rendering *chevaux-légérs-lanciers* into its shorter (and later) English equivalent of 'lancers'.

★ ★ ★

I must acknowledge the help I have received from Professor Pericoli, who made available to me the notes he had made in his years of research into the uniforms worn at Waterloo, from the late René North, from Stephanie Glover and the rest of the staff of the Royal United Services Institute. Most of all, I am indebted to my wife, whose knowledge of uniforms has steered me clear of many pitfalls and who, in this book, has contributed even more in advice, assistance and encouragement than she has to my previous works.

Part 1
The Campaign

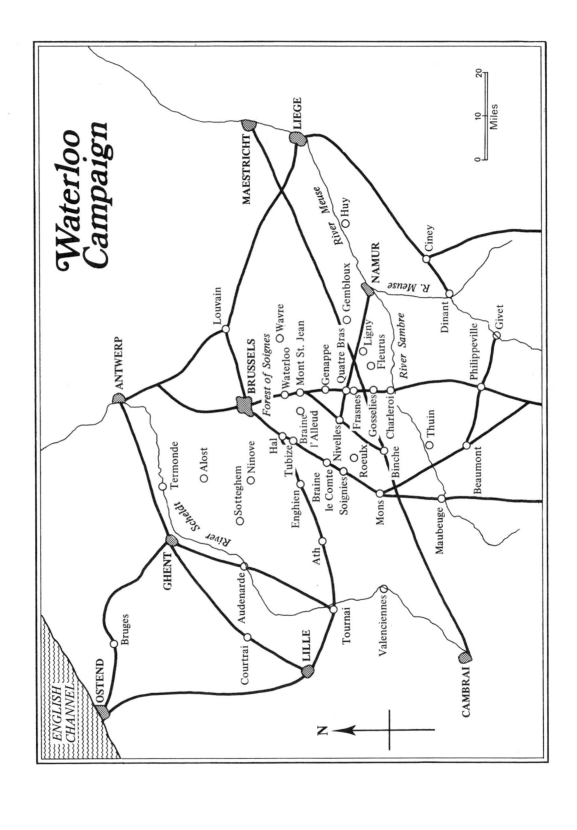

'I have been brought back to the throne by my anger at seeing sacred rights, won by twenty years of victory, scorned and cast aside, by the cry of injured honour, by the will of the people.'

THE EMPEROR NAPOLEON 1 June 1815

1. Advance to Contact

At Easter, 1814, peace came to Europe after more than twenty-two years of war. From Moscow to Lisbon all governments and most peoples congratulated themselves that the French domination of Europe had been broken and that Napoleon Bonaparte had been exiled. In Vienna a congress assembled to decide the political geography of the continent. Little progress had been made when, on 7 March 1815, news reached Vienna that Napoleon had decamped from Elba.

In the nine and a half months he had spent on the island the former Emperor had kept closely in touch with opinion in France. He knew that the restored Bourbons had failed to establish themselves in either the respect or the affections of their people. He knew that few actively liked their government and that two substantial minorities, the Bonapartists and the Republicans, would never be reconciled to it. He knew that his old soldiers were praying for his return. He knew that the Bourbons had no intention of paying the pension he had been promised and that, in consequence, his Elban subjects were becoming restive at having to support by their taxes an imperial court in miniature. On 26 February he embarked on the brig *L'Inconstant*, flagship of the Elban navy, and sailed for France, accompanied by three generals and 1,050 soldiers. On 20 March he re-entered Paris as Emperor. As he climbed the crowded staircase at the Tuileries, 'he moved slowly, his eyes closed, his hands outstretched, walking like a blind man. Only his smile showed his happiness.'

There was no happiness in Vienna when the news arrived. There was, however, a unanimity in the discussions of the Congress which had earlier been notably absent. Napoleon was declared to be 'the enemy and disturber of the peace of the world'. To extirpate the menace he represented, the four great powers agreed to raise armies with which to invade France. How these armies were to be deployed was still being discussed when Waterloo was fought, but it was unanimously agreed that, as had become traditional, Britain should pay most of the expenses. The British representative, the Duke of Wellington, reported that, 'We are all zeal and, I think, anxious to take the field. I moderate

15

these sentiments as much as possible and endeavour to get them on paper.' Since Wellington was the only allied commander who had never been beaten by the French, the Czar invited him to act as adviser to the Russian armies. Wellington declined politely, remarking privately that 'I should prefer to carry a musket'. In due course he was appointed to command the small British army in the Netherlands. Whether this force could be expanded depended on the time it would take to bring the experienced British infantry back from the useless and largely unsuccessful war in America.

In Paris Napoleon was busy rebuilding his government. He granted a constitution more liberal than that granted by Louis XVIII (and equally inoperative). He abolished the slave trade. He made gestures of conciliation to every shade of French opinion. Those who had supported the Bourbons during the short peace were forgiven as readily as those who had never ceased to work for a republic. Above all he strove to reconstitute his army.

It was on the army that the restored empire relied for support. The mass of the French people wanted peace and would tolerate any government that seemed able to give it to them. The extremists, both royalist and republican, would accept nothing but their own solutions. The army actively wanted a return of the empire. Under the Bourbons the soldiers had been slighted. Too many commissions had gone to inexperienced *emigrés*. Too many veterans had been put on half-pay or sent on indefinite leave. The state of the French economy was such that jobs could not be found even for those who were prepared to be absorbed into civilian life. The soldiers and the junior officers longed for the return of the man who had so often led them to victory. Above all they wanted him to lead them to new successes which would wipe away the trauma of invasion and the defeat of 1814. The senior officers were less enthusiastic. They had achieved rank and position. Peace gave them a chance to enjoy what they had gained. A French historian wrote, 'The generals saw things as they really were. The soldiers harked back to dreams of *La Gloire* from which they had been awakened. They would not believe that the dream was over.'

After two months of intensive work Napoleon had a field army of 284,000 men backed by a quarter of a million embodied National Guards and other second line troops. The arming, mounting and clothing of this vast force was an administrative work of genius, even if it was not as complete as it appeared to be. There were some shortages in equipment and orders had to be given for the manufacture of pikes for the National Guard, thus releasing muskets for the regulars. The field army was, potentially, the finest in the world. A high proportion of the men in the ranks had been trained in victorious campaigns all over the continent. Their devotion to the emperor was absolute, fanatical. Their detestation of foreigners, a hatred nurtured in prison camps and in rotting hulks off the English coast, gave them an unrivalled will to victory. At the same time, their discipline was uncertain. They could not fail to sense the reservations of their seniors. They could be trusted to obey orders to attack at any odds but they looted abominably. They saw treason in everyone who did not have their own blind faith in the Emperor. 'Never,' said the same historian, 'did Napoleon have so formidable or so fragile a weapon in his hand.'

Napoleon had to choose whether to use this army for a pre-emptive strike or to wait until he was attacked. The latter course had many attractions. An 'un-provoked' attack on France would rally to his side many Frenchmen who would otherwise be indifferent to his government. The coalition against him might collapse, especially if Britain, the paymaster and known to be war-weary, could be detached from the others. The rest of the powers could be dealt with separately by diplomacy or by force. He believed that the Czar was still susceptible to his influence. The Emperor of Austria was his father-in-law. Even if the great joint invasion was launched, his experience of 1814 told him that the movements of the four invading armies would be poorly co-ordinated*. Napoleon was, or had been, the great master of manoeuvre and there was a good chance that they could be defeated in detail.

On the other hand a bold offensive, a short sharp victory, would do much to consolidate the empire. Many Frenchmen who were not Bonapartists believed that Belgium was French. To secure it by conquest could be considered no more than natural justice. To defeat the British and Prussians in Belgium would re-establish *La Gloire*, would probably bring down the Tory government in London (and stop the flow of British subsidies) and might well deter the Austrians and Russians from invading.

The political arguments for the alternatives were equally balanced. The military arguments tipped the scale in favour of the offensive. The troops were thirsty for victory. Their enthusiasm was at fever pitch and they were in no mood for a long, uneventful defensive. The longer war was postponed, the more the edge of the army's enthusiasm would be blunted. In mid-May Napoleon took his decision. He would drive at Brussels at the head of 124,000 men, leaving covering forces on the other frontiers.

Against him in Belgium were two armies amounting, apart from garrisons, to about 200,000 men. To the east was a Prussian army with the formidable strength of 120,000. This figure was more impressive than the quality of the troops warranted. More than half the infantry and much of the cavalry were militia *(landwehr)* who, although tough, were sketchily trained and short of experienced officers. Many of the troops came from territories newly acquired by Prussia and were unenthusiastic about their new rulers. A contingent of Saxons, 14,000 strong, mutinied in May and had to be sent to the rear. There

---

* In 1814 Napoleon, in his defence of Paris, had fought one of his most brilliant campaigns attacking and defeating in succession a series of numerically superior armies. Without detracting from Napoleon's tactical skill, it must be admitted that the eastern allies behaved most imprudently in their unco-ordinated advances. Wellington commented that he 'would not march a corporal's guard on such a system'.

was a shortage of arms and some regiments were issued with muskets of three different calibres – a quartermaster's nightmare in battle. The Prussian army's greatest asset was its commander, Prince Blücher, who although seventy-three years old combined a ruthless determination to get at his enemy and destroy him with a genius for inspiring his men to follow him. Blücher was no scientific soldier, he had suffered more defeats than he could claim victories, but nothing, except occasional bouts of insanity, could curb his offensive spirit. To try to compensate for his defects, he had been allocated as chief of staff, Count Gneisenau, a highly trained and efficient officer. Where Blücher was rash, Gneisenau was cautious. His first scheme for defending Belgium proposed that the Prussian army should take up a position with Brussels between them and the French. While Blücher was determined to work in the closest cooperation with his British ally, Gneisenau regarded Wellington as 'a master of the art of duplicity'. Since the Prussian system of command gave so much importance to the chief of staff everything had to be settled between Blücher and Gneisenau by endless discussion.

On the Prussian right, the Duke of Wellington commanded a field army of 88,000 men. This total again was misleading. One third of the number were from the newly founded Kingdom of the Netherlands, an unhappy and short-lived union of Holland and Belgium. Such of these troops as had military experience had gained it under Napoleon's leadership and the emperor confidently expected that the Belgians would desert Wellington and join their old commander. The loyalty of the Dutch troops was less suspect but their training was minimal and their officers inexperienced. As for the Belgian officers, the Duke remarked that 'I would not trust one of them out of my sight'.*

Almost a third of the army came from Germany. Nearly 6,000 of these were members of the King's German Legion, a part of the British army drawn from the remnants of the Hanoverian army which had been disbanded when France invaded King George's other realm in 1803. These were thoroughly reliable troops, but the remainder of the Germans were Hanoverian militia and contingents from Brunswick and Nassau. The most that could be expected from these troops was stolidity. None of them had sufficient training to manoeuvre under fire.

The hard core of the army was the British force, 17,000 infantry and 6,000 cavalry. Far too few of these were what Wellington referred to as 'my old Spanish infantry', the men he had led in the Peninsula. Most of the rest were either without battle experience or had served only in the ill-fated attempt to take Bergen-op-Zoom in 1814.

As in the Prussian army (and of course the French) the chief asset of the Anglo-Netherlands army was its commander. Wellington was forty-six, the

* Wellington's suspicions were, on the whole, justified but exception must be made of Lieutenant General Baron Chassé, who greatly distinguished himself at Waterloo although his previous employment had been as one of Napoleon brigade commanders.

same age as Napoleon, although he was in better physical shape. He had defeated a string of Napoleon's marshals in the Peninsula and had shown himself to be an eminently safe general with the ability to take great risks when occasion demanded. He ruled his troops with a rod of iron but they well knew his detailed care for their health and their lives. They had absolute trust in his competence in battle. He had never been defeated and, as one of his officers remarked, 'We had a notion that while he was there nothing could go wrong'.

Napoleon's army was superior in numbers to each of his opponents taken singly*. In quality it was almost a match for the two of them together unless some setback should occur to crack its over-tempered spirit. The Emperor's aim must be to defeat Blücher or Wellington separately, meanwhile holding the other in check. Their armies were cantonned, as he knew, in a single line, a hundred miles long, at right angles to his line of advance. The two armies joined hands south of Brussels but each lay along its lines of communication with its home base, the Prussians stretching to Liège, the British to Audenarde on the road to Ostend. Napoleon was convinced that each of the opposing commanders would fall back on their communications if seriously threatened and decided to strike at their point of junction, to advance on the line Charleroi-Brussels.

By the evening of 14 June the French army was concentrated behind the frontier in the area Beaumont-Philippeville. As an Imperial Order of the Day proclaimed, it was the fifteenth anniversary of the battle of Marengo. This was, perhaps, an unfortunate augury. Marengo was the culmination of Napoleon's grandest strategic design but the battle itself was all but lost through his own mistakes and was only saved by the intervention of Desaix, acting against his orders. Desaix had died at Marengo. He had no successor.

If Napoleon's plan was to succeed it must be executed immaculately. There must be no mistakes, no miscalculations. Every subordinate commander must contribute punctual obedience and intelligent initiative. The French generals of 1815, though uniformly brave, were not up to such a task. Soult, now chief of staff, was better as a planner than as an executant; Ney, who at the last moment was given command of the left wing, understood, in Napoleon's words, 'less of my plans than the youngest drummer boy in the army'; Grouchy, who assumed command of the right wing, was a cavalry general of talent but had never handled a large force of all arms; D'Erlon, in charge of 1st Corps, was described by a colleague as 'a mixture of kindness and inadequacy'. These men were not competent to carry out a plan which called for skill and judgment of the highest order. The Napoleon of a decade earlier might have galvanized them into a victorious combination – if he was still the man of Austerlitz and Friedland. His basic plan was brilliant. Had he the stamina to execute it?

* The French army totalled 123,665 men of all arms with 286 guns. The Prussian strength was 116,000 and 296 guns. Wellington had 88,000 all ranks and all arms with 174 guns.

At first everything went well, better than could have been hoped. Attacking at dawn on 15 June the French, aiming for Charleroi, drove in the Prussian outposts south of the River Sambre. Incredibly the Prussians made no stand on the river line. The bridges were not destroyed and were only defended with barricades and musketry. By noon the French were across the river and held Charleroi. The next objective was the Nivelle-Namur road, the only forward lateral road by which the Prussians and the British could communicate. On the right Grouchy was sent forward to Sombreffe. On the left, Ney marched for Quatre Bras. Before one o'clock the Emperor rode into Charleroi and dismounted outside an *estaminet* called La Belle Vue. A chair was brought out and he sat down to watch the troops march through to the north. As the long columns wound through the town the cries of '*Vive L'Empereur*' drowned the roll of the drums and the trumpet calls. Napoleon heard none of these sounds. He had dropped off to sleep.

At dusk neither of the French thrusts had reached the vital road. Seven Prussian battalions had fought a stout delaying action at Gilly which meant that at nightfall the French outposts were no further south than Fleurus. On the left, Ney's advanced guard had been so impressed by the formidable appearance of the Nassauers at Quatre Bras that they had retired to Frasnes to await re-inforcements. The success of Napoleon's plan depended on the allies not having time to concentrate. The failure to seize the road by which they could most easily combine was a setback of a severity not immediately appreciated by the French. By the following day Blücher would be able to concentrate three of his four corps, more than 80,000 men, on a position he had chosen behind the Ligny stream. Napoleon estimated that the Prussians could not have more than 40,000 men on the field on 16 June and, since not a single British soldier had so far been seen, believed the game still to be in his hands. On the following day he would make his main attack on Blücher's position while Ney, having cleared Quatre Bras, would swing round on the Prussian flank and complete their ruin. Then there would be time to deal with Wellington.

★ ★ ★

Brussels was a gay city in the first half of June. 'Balls are going on here,' wrote Lady Caroline Capel, 'as if we had had none for a year.' Wellington was anxious that the air of gaiety should be maintained. He gave a rout on 3 June and was sending out invitations to a ball for the second anniversary of Vitoria on 21 June. When the Duchess of Richmond wished to give a ball on 15 June she felt that 'it might appear extraordinary her giving a ball at such a time, when all the papers, as well as private communications announced that the French army had for several days after being reviewed by the French Emperor marched to the frontier, and when it was not known the moment our army might be ordered to meet them. I said to the Duke of Wellington, "Duke, I do not wish to pry into your secrets, nor do I wish to ask what your intentions may be; I wish to give a ball, and all I ask is – May I give a ball? If you say – Duchess, don't give your ball, it is quite sufficient – I ask no reasons". The Duke's answer was "Duchess, you may give your ball with the greatest safety, without fear of interruption".' Nevertheless, at about the same time, when her daughter, Georgiana, asked him if it would be safe for her and a party of officers to go on 'a party of pleasure in the neighbourhood, either to Tournay or Lille, he at once said, "No, better let that drop".'

The Duke was an adept at concealing his true feelings and it was in the public interest that the British in Brussels should appear unruffled. To Wellington, as to Napoleon, it was probable that the Belgians would change sides if it seemed in their interests to do so and he went to great lengths to maintain an air of confidence. He must, on occasion, have overacted his part for his public pronouncements were so complacently optimistic that busy, bumbling Mr Creevey remarked caustically about them to the British Minister in Brussels. 'Then,' replied the diplomat bluntly, 'he is damned different with you from what he is with me.'

Wellington was worried. For weeks information had been pouring into his headquarters of French movements. Much of it was contradictory. Some of it was absurd. 'There is,' he grumbled, 'a good deal of *charlatanism* in what is called procuring intelligence.' For a week an intelligence picture had been building up of a great French concentration beyond the frontier. It was not the first time that all reports had pointed to such a gathering. What concerned the Duke was not that the concentration existed but the way in which it would move. On 6 June there was a report from a credible source that the French plan was to feint at Charleroi and make a serious attack on Mons. Had Wellington been in his adversary's place, this is the plan he would have followed. The Anglo-Netherlands army was the smaller, the more widely dispersed and the more exposed to defeat in detail. Not realising fully Napoleon's urgent need for a quick, spectacular victory, Wellington found it hard to credit that so able a general would set out to bludgeon his way through.

To add to the Duke's trouble there were breakdowns in the transmission of information. A vital message from his most trusted intelligence officer, Colquhuon Grant, was intercepted by an officious Brunswick general at Mons. The Prussian commander of the advanced corps, who had been punctilious in forwarding information as long as nothing was happening, stopped sending messages as soon as the first skirmishing shots had been reported. Consequently, Wellington spent the morning of 15 June ignorant of the fact that war had broken out within thirty miles of his headquarters. It was a delay his widely dispersed army could barely afford.

At 3 pm the Duke was dining in Brussels with the Prince of Orange, who commanded the left corps of the army. The Prince had visited his outposts early in the morning and had found all quiet. At dinner a message arrived from the Prince's headquarters saying that the nearby Prussian outposts had reported that their infantry south of the Sambre had been attacked and that alarm guns had been fired all along their front. All was still quiet in the Anglo-Netherlands sector. The news was not necessarily serious since shots had been exchanged across the frontier on previous occasions as a result of local errors. About 4 o'clock a Prussian report reached Brussels announcing that their outposts had been engaged. This message had taken six hours to cover 34 miles*. So far nothing had arrived to contradict the Duke's belief that Napoleon would feint at the Prussians and advance on Brussels through Mons. Later a message from Blücher repeated the information Wellington already had and asked him to concentrate his army on his left. This the Duke was not prepared to do. The Prussians gave no information that suggested that the attack on them was a serious thrust. If it was, Wellington would have to concentrate eastward. 'Should, however, a portion of the enemy's force come by Mons, I must concentrate more towards my centre. For this reason I must positively wait for news from Mons before I fix my rendezvous.' Warning orders were sent to every formation at 6 pm but only those on the extreme west were actually told to move inwards.

Information that there were no French in front of Mons arrived about three hours later and at 10 pm 'after-orders' were issued for the army to concentrate at Nivelles and Quatre Bras. No messages had been received from the Prussian front dated less than twelve hours earlier.

Historians, especially French historians, have been critical, even contemptuous, of Wellington for going at midnight to the Duchess of Richmond's ball. It was, like all his actions, a well thought out gesture. In the first place, there was nothing else he could usefully do that night. The necessary orders had been given. All that remained was to wait until the troops completed their marches to the concentration area. It was essential to maintain the calm in Brussels that he had worked so hard to establish. As he remarked to his Prussian liaison officer, 'The numerous friends of Bonaparte who are in Brussels will raise their heads: the well-disposed must be reassured, let us therefore go to the ball'. Most important, however, was the fact that at the ball he would find most of his senior commanders and staff officers.† If more orders became necessary, the ballroom was a convenient place to give them.

The ballroom in the house the Richmonds had hired in the Rue de la Blanchisserie, which Wellington 'always called the "wash house"', was, according to the hostess's daughter, 'a large room on the left of the entrance, connected

---

* According to Wellington the reason for the delay was that the message had been entrusted to the fattest officer in the Prussian army.

† Invitations had been sent to both corps commanders, the cavalry commander, three divisional commanders and eight brigade commanders from outside Brussels, the commander of the artillery, the Quartermaster and Adjutant Generals and most of their senior subordinates.

with the rest of the house by an ante-room. It had been used by the coach-builder, from whom the house was hired, to put carriages in, but it was papered before we came there; and I recollect the paper – a trellis pattern with roses. My sisters used the room as a school room, and we used to play battledore and shuttlecock there on a wet day. When the Duke arrived, rather late at the ball, I was dancing, but at once went up to him to ask about the rumours. He said, very gravely, "Yes, they are true; we are off tomorrow".'

Wellington, despite his gravity in response to the direct question, maintained his unruffled facade. According to his Prussian liaison officer, he 'appeared very cheerful'. He chatted 'playfully' to the Richmond daughters. The strain was beginning to show, however, and Lady Hamilton Dalrymple noted in her diary that although he 'affected great gaiety and cheerfulness, it struck me that I had never seen him have such an expression of care and anxiety on his countenance. I sat next to him on a sopha a long time, but his mind seemed quite pre-occupied; and although he spoke to me in the kindest manner possible, yet frequently in the middle of a sentence he stopped abruptly and called to some officer giving him directions.'

At about one o'clock in the morning, he took his place at the supper table, sitting on the left of the Duchess of Richmond. Her right-hand neighbour, the Prince of Orange, had been called from the table by the arrival of an ADC from his headquarters. The message he received was dated 10.30 pm and announced that French troops had, late in the afternoon, pushed up to Quatre Bras but had retired on finding it held. The Prince's chief of staff, an old-Etonian Dutchman, added that he had given orders for the crossroads to be reinforced. It was now clear that the French were across the Sambre at Charleroi in great force and that the Prussians had been driven back.

Coming back into the supper room, the Prince whispered this news in Wellington's ear. '"I have no further orders," answered his Grace, aloud; then added kindly, "I think the best thing you can do is to go to bed." The Prince attempted no other communication; he at once retired.' Wellington had already done everything that could be done. Although his allies had left him ignorant of the state of the battle, he had taken the right decision and ordered the right moves. He, therefore, resumed his conversation with the Duchess and, according to her son, 'surrendered himself to the pleasures prepared for him, with perfect confidence and ease of manner for full twenty minutes. He then rose from his seat, and leaving his place at the supper table, advanced on his host, to say "Good night". This having been done in his usual manner, he suddenly sank his voice so as not to be overheard, and asked, "Have you got a good map of the country between here and the French frontier?" His host quitted the table, as the Duke paid his *adieux* to my mother and such members of the family as happened to be near her, and accompanied his guest out of the room; but instead of proceeding to the street door, my father led him into his private sitting room. **23**

'"Bonaparte has gained a day's march on me," said Wellington, when the door closed behind them. My father anxiously desired to know what his friend intended to do. The map was found and spread out before them. The Duke scrutinised it closely. "I have made arrangements to meet him at Quatre Bras," he observed, "and if I find myself not strong enough to stop him there, I shall fall back towards Blücher and fight him there." The Duke pointed to the open country, where he made a mark with his thumbnail.'* Then he left the house with his Military Secretary who remarked, 'No doubt we shall be able to manage those fellows.' 'There is little doubt of that,' replied Wellington, 'provided I do not make a false move.'

'I don't like lying awake; I make it a point never to lie awake,' said the Duke later in his life, and he was certainly asleep at 4.30 am, when General Dörnberg arrived from Mons where he had already caused enough trouble by failing to forward Colquhoun Grant's intelligence report. He insisted on seeing the Duke who was wakened accordingly and received him in his nightshirt. Having heard Dörnberg's report, he merely remarked, 'Ah! taken Charleroi? I dare say they have.' Then he paused. 'Well,' he continued, 'I have done all a man can do. I shall be at Quatre Bras tomorrow morning.' He bowed the Brunswicker out and returned to bed. Two minutes later he was heard to snore. At 10 am he reached Quatre Bras.

★ ★ ★

Wellington's delay in ordering the concentration of his army gave Napoleon a chance to catch up on his timetable. The Prussian army was still isolated. If the Emperor used his time to the best advantage it could be destroyed on 16 June without interference from Wellington. It seems that no idea of urgency crossed Napoleon's mind. He believed that his right was opposed by little more than a single Prussian corps and his left by only a light screen. Contrary to his usual practice he issued no orders overnight. None were sent out until 7 am and even then they did not give the impression that time was all-important. On the left, Ney was to advance his two corps to Quatre Bras from where he should send out reconnaissances. Later, either at 3 pm or in the evening, he was to be prepared to march on Brussels. From the time this march was estimated to take it was clear that the advance was expected to be unopposed. On the right Napoleon was to take the Guard to support Grouchy, with three corps, in an attack on the Prussians at Sombreffe and Ligny. No major action was expected. 'All the reports I have show that the Prussians cannot oppose us with more than

* This account of the interview between Wellington and Richmond is that of Lord William Pitt Lennox, who, having a broken arm, was at the ball to the end. Presumably he heard it at once from his father's mouth. The more usually quoted version is that of Lieutenant & Captain George Bowles. Lord William omits the oft-quoted phrase, 'Napoleon has *humbugged* me, by God'. If Wellington had actually said this, Lord William would scarcely have forgotten it. According to Lady Louisa Lennox the map was spread out on her mother's bed.

40,000 men.' The hope was that the battle would be over by mid-afternoon, whereupon the Guard would follow Ney's corps on its triumphant march into Brussels. Against this great occasion the guardsmen carried their full-dress uniforms in their packs. It was almost three o'clock before the attack on Ligny was launched. By that time Blücher had 80,000 men in position.

Communications between the British and the Prussians were re-established during the morning. Having seen that all was quiet at Quatre Bras, Wellington rode the five and a half miles eastward to the windmill at Bussy where Blücher had his command post in the centre of the convex position of his army. The meeting, although it convinced the two commanders of their mutual resolve to give each other all possible support, was not as productive as it could have been. The trouble was created by Gneisenau, largely because he disagreed with his own commander-in-chief as to how the battle should be fought. He refused to understand the length of time it would take the Duke's troops to intervene in the Ligny battle, even if, as he insisted on assuming, there was no substantial attack on Quatre Bras. His own representative at Wellington's headquarters laboured to convince him that it was physically impossible for the British troops to march to the rear of the Prussian position, where Gneisenau wished them to act as a reserve, before the battle at Ligny would have been decided one way or the other. Gneisenau refused to believe this self-evident truth and considered Wellington's refusal to commit himself to such a course as further evidence of British perfidy. The meeting reached no conclusion, but Gneisenau chose to interpret Wellington's parting words, 'Well, I will come, *provided I am not attacked myself*', as an unconditional pledge of British support at an early hour. The Duke started to ride back to his own sector at about two o'clock.

The battle of Ligny was one of attrition. The Prusians had some 10,000 more men than the French but could not match them for quality and experience. They fought stubbornly but they were badly placed, drawn up on a forward slope fully exposed to the greatly superior French artillery*. Until about half past six, they held their ground, the key villages on their front changing hands several times. Then Napoleon committed the Imperial Guard to break their centre. Blucher had no infantry reserves left and counter-attacked with his cavalry. Mounted on a charger given him by the Prince Regent of Britain, he led the 6th Uhlans in a final despairing charge. The attack broke on the steady volleys of the 4th Grenadiers. Blucher's horse was shot and the old marshal was twice ridden over by cavalry. He was rescued by a staff officer and taken to a farm house with a crowd of other wounded. For several hours his headquarters did not know where he was. Command of the army passed to Gneisenau.

Darkness and a thunderstorm brought the battle to an end. The French had

---

* Wellington had hinted to Blücher that his men were over-exposed, but the bellicose old man had replied that his men liked to see their enemy. As Wellington rode away he remarked to his staff, 'If they fight here they will be damnably mauled'.

driven their enemy from their position and inflicted a heavy loss, about 12,000 men. They had not routed them. Covered by a rearguard under Major General von Jagow, the Prussians were able to retreat in confusion but not in chaos. Their commanders could still choose the direction in which the retreat would be made. Gneisenau had to take the vital decision. His instincts told him to make eastward for Liège and his communications. Allied co-operation demanded that he continue to cover Brussels and keep in touch with Wellington but at Ligny not a single British soldier had appeared to support the Prussians. He compromised. The army should fall back to Wavre, fifteen miles due north. Once there a final decision could be taken. It was certainly his intention that the next move should be to the east but at least the options were still open. The decision to retreat on Wavre meant that Napoleon could, and probably would, be beaten. It was, said Wellington, 'the decisive moment of the century'.

Not all those serving under Gneisenau were prepared to leave the options open. A vast crowd of stragglers and deserters, mostly men of the *Landwehr*, shaken by their first battle, decided that they had had enough and made for home, streaming along the roads and across the fields towards Namur and Liège. Their contribution to the campaign was immeasurable. So large were their numbers that, during the night, reports from his cavalry patrols assured the Emperor that the Prussian army was in rapid retreat eastwards. Since this was exactly what he wished to believe, Napoleon had no difficulty in accepting this opinion. He ·convinced himself that he had broken Blücher's army, that Wellington was now isolated and ripe for destruction. Without making any serious efforts to discover what was happening to the north of Ligny, he clung to this illusion for thirty-six hours.

★ [★] ★

With his right wing Napoleon had achieved a victory even if it was not the victory he hoped and believed. On his left, things went very ill. If it had been possible for Ney to have brought his infantry forward late on the afternoon of 15 June, the light allied guard on Quatre Bras could easily have been overwhelmed. Through nobody's fault this had been impossible and by the following morning the situation had changed for the worse. Prince Bernard of Saxe-Weimar, the local commander, and Constant de Rebecque, chief of staff to the Prince of Orange, acting in the spirit rather than the letter of Wellington's orders had ensured that 6,500 men were in position at the vital crossroads on the morning of 16th. They were not very reliable troops but, since the country was undulating and woody, Ney was not in a position to appreciate the fact.

The first orders Ney received, to occupy Quatre Bras and be ready to march on Brussels, reached him soon after 8 am. They gave no hint of urgency. The marshal accordingly allowed his troops time to cook and eat. Since the supply arrangments were inadequate, many soldiers went scavenging and it was 11 o'clock before his leading division was ready to march from Mellet, more than four miles from the crossroads. At about this time, a letter from Soult reached him telling that cavalry reported Quatre Bras to be strongly held and urging him to keep his two corps, those of Reille and D'Erlon, and his cavalry well together, (*réunissez les corps*) and to defeat and destroy the enemy in his front. Ney was a notoriously rash general and, in thus phrasing the order, Napoleon hoped to curb his impetuosity. As things turned out, it was fatal to French plans. Ney's infantry, when he received the order, was spread over fifteen miles of road. D'Erlon's two rear divisions had only just crossed the Sambre. It would take most of the day to concentrate them near Quatre Bras. Ney decided not to wait until D'Erlon's corps was up but the caution enjoined on him did stay in his mind.

Soon after noon Reille's leading division came in sight of Quatre Bras. It was difficult to estimate the strength of the opposition. There were woods on either flank and in the fields the corn stood shoulder-high. Behind the Nivelle road there was a low ridge which might conceal a typical Wellingtonian reverse-slope position. Ney and Reille had both fought in the Peninsula. Ney could remember the abrupt appearance of the Light Division at Busaco, where the redcoats had risen unexpectly from a sunken road and routed his leading troops. Reille had been at Vitoria and the Pyrenees. He said to the marshal, 'This could well be like one of those battles in Spain when the English show themselves only at the critical moment. We would be wise to wait until we can attack in strength'. At this moment Wellington was at Bussy with Blücher. His reputation was fighting for him in his absence. It won him two vital hours. Ney, uncharacteristically cautious, remembered Soult's report that the crossroads were strongly held and waited until two more divisions were available.

By 2 o'clock 1,500 more Netherlanders and a battery had joined the defence but when Ney attacked with three divisions and cavalry the allied force, only 8,000 men and 16 guns, could not hold its ground. As Wellington returned from Bussy all seemed lost but, just in time, Picton's division with eight Peninsular battalions, arrived from Brussels. Wellington was still greatly outnumbered but without hesitation he counter-attacked and held the French advance. Ney paused for further reinforcements to arrive.

This pattern repeated itself throughout the afternoon. Again and again the French gathered enough strength to break through but, as they were on the point of doing so, allied reinforcements arrived to save the situation. At last the supply of French reserves dried up. Since 2 pm Napoleon had been sending orders of mounting urgency pressing Ney to break through and swing east on to the Prussian flank. The first of these orders arrived at the moment when they became impossible to perform, just as Wellington's first counter-attack checked Ney's advance. When Ney's fieriness would have been invaluable, Napoleon had urged him to caution. When no amount of daring could succeed, Napoleon demanded dash. Having no infantry available, Ney flung a brigade of Kellermann's cuirassiers at the allied infantry. They did all and more than could have been expected from them. They decimated two Highland regiments. They caught an English regiment in extended order and captured one of its colours. Another English battalion broke and fled for the woods. The horsemen actually reached the Nivelles road before they were halted and driven back. They had inflicted heavy casualties but they achieved nothing. There was no more infantry to exploit their temporary success. D'Erlon never arrived to support Reille.

D'Erlon's leading division had almost reached the battlefield when one of Napoleon's orderly officers ordered them to countermarch so as to intervene at Ligny. It is not clear whether this order emanated from the Emperor or whether the orderly officer attempted an intelligent anticipation of the orders he carried for Ney. What is certain is that D'Erlon turned away and marched towards Ligny. It is also certain that the imperial messenger failed to tell Ney what he had done. When, too late, the news reached the marshal he lost his temper. He sent a staff officer galloping after D'Erlon with peremptory orders to return. D'Erlon's leading division was already in sight of Ligny when this second counter-order arrived but he obeyed it, leaving one division in observation to the east. By the time he reached Ney it was dark and the battle was over. 20,000 French infantry had succeeded in missing both battles. Their presence in either would have been decisive.

* * *

By maintaining his tenuous hold on Quatre Bras throughout the day, Wellington had made up the time he had lost by his misappreciation of Napoleon's plan on the previous day. By the morning of the 17th his army would be all but complete at Quatre Bras and, assuming that Blücher had held Ligny, the combined armies could take the offensive. News of the Prussians was inadequate. Before 6 pm on the 16th Gneisenau had sent two officers to Quatre Bras with information. One was wounded on the road and never arrived. The other could only report that the Prussian front was still intact but that their losses had been heavy and the most that could be expected was that they would hold their ground until nightfall.

At 3 am on the 17th there was still no more news and the Duke sent one of his ADCs, Colonel Gordon, to Ligny to discover the situation there. Gordon returned at 7.30 having found the French bivouacked on the battlefield. Working round to the south, he had contacted the Prussian rearguard from whom he learned that the army was falling back on Wavre. This caused consternation in the British staff. Their maps did not stretch that far and Müffling, the Prussian liaison officer, had to tell them how far his compatriots had retreated. Wellington appeared unmoved. To a Guards officer standing by, he said, 'Old Blücher has had a damned good licking and gone back to Wavre, eighteen miles. As he has gone back, we must go back too. I suppose in England they will say we have been licked. I can't help it; as they are gone back, we must go too.' Then he retired to the hut which was serving as headquarters and gave orders for the retreat.

Wellington's position was uncomfortably exposed. To his front was Ney's wing of the French army. Despite having suffered more than 4,000 casualties, Ney still had about 45,000 men. To the east, straight along the Nivelles – Namur road, were 60,000 more Frenchmen with nothing to engage their attention except the rapidly retreating Prussians. Wellington, whose losses at Quatre Bras were almost 5,000, had about 50,000 men with him. Less than half were British and some of them had been badly shaken on the previous day. If Napoleon moved quickly he could bring almost double numbers against Wellington. If that happened the Anglo-Netherlands army would be lucky to escape at all. Such part as managed to escape would have to move westward, directly away from Blücher.

At 9 o'clock a letter arrived from Blücher, who had been found and brought to his headquarters. He confirmed that his army was to rally on Wavre and asked to know the Duke's intentions. The officer who brought the letter spoke English and Wellington questioned him closely. Satisfied with his replies, Wellington declared that he would fall back on a position south of the Forest of Soignes where he would stand and fight provided that Blücher would undertake to come to his assistance with at least one corps.

All this time squadrons of cavalry had been dismounted and their horses used to bring in the wounded from the previous day and transport them to the rear. When this was completed, about 10 o'clock, the infantry started to fall back. The hours which followed were the most critical of the campaign. If the French struck at the army from flank and rear while the infantry was strung out between Quatre Bras and Genappe there was every chance of a disaster. Outwardly Wellington seemed quite unperturbed. Much of the time he sat on the grass and chatted to his staff. For a time he lay down and slept with a newspaper over his face. His anxiety was apparent to close observers. For about an hour he walked up and down alone. 'His left hand was thrown carelessly behind his back. He had a small switch in his right hand, the one end of which he frequently put to his mouth, apparently unconscious that he was doing so.'

Napoleon wasted most of that morning. At 8 am no orders had been issued and when Marshal Grouchy rode to Fleurus to ask what the right wing's task was to be, he was taken on a tour of the Ligny battlefield where the Emperor showed his usual keen concern for the wounded. Meanwhile Soult was writing orders to Ney telling him to move on, if he could, and occupy Quatre Bras. If that was impossible, the Emperor was to be informed so that a combined operation could be mounted. The orders, despatched soon after 8 am, concluded, 'If there is only a rearguard there, attack it and take up a position. Today is to be devoted to mopping up, completing with ammunition and rallying stragglers.' Ney could hardly be expected to get any impression that speed was necessary and he reacted accordingly. He had not moved a man at midday. When Grouchy pressed for orders, he was curtly told, 'I will issue orders when I see fit'.

It was after 11 am when a definite order was sent to Ney telling him to attack Quatre Bras and promising the assistance of 30,000 men who would strike at Wellington's left flank along the Namur-Nivelles road. Before this attack could be mounted, all but the allied rearguard had marched away. When news that the crossroads had been evacuated was brought to the Emperor he snapped, 'On a perdu la France'. By his dilatoriness he had created a situation where only a miracle could save his empire.

Soon after Ney's final orders were dispatched Napoleon sent instructions to Grouchy and the right wing. Although it had been reported that at least some part of Blücher's army was heading for Wavre, that town was not mentioned in Grouchy's orders. He was ordered to move with two corps of infantry, a spare division and a large force of cavalry to Gembloux, to the north-east of Ligny, keeping the infantry 'concentrated within a square league of ground'. From Gembloux, 'You will reconnoitre in the direction of Namur and Maastricht, and you will pursue the enemy'. Namur is south-east from Gembloux and Maastricht is north-east, so that it is hardly surprising that Grouchy set his eyes eastward, rather than north, the Prussian's actual direction. A later section of the orders stressed that 'It is important to discover the enemy's intentions. Either they are leaving the English or they intend to unite, covering Brussels and Liège, and chance another battle.' This, although mentioning Liège, again to the east, as a possible direction to search for Blücher, did suggest that the marshal should search widely but it is quite clear that the Emperor believed Blücher to be to the east and only natural that Grouchy should be influenced by this fact. To make a wide search more difficult, Napoleon, within an hour of issuing Grouchy's main orders, sent him a supplementary instruction depriving him of fourteen regiments of cavalry. Grouchy, therefore, marched off eastward with 33,000 men who, for all the effect they had subsequently on the campaign, might as usefully have dispersed to their homes.

All that was left to Napoleon on 17 June was to inflict the greatest possible damage on the allied rearguard. In effect, only the British cavalry and their accompanying horse batteries were within his reach since the infantry had passed the dangerous defile at Genappe before the French could come within striking distance of them. Indeed, before Napoleon's attack could develop only the light cavalry rearguard and some guns were on the ground. Any damage that might have been inflicted was prevented by a quirk of the weather. The gunner officer who was with the ultimate rearguard on the left wrote a graphic description of how the engagement started. Looking up the Namur road, he saw the French coming on in dark masses, while the British hussar piquets galloped passed him to the rear and 'up came Lord Uxbridge, "Captain Mercer, are you loaded?" "Yes, my lord." "Then give them a round as they rise the hill, and retire as quickly as possible. – Light dragoons, threes about! at a trot, March!"' and as the cavalry rode smartly away, Uxbridge continued, '"Let them get well up before you fire. Do you think you can retire quick enough afterwards?" "I am sure of it, My Lord." "Very well then, keep a sharp look out and point your guns well." I had often longed to see Napoleon. Now I saw him. The sky had become overcast since the morning and at this moment presented a most extraordinary appearance. Large isolated masses of thundercloud, of the deepest, almost inky black, their lower edges hard and strongly defined, lagging down, as if momentarily about to burst, hung suspended over us, involving our position and everything on it in deep and gloomy obscurity: while the distant hill lately occupied by the French army still lay bathed in brilliant sunshine. Lord Uxbridge was still speaking when a single horseman, followed by several others, mounted the plateau, their dark figures thrown forward in strong relief from the illuminated background, making them appear much nearer to us than they really were. For an instant they pulled up and regarded us, when, several squadrons coming rapidly on the plateau, Lord Uxbridge cried out, "Fire! Fire!" and, giving them a general discharge, we quickly limbered up, as they dashed forward. The first gun that was fired seemed to burst the clouds overhead, for its report was instantly followed by an awful clap of thunder and lightning that almost blinded us, whilst the rain came down as if a waterspout had broken over us. Flash succeeded flash, and the peals of thunder were long and tremendous: whilst, as if in mockery of the elements, the French guns still sent forth their feebler glare and now scarcely audible reports – their cavalry dashing on at a headlong pace, adding their shouts to the uproar. We galloped for our lives through the storm, Lord Uxbridge urging us on, crying, "Make haste! Make haste! for God's sake gallop, or you will be taken!" We did make haste, but with the French advance close on our heels. However, observing the *chaussée* full of hussars, they pulled up.'

It was the only real excitement of the day. Soon the torrential rain made the fields impassable, horses sinking to their knees in the mud, and all movement was confined to the roads. According to a hussar officer, even 'the road was one mass of liquid mud and when we were halted and fronted, the men were so covered in mud that it was utterly impossible to distinguish a feature in their faces or the colour of the lace on the dress.' Apart from skirmishing, only one incident amounted to an engagment. Wishing to check the pace of the French pursuit, Lord Uxbridge decided to turn and attack their advance guard as it debouched from Genappe. Although he had several heavy cavalry regiments available, his lordship decided to employ the 7th Hussars, the regiment of which he was colonel, for this task. The hussars failed. They could hardly have done otherwise. The leading French regiment, 2nd Lancers, were drawn up, knee to knee, between the houses at the north end of the village street. Their supports closed up behind them and the front rank became so jammed that they could not have given ground even if they wished to. 'A few minutes before we charged, one of the heaviest showers of rain I can ever remember fell which rendered fire-arms useless, and though the French fired a few pistol-shots, I don't think they did any damage; our engagement was therefore one of lance and sabre. Of course, our charge could make no impression,' wrote one of the officers, 'but we continued cutting at them, and we did not give ground, and nor did they.' One of his brother officers commented, 'We might as well have charged the side of a house. They kept poking at us with their lances, and our men were unable to reach them with their sabres.' When the 7th had suffered more than forty casualties, Uxbridge ordered them to retire. There was a pause, during which he tried to order a light dragoon regiment to repeat the experiment, a suggestion against which their colonel remonstrated. Then the French advanced from their well protected position. 'Very well,' said Uxbridge, 'the Life Guards shall have this honour,' and two squadrons of the 1st Life Guards hurtled down on the unfortunate lancers. 'It did one's heart good,' wrote a watching Rifleman, 'to see how cordially they went at their work: they had no idea of anything but straight-forward fighting, and sent their opponents flying in all directions.'

For the rest of the day the French kept at a respectful distance until the retreat stopped on reaching the ridge of Mont St Jean. Before nightfall, Wellington had his fighting force on the position in which, given an assurance of Prussian support, he intended to defend Brussels and the future tranquillity of Europe.

He had not gathered all his troops together. He stationed 17,000 men, mostly Netherlanders but including one British and one Hanoverian brigade, at Hal and Tubize, ten miles and more beyond his right flank. These took no part in the battle on 18 June and none of Wellington's actions has been subjected to so much subsequent criticism, one British historian going so far as to suggest that, having stationed them on the 17th to meet a possible emergency, he then forgot about them. The Duke seldom forgot about anything to do with his army in battle and since he claimed, with every justification, that, 'you may depend upon it that there are few of the general arrangements of the army which have not been maturely considered by me; and that, although some inconveniences may attend some of them, they are the smallest that, after full consideration, it was found would attend any arrangements of the subjects to which these arrangements relate', it can be assumed that he had very good reasons for this detachment. His earlier pre-occupation with a French advance on the Mons road to Brussels may have played some part in his decision but much stronger was his belief that Napoleon would not be so foolhardy as to make a frontal attack on British infantry settled in a position chosen in advance. A few weeks after the battle he remarked, 'I think that, if I had been Buonaparte, I should have respected the English infantry more after what I must have heard of them in Spain; and that I should not have taken the bull by the horns.' If Napoleon was not to attack frontally, he seemed likely to manoeuvre on Wellington's right. To attempt to turn the left would be suicidal since the turning force would expose its rear to Blücher.*

Another possibility was that Napoleon might combine a frontal assault with a left hook. Wellington had no means of estimating the strength of the French army attacking his troops. He believed it to be between 90 and 100,000 strong.† His own army at Mont St Jean was less than 68,000, many of whom were of dubious reliability in the calculation of both himself and Napoleon. If Napoleon attacked him in front with equal numbers, a strong corps could swing wide round his left and be in Brussels while he was still engaged. If, moreover, the French broke his centre, and with more than 90,000 men they well might, the right wing of his army would have to fall back westward, where a fresh force of 17,000 men would be an invaluable 'firm base'.

He realised also that Napoleon might be tempted to turn his right since to do so would threaten the shortest sea communication with England, through Ostend. It was known that British sensitiveness about their route to the sea was an article of faith in the French army. Ostend, in fact, was not an object of concern to Wellington. He had earlier decided that it was less vital to him than co-operation with Blücher. If he had to fall back to the sea he would go to Antwerp. His arrangements had been made. A large depot of reserve ammunition had been established at Maastricht and orders given that, in case of danger, the magazines at Alost and Termonde should be evacuated to Antwerp. The exiled court of Louis XVIII had been advised to make for the same port and, on 17 June, the wounded from Quatre Bras were ordered to be evacuated through Antwerp rather than Ostend. His westward communications, though convenient, were expendable and played no part in influencing his decision. His right flank, on the other hand, was in the air in the presence of superior numbers. Four years earlier, Wellington had had his right flank in the air at Fuentes de Oñoro. After a hard fought battle he had remarked, 'If Boney had been there we should have been beat'. In 1815 Boney was there and Wellington was not the man to make the same mistake twice. A British brigade and some dubious foreigners was a small insurance premium to pay when the risk appeared so great.‡

As the army settled into its position, the rain continued to pour down, although the thunder and lightning had stopped, 'We considered in what way to pass the night; to lie down was out of the question, and to stand up all night

* Wellington could not be expected to realise that Napoleon was ignorant of the Prussian position.
† In the Waterloo despatch, written on 19 June, Wellington still believed that he had been attacked by the whole French army 'with the exception of the 3rd Corps'. The 3rd corps amounted to about 20,000 all arms. The Prussians believed they were only being shadowed by 15,000 men. The original French total of about 125,000 was known.
‡ Napoleon also did not bring forward his full strength. Girard's division was left at Quatre Bras, to protect the communications.

was almost equally so. We endeavoured to light some fires, but the rain soon extinguished them, and the only plan we could adopt was to gather arm-fulls of the standing corn, and, rolling it together, made a sort of mat, on which we placed the knapsacks; and sitting on that, each man holding his blanket over his head to keep off the rain, which was almost needless, as we were so thoroughly drenched.' 'Midnight approached, and all the fields were hid in darkness. At this time a very heavy shower poured down upon us and occasioned some movement or noisy murmur in the French army. This induced our sentries to give an alarm. In an instant every man of the brigade stood by his musket; the bayonets were already on the pieces, and these all loaded, notwithstanding the rain. We thus stood to our arms for nearly an hour, sinking to our ankles amongst the soft muddy soil of the field, when the alarm was found to be false, and we again sat or lay down to repose.'

If the British troops were having a miserable night, the French were worse off. Their infantry spent most of the night marching up to the next day's battlefield. One French soldier, whose battalion did not pass Genappe until 11 pm 'thought every moment I should have dropped down from exhaustion: but matters became worse when we overtook the baggage, for then we had to march by the side of the road, in the fields, and the more we advanced, the deeper we sank into the mud.' Every time the column halted, many men broke ranks and went into the roadside gardens, 'in spite of the shouts of the officers; every one dug up what he could with his bayonet, and in a few minutes there was not a root left in the ground. At last, moving on, we mounted a little ridge and, in spite of the rain, we could see the bivouacs of the English. We were told to take up our position in a cornfield, among several regiments we could not see, because the orders were that we should light no fires, lest we should frighten the enemy into continuing his retreat. Fancy to yourself the feelings of men, lying under cornstalks like gypsies, their teeth chattering with cold, thinking themselves lucky if they had a turnip, a carrot, or anything else to keep themselves going.' That evening the Provost Marshal of the French army resigned his post. While there was no doubt that the army would fight when ordered, he despaired of stopping them from pillaging. The spirit of the troops was at its height. Their discipline was disintegrating. They would obey only orders which sent them against the enemy. If, on the following day, they met anything but overwhelming victory they would stop being an army and become an armed mob.

The Emperor set up his headquarters at Caillou Farm, a mile and a half behind his forward troops. He had ordered a cavalry demonstration against the allied lines before darkness fell. The Cuirassiers, eight regiments of them, had drawn artillery fire from the whole length of the position. Content, Napoleon went back to Caillou. Now he knew that Wellington was at Mont St Jean with his whole army. Napoleon's greatest fear was that it was nothing but a rearguard and that Wellington's main body was withdrawing on Brussels. 'I returned to

34

my headquarters delighted that the enemy commander was making so great a mistake and concerned only lest the weather should prevent my taking advantage of it. The next day would see the overthrow of the British oligarchy. That day France would become more glorious, more powerful, greater than ever.'

Napoleon's thoughts ran only on Wellington and his army. He was convinced that the Prussians could not intervene. The evidence was mounting that he was wrong. At 9 pm General Milhaud reported that his cavalry patrols had seen a column of Prussian artillery marching due north towards Wavre. At 2 am the following morning a despatch arrived from Grouchy, written four hours earlier. The marshal was uncertain of the Prussian intentions. It seemed that Blücher's army had divided into two columns. One seemed to be moving on Wavre, the other on Liège. If further reports confirmed that the bulk of the Prussians were moving on Wavre, Grouchy would follow them 'to keep them from joining Wellington'. In principle, this was satisfactory. In practice, it was impractical. Grouchy was at Gembloux, amongst his leading troops. From Wavre to Mont St Jean is nine and a half miles. From Gembloux, the distance is seventeen miles. The roads on either route were equally abominable. The Prussians could only be overtaken if Grouchy marched his men all night. This Napoleon knew he had no intention of doing. He had announced his intention of waiting for further reports during the night. Napoleon sent Grouchy no orders in the small hours. He had made up his mind about Blücher. On the evening of 17 June some of the senior officers of Reille's corps dined at the 'King of Spain' Inn in Genappe. 'The waiter who served us told us that Lord Wellington had dined there the previous day* and that one of his aides-de-camp had let slip that the English army would stand and await the French outside the Forest of Soignes and that there they would be joined by the Prussians, who were marching on Wavre.' One of the French officers present was Prince Jerome Napoleon and next morning he passed this news to his brother. The Emperor replied, 'After having been beaten in a battle like Fleurus†, and being pursued by a substantial body of troops, it is impossible for the Prussians to join the English in less than two days.' He added, 'We should be delighted that the English are standing their ground. The coming battle will save France and be renowned in history. I shall bombard them with my great weight of artillery, I shall charge them with my cavalry, so that they show themselves and, when I am quite sure where the English troops are, I shall march straight at them with my Guard.'

Meanwhile, the four corps of the Prussian army were closely grouped round Wavre. Despite their defeat at Ligny, their morale was high. The swarm of deserters who had misled the French cavalry by making off to the east were, for

* Wellington had dined at Genappe that afternoon and it must have been then that the ADC had made his indiscretion. Wellington was in Genappe the previous evening but he did not then know that Blücher had been defeated and had retired.
† Fleurus was, and is, the French name for the battle of Ligny.

the most part, men who had only recently become Prussians under orders from the Congress of Vienna and the fighting quality of the remainder was higher for the absence of those with no stomach for the fight.

About midday on 17 June, Blücher had received Wellington's letter undertaking to fight in front of Waterloo, provided that he was assured of the support of at least one Prussian corps. The next twelve hours were spent in continuous argument between Blücher, supported by von Grölmann, his quartermaster general, and Gneisenau. Gneisenau was for retreating on Liège, *reculer pour mieux sauter*. No Prussian territory was so far in danger. The Austrians and Russians would soon be ready on the Rhine to sweep into France in a grand, irresistible advance, the kind of advance which had brought them to Paris the previous year. Experience had shown that Napoleon could only be conquered by overwhelming numbers. Why should Prussia's only army be risked to help Wellington? What had Wellington done to help them the previous day at Ligny? Was it not probable that Wellington only asked for Prussian help in order to cover his own retreat to Ostend? The British always made for their ships when the going got tough. If they run for it again, we shall have no hope of escape. Our army will not just be defeated, it will be destroyed.

Blücher did not agree. He was in poor physical shape. He was bruised from head to foot but he had been rubbed down with brandy and had dosed himself with a medicine in which he had great confidence – gin and rhubarb. Between him and Wellington there had grown up a confidence and respect astonishing in two men of such different tastes and temperaments. If the Duke had said he would stand and fight then Blücher believed that he would do so. They might be beaten but if the Prussians went to their aid the chances were in favour of victory. Rather than miss the coming battle, he would be tied to his horse. At 11 o'clock at night the argument was still going on when a letter arrived from Müffling. The Duke, he reported, had concentrated his army on the ridge of Mont St Jean and was evidently determined to await the French attack.

This turned the scale. In Blücher's anteroom Colonel Hardinge lay on a truss of straw, nursing the stump of his newly amputated arm. He was Wellington's representative with Blücher, the British counterpart of Müffling. He had not been admitted to the long discussion. It was almost midnight when Blücher called him in and said, 'Gneisenau has given in. We are to join the Duke.' At once the old marshal dictated a letter to Müffling telling him to let Wellington know that two corps would march at dawn to attack the French right flank. 'The exhaustion of the troops, some of whom have not yet arrived, makes it impossible to advance earlier. Let me know in good time when and how the Duke may be attacked so that I may make my dispositions accordingly.'

Meanwhile, Gneisenau was writing detailed orders to the corps commanders. It was unfortunate that the corps he chose to lead the advance was that of von Bülow, the corps furthest from Waterloo. To reach the battlefield it would have to march through Wavre, traversing the bivouacks of two other corps. Gneisenau was not anxious to become involved in the battle earlier than necessary. The later the Prussians arrived, the clearer it would be whether Wellington really intended to fight.* Before the Prussians had come to a decision, Wellington had gone to bed at the inn in Waterloo village. He had heard nothing from Blücher and he could not give definitive orders to stand for battle until he had a firm promise of Prussian support. As long as the rain lasted he could leave the decision open. The French would not fight a battle tied to the roads.

He was woken about 3 am. It was still raining and there was no word from Wavre. The heavy going would have delayed Blücher's messenger. He settled at a table to write some essential letters. Since nothing had been heard from Blücher, he must face the possibility that he never would hear. If retreat became necessary something must be done to warn the French Royal family at Ghent. They were told that 'It is possible that the enemy may turn us through Hal, although the weather is terrible, the roads detestable and despite a corps I have stationed between Hal and Enghein.' The royalist troops at Ghent, although regarded by the British as somewhat comic, would be sufficient to escort the King to Antwerp. A further note was written to the Governor of Antwerp authorizing him to admit the King and his party. He had also to be warned against 'the *crochets* which I find in the heads of the King's governors at every turn'. Next, the crowd of British civilians in Brussels must be alerted but not alarmed. To the British Minister, he wrote, 'Pray keep the English quiet if you can. Let them all prepare to move, but neither be in a hurry or a fright as all will yet turn out well.' There was still no Prussian messenger when the official letters were written so, to fill in the anxious time, he wrote to a friend in Brussels who was imminently expecting a baby. 'The course of operations may oblige me to uncover Brussels for a moment and may expose that town to the enemy; for which reason I recommend that you and your family should be prepared to move to Antwerp at a moment's notice. I will give you the earliest intimation of any danger that may come to my knowledge: at present I know of none.'

By six o'clock the rain cleared and there were signs that the sun might soon be shining. A decision, to fight or to retreat, must soon be taken. Wellington mounted his horse and started to ride towards Mont St Jean. His staff followed him, a glittering cavalcade of British and foreign uniforms. A Prussian officer, mud-spattered, on a tired horse, rode up, saluted and handed a letter to Müffling. He tore it open and told the Duke of Blücher's promise. Two Prussian corps were on their way. 'Now,' said Wellington, 'Buonaparte will see how a general of sepoys can defend a position.'

---

* The reason given by Gneisenau's apologists for this clumsy move is that von Bülow's corps had not been engaged at Ligny and was fresher than the others. While this is true, von Thielmann's corps had been only lightly engaged in the battle and was fresher since it had not marched so far. It was stationed five miles closer to Mont St Jean.

*'The history of a battle is not unlike the history of a ball.
Some individuals may recollect all the little events of which
the great result is the battle won or lost; But no individual
can recollect the order in which, or the exact moment at
which, they occured which makes all the difference as to
their value or importance.'*

THE DUKE OF WELLINGTON   18 August 1815

2. The Battle 18 June 1815

'The position which I took up in front of Waterloo,' wrote Wellington in his despatch, 'crossed the high roads from Charleroi and Nivelles, and had its right thrown back to a ravine near Merbe Braine, which was occupied, and its left extended to a height above the hamlet of Ter La Haye, which was also occupied.' The main line of the position is a ridge about three miles long lying east and west, except at the western end where it swings forward giving a concave front to the whole line. The front of the ridge is smooth and fairly steep but not steep enough to check the pace of a galloping horse. The reverse slope is gentler and offers no obstacle to the transverse movement of troops or guns. The front of the ridge is most marked at the left, eastern, end and in front there is a scatter of farms, Papelotte, La Haye, Frischermont, and the hamlet of Smohain, astride a small stream running in a valley which, while not impassable, was not easy to cross for formed bodies of troops. In front of the left centre was the farmhouse of La Haye Sainte, on the right hand side of the Brussels-Charleroi road. The house and its outbuildings form a square and to north and south were hedged enclosures. A much more substantial building stood in front of the right centre. This was the manor house of Hougoumont, a heavily built chateau, in a rectangle of residential and agricultural buildings. On its left was a walled garden and an orchard and to the south some woodland and fields, the whole making an enclosed area more than 500 yards square.

Some 1,200 yards to the south of the ridge is another, very similar in height, with the inn of La Belle Alliance on its crest standing beside the Brussels-Charleroi road. It was on this ridge that Wellington had planned to fight, but William de Lancey, who as acting Quartermaster General, was sent back from Quatre Bras on 17 June to fix the positions of the troops, decided that it was too extensive for the number of men available. He chose instead the more northerly ridge behind which stands the farm of Mont St Jean. The ridge of La Belle

Alliance thus became the position on which the French drew up their army before the battle opened.

There can be no doubt that De Lancey was right to choose the northern ridge. The left flank is strengthened by the valley of the Smohain stream and on the right the end of the position is marked by a well-defined re-entrant running north-west up to Braine l'Alleud. While in modern terms this is not the ravine Wellington called it, its eastern slope gave a good defensive position from Merbe Braine to Hougoumont which would have been invaluable had Napoleon, as Wellington expected, attempted to turn the allied right.

Between the ridges of Mont St Jean and La Belle Alliance the ground is open. There were no hedges or ditches except for the enclosures round the groups of buildings. Most of the ground was under rye which stood up to the girths of the horses until it was trodden down. Looking from the northern ridge across the valley towards La Belle Alliance the ground appears a steady concave. In fact there is, at the bottom of the valley, a slight swell. It is imperceptible to the observer but very noticeable to a heavily laden infantryman plodding forward under cannon fire.

Mont St Jean was the best position available. It had not the topographical grandeur of some of Wellington's Peninsular defensive positions such as Busaco or Sorauren but there was nothing better between Brussels and the French frontier. It bore a strong resemblance to the ridge Wellington had chosen for Beresford at Albuera in 1811. Beresford's misfortunes in that position may have had something to do with Wellington's constant, almost obsessive, pre-occupation with the right flank.

Napoleon subsequently said that it was an unforgiveable fault of Wellington's to have fought so crucial a battle with the Forest of Soignes so close to his rear as it would have been very difficult to retreat under pressure through the thickly wooded stretch. This criticism misses the essential point. Wellington had no intention of retreating under pressure. He did not intend to fight at all unless he had Blücher's promise of support. When, at 6 am, he received Blücher's undertaking to come with two corps, the idea of retreat was utterly abandoned. He would stand on his ridge until the Prussians came or until his army was destroyed. There could be no middle course. To retreat would leave the Prussians exposed to the full strength of the French army, having first drawn them away from the safety of Liège and their communications. Such a betrayal was unthinkable to a man of the Duke's character.

To Napoleon, even more than to Gneisenau, such reasoning was incomprehensible. Moreover he did not believe it possible for Blücher to join Wellington. During the night the Emperor's main concern was that the English might slip away. When he saw them still on their ridge at eight o'clock he said with relief, 'There is no longer time for them to retreat. Wellington has gambled and lost. He has made defeat certain.' Under his hand Napoleon had more than

65,000 infantry and cavalry and 266 guns. Except in artillery it was not a great numerical superiority, about 3,000 infantry and 2,500 cavalry but in quality he was immensely stronger. Only 30,000 British and German Legion troops could match the French. To Napoleon the odds were more than satisfactory. During the night, Soult urged him to order Grouchy to detach a corps to the main army. No orders were sent. Soult re-opened the subject in the morning, only to be brutally snubbed. 'Just because Wellington has defeated you, you think he is a great general. I tell you Wellington is a bad general, that the English are bad troops and that this is going to be a picnic *(l'affaire d'un déjeuner)*.'

The French army had been ordered to be ready to attack at 9 am. No corps was ready and some battalions had barely reached their position. Moreover the ground was so sodden that the heavy guns could scarcely be moved. Final orders were issued at 11 am giving the start time as 1 pm. Above all things Wellington needed time. Napoleon and the weather had given him four hours, four hours freedom from bombardment, four hours for the Prussians to march towards him. The attack Napoleon planned was a frontal assault aiming for Mont St Jean farm. It was to be made by D'Erlon's corps after a heavy artillery preparation. While the orders were being written out they were given verbally to the two front-line corps commanders, D'Erlon and Reille. They and the other officers who had fought in Spain were appalled but they knew how the Emperor had dealt earlier with Soult's protest. They kept silent until Napoleon asked Reille how he thought the day would go. Reille was in a quandary. He also had been beaten by Wellington in Spain and his advice would in any case, be suspect. It was he who had persuaded Ney to be cautious at Quatre Bras two days earlier, advice which turned out to be unnecessary and disastrous. Nevertheless, Reille was a professional and gave his opinion. 'In the kind of position which Wellington is so good at choosing, I regard the English infantry as impregnable because of their quiet steadiness and the superiority of their fire discipline. We shall lose half our assault force before we can get at them with the bayonet. On the other hand, they are more ponderous, less flexible than we are. They may not be susceptible to frontal attack but we could beat them by manoeuvring.' The Emperor shrugged and turned away. Nevertheless, soon afterwards Reille was told to use his corps to clear D'Erlon's flank and draw off Wellington's reserves by capturing Hougoumont.*

Across the valley the Anglo-Netherlands army was taking up its positions. The troops had not been put in order of battle on the previous evening since the rain was heavy and there was an even chance of the retreat being continued on the 18th. A stong screen of piquets and videttes had covered all the approaches and

---

* There is no mention of the attack on Hougoumont in the 11 am orders and Reille received his instructions verbally. It has never been clear how many troops Napoleon intended him to use. Reille has frequently been blamed for tying up too many men in what was intended mainly as a diversion. Certainly Napoleon made no attempt to restrain the general when he saw how many men he was committing and, far from remostrating, sent him reinforcements of artillery.

the main danger points, such as Hougoumont and La Haye Sainte had been garrisoned with reliable troops, but the bulk of the army had been roughly grouped behind the ridge, ready to move either towards Brussels or to their fighting posts. 'As morning dawned,' wrote an officer of the Thirty-second Foot, 'the men procured some wood, and made large fires; biscuits and spirits were served out and our clothes were nearly dry when the enemy appeared on the heights opposite us, standing to their arms.' It was not until 9 am that the baggage was ordered to the rear and a quarter of an hour later a gunner officer was dashing off a letter. 'All quiet on both sides – all getting into order. Ammunition coming up. I expect we shall have some cannonading today.' The Gordon Highlanders had 'stood to' at daylight and a sergeant recalled that 'I never felt colder in my life; every one of us was shaking like an aspen leaf'. A corporal of the Greys, who was sent on vidette 'after I had eaten my ration of stirabout, ... could see the French army drawn up in heavy masses opposite me. They were only a mile from where I stood; but the distance seemed greater, for between us the mist still filled the hollows. There were great columns of infantry, and squadron after squadron of cuirassiers, red dragoons, brown hussars and green lancers with little swallow-tail flags at the ends of their lances. The grandest sight was a regiment of cuirassiers dashing at full-gallop over the brow of the hill opposite me, with the sun shining on their steel breastplates.' At 8.30 Lambert's brigade, three fine Peninsular battalions just back from America, marched on to the ridge, headed by the Fourth (King's Own) with its 'band playing and colours flying'.

All along the ridge the troops were moving into position, tramping through the poached ground, ankle deep in mud. 'The grain, I can't say whether wheat or barley, was above our heads but it was soon trodden down.'

Wellington rode from end to end of the line accompanied by his staff and the Prussian liaison officer. Near La Haye Sainte he stopped to drink a cup of tea brewed by the Rifles against the wall of the cottage in which their colonel had spent the night. Twice he visited Hougoumont, to see how the garrison was getting on making loopholes in the garden wall, as he had ordered the previous evening. Müffling considered this to be the weakest point in the line. 'I deemed it untenable against a serious attack. This the Duke disputed as he had put the old château in a state of defence and caused the long garden wall to be crenellated; and, he added, "I have put Macdonnell in charge of it".'

Captain and Lieutenant-Colonel James Macdonnell was a huge Highlander who had fought at Maida and in the Peninsula. He commanded the light companies of the Coldstream and Third Guards. He was entrusted with the defence of the buildings of Hougoumont and to support him in the grounds were the light companies of the First Guards. Defending the perimeter of the enclosure were Hanoverian and Nassau light infantry, but the fact that he put the Guards into Hougoumont was the measure of Wellington's concern for that point. The main body of his Guards division was on the ridge in rear of the château. One other part of the front seemed particularly threatened, the place where the Brussels road crosses the ridge at its lowest, smoothest part. Here he stationed the best of his infantry under his best divisional generals. Sir Charles Alten, a Hanoverian who had greatly distinguished himself in Spain, held the right of the road with a battle-tried brigade of the German Legion, flanked by a Hanoverian brigade and four British battalions. The left was entrusted to eight Peninsular battalions, four of them Scottish, under Sir Thomas Picton, probably the strongest combination of troops and commander on either side. With them was a Netherlands brigade which had suffered badly at Quatre Bras, where it had shown creditable staunchness.

A complete Anglo-Hanoverian division was in reserve behind the right wing and Lambert's newly arrived veterans were behind the centre, where were also stationed the two British brigades of heavy cavalry. The remaining Netherlands and Hanoverian formations held the gaps in the line, closely interwoven with the more experienced troops, or were in reserve. A single British brigade held the extreme right flank beyond Hougoumont.

Soon after 11 o'clock a Prussian officer arrived at the light cavalry on the allied left flank with the news that von Bülow's corps was 'three-quarters of a league' away and was coming up to join the Duke. No news could have been more welcome. Wellington was confident as always but now it seemed that Blücher's army would be in action against the French flank early in the afternoon. 'One of his staff said, "I do not think the French will attack today." "Nonsense," the Duke replied, "The columns of attack are already forming, and I think I have discerned where the weight of the attack will be made. I shall be attacked within the hour and I shall soon want every man".' He was observed to be 'in high spirits, very animated, but so cool and so clear in the issue of his orders, it was impossible not fully to comprehend what he said.' The newly appointed Spanish ambassador to the Netherlands, an old friend of the Duke's, who had served for years on his staff in the Peninsula, decided, 'although I had received no orders to that effect,' to join the army on the morning of the 18th. He arrived in some alarm but was reassured by Wellington's first casual remark – 'Were you at Lady Charlotte Greville's last evening?' Soon afterwards, he added, 'The French are going to get the devil of a surprise when they see how I defend a position.'*

Across the valley, Napoleon was taking up his station on a mound near La Belle Alliance. Through his glass he watched the allies taking up their ground. 'How steadily they form,' he remarked. 'See those grey horses! What splendid horsemen! Those are fine troops but I shall cut them to pieces in half an hour.' Then he rode along the line of his two forward corps. A soldier in the ranks

* The ambassador, Major General Don Miguel de Alava, was the only man to be present at both Trafalgar and Waterloo. At the first he had been a midshipman in the Spanish Navy.

remembered that, 'There rose on our left a sudden tempest of shouts, *"Vive l'Empereur"*, and the shouting came closer and grew louder and louder. We all stood on tip-toe and craned forward. Excitement spread through the ranks, even the horses behind us neighed as if they wanted to join in the shouting. Suddenly a cloud of generals galloped past us. Napoleon was among them. I think I saw him. He was riding so fast and so many men hoisted their shakos on their bayonet points that there was hardly time to glimpse his round back and grey overcoat in the midst of the embroidered uniforms. Our captain just had time to cry, "Shoulder arms! Present arms!" and they were gone. That's the way one always saw him unless one was in the Guard.'

★ ★ ★

The bombardment opened at twenty past eleven. Eighty French guns had been dragged, axle-deep in mire, on to the forward slope. An officer on the ridge above La Haye Sainte remarked aggrievedly that the first round 'took off the head of our right hand man'. Soon afterwards light cavalry probed down towards Smohain on the allied left and a column of infantry, thickly screened by skirmishers, moved against Hougoumont. Reille had sent his strongest division, commanded by Prince Jerome, the Emperor's brother, against the château. Their *voltigeurs* were briskly engaged by the Hanoverian and Nassau light infantry who held the wood but the French numbers were overwhelming and the trees were not a serious obstacle. 'There was no underwood and it is easily traversed in all parts by light infantry, and the communication of files kept up with the greatest facility.' The Germans were forced back.

When the *voltigeurs* reached the orchard, it was a different story. The loop-holed garden wall was lined with a company of the Coldstream. It would need more than skirmishers to dislodge guardsmen. A heavy column, Bauduin's brigade, was formed under cover of the wood ready for the assault. On the ridge above, Wellington saw the danger. He ordered up a troop of howitzers and said to the commander of the horse artillery, '"Colonel Frazer, you are going to do a very delicate thing. Can you depend on the force of your howitzers? Part of the wood is held by our troops, part by the enemy." I answered that I could perfectly depend upon the troop.' As a rain of shrapnel and common shell began to burst among the trees, the Duke sent down a reinforcement of four companies of the Coldstream, saying briskly, 'In with you, my lads, let me see no more of you'.

The orchard was re-captured but the French renewed again and again their attempt to storm the garden wall.

The fight round Hougoumont became almost a separate battle from the action on the rest of the field. As the afternoon wore on Reille fed in battalion after battalion in an attempt, always unsuccessful, to take the buildings. Wellington answered by sending down a few more companies of guards. On the French side, three brigades were absorbed, on the British eighteen companies, less than two battalions.* Firing from the loop-holed garden walls and from the solidly built farm buildings the guardsmen could not be dislodged. Once a party of Frenchmen, headed by the giant Sous-Lieutenant Legros, forced their way into the courtyard. Macdonnell with three officers and a sergeant forced the great gate shut behind them and soon there was not a live Frenchman left inside except a forlorn, wounded drummer boy. Macdonnell, bleeding from the cheek, found 'a large piece of wood or the trunk of a tree' to wedge the gate shut. Later, the barn was set on fire. In the confusion 'three or four officers' horses, rushed out into the yard and in a minute or two rushed back into the flames and were burnt.' As many wounded as possible were removed from the barn but some had to be left behind and shared the fate of the chargers. The fire burned up to the foot of the cross in the chapel and then went out, 'which in so superstitious a country made a great sensation'.

Ammunition was a constant problem. Supplies could only be taken to the château down the forward slope of the ridge – no light undertaking under the storm of shot that was falling there from the great battery. Late in the day, one of Lord Uxbridge's ADCs 'was called to by some officers of the Third Guards defending Hougoumont, to use my best endeavours to send them musket ammunition. Soon afterwards I fell in with a private of the Waggon Train† in charge of a tumbril on the crest of the position. I merely pointed out to him where he was wanted, when he gallantly started his horses, and drove straight down the hill to the gate, where I saw him arrive. He must have lost his horses, as there was a severe fire kept on him. I feel convinced to that man's service the Guards owe their ammunition.' The fighting at Hougoumont was still continuing shortly before dusk when the result of the battle was settled elsewhere.

⋆ ⋆ ⋆

Just before one o'clock an aide-de-camp from Ney rode up to tell the Emperor that all was ready for the great attack by D'Erlon's corps on Wellington's left centre. The Emperor was dictating a letter to Grouchy. At eleven o'clock a despatch, written by Grouchy at 6 am had arrived saying that 'All my reports and information confirm that the [Prussian] enemy is retiring on Brussels intending to concentrate there or to join Wellington and offer battle again.' He added that he was following them towards Wavre. The letter was written at Gembloux, eleven miles from Wavre by passable roads. From Gembloux to La Belle Alliance was more than fifteen miles across the grain of the country.

---

* The original garrison consisted of four light companies, two from the First Guards and one each from the Coldstream and Third. During the afternoon seven more companies of each of the two latter regiments were added, leaving two battalion companies on the ridge to guard the colours.

† He was, in fact, Corporal Gregory Brewster.

Having left Grouchy's letter unanswered for two hours, Napoleon wrote to assure him that his movement on Wavre, 'conforms with the orders you have been given.' In addition, the marshal was urged 'to bear in mind the need to manoeuvre in our direction and to move nearer to us before any Prussian corps can intervene between our two forces. The battle is beginning at this moment on the line of Waterloo, in front of the forest of Soignes. The enemy's centre is at Mont St Jean. Manoeuvre, therefore, so as to join our right.'

By the most optimistic calculation this letter could not have reached Grouchy before 4 pm, by which time he would be at or near Wavre. Even if he could obey instantly, none of Grouchy's men could have reached the battlefield before dark. Nor were his orders clear. Two contradictory courses were prescribed. He was to march on Wavre *and* to join the Emperor's right. As the Prussian army was three times his own strength, either course would take all his force to have any hope of success. In the event, communications were much worse than could have been expected. It was not until 4 pm that he received Napoleon's earlier, 10 am, letter which told him unequivocally to 'direct your movements on Wavre.' Some of his subordinates pressed him to march to the sound of the guns which could be heard to the west but Grouchy believed his orders to be clear and decided to obey them. Napoleon's second, 1 pm, letter did not reach him until 6 pm. By that time any action he took was irrelevant.

The second letter was held up before being despatched. As it was completed a staff officer looking through his glass to the east saw a body of troops emerging from the woods beyond Wellington's left. For a moment there was a hope that Grouchy had acted on his own initiative and come to roll up the allied flank. Then a captured warrant officer of the 2nd Silesian Hussars was brought to Napoleon. He carried a letter from Gneisenau to Müffling making it clear that Bülow's corps was marching against the French right. The hussar admitted that most, if not all, the Prussian army was following Bülow. A postscript was added to Grouchy's orders. 'A letter has been taken saying that General Bülow will attack our right flank. We think we see this corps on the heights to the east. Do not lose a moment in joining us so that Bülow, whom you will catch red-handed, can be crushed.' To Soult, Napoleon remarked, 'This morning the odds were nine to one in our favour. Now they are six to four. If Grouchy rectifies the appalling mistake he made in dallying at Gembloux and gets here quickly, our victory will be even more decisive as we shall destroy Bülow's corps as well.' Meanwhile he ordered two light cavalry divisions to be wheeled to the right to observe Bülow. During the afternoon the two infantry divisions of Lobau's corps were moved to support them. Napoleon's only remaining reserve of infantry was the twenty-three battalions of the Imperial Guard.

At 1.30 pm the bombardment from D'Erlon's front burst into life again. 'The gunners were standing in line, inserting the charges, ramming them home, swinging the slow matches to make them burn more brightly. They seemed to move as one man. Behind them stood the captains of the guns; nearly all of them were elderly and they gave their orders as if on parade. Eighty guns fired together, blotting out every other sound. The whole valley was filled with smoke. A second or two later, the calm clear voices of the captains could be heard again, "Load! – Ram! – Aim! – *Fire*!!" This continued without a break for half an hour. We could scarcely see our comrades but across the valley the English had also opened fire. We could hear the whistle of their cannon-balls in the air, the dull thud as they struck the ground and that other noise when muskets were smashed to matchwood and men hurled twenty paces to the rear, every bone crushed, or when they fell with a limb gone.'

The cannonade was impressive but it did little harm. Unlike Blücher at Ligny, Wellington had not posted his men on the forward slope. Only the light companies and the guns were in sight of the French except to the east of the Brussels road where Bijlandt, with his continental training, drew up his brigade of Netherlanders in front of the crest. They had already suffered badly at Quatre Bras and now they were terribly pounded. For the rest, the noise was worse than the damage. The weather was still fighting for Wellington. The sun was out but the ground, from the earlier rain, 'was so deep that numberless shells burst where they fell and did little injury from being buried in the ground, and many round shot never rose from the place they first struck, instead of hopping for half a mile and doing considerable injury.' Sergeant Morris, lying down with his battalion had a short sleep 'as comfortably as ever I did in my life'.

At about two o'clock the bombardment lifted for a few moments while D'Erlon's 16,000 infantry marched through the intervals of the guns and started down the slope. They came on echelonned in four vast masses from their left on the Brussels road to their right moving on Smohain. 'Each regiment rent the air with shouts of "*Vive l'Empereur!*" and backed by the thunder of their artillery, and carrying with them the *rubidub* of drums and the *tantarara* of trumpets, in addition to their increasing shouts, it looked at first as if they had some hopes of scaring us off the ground; for it was a singular contrast to the stern silence reigning on our side where nothing, as yet, but the voices of our great guns told that we had mouths to open when we chose to use them.'

The French came on with incredible gallantry. Massed as they were, every allied shot could hardly miss and yet they never faltered. Some of them inclined to their left and swarmed round La Haye Sainte, forcing the German defenders to take cover in the buildings. A Hanoverian battalion sent up to reinforce them was cut to pieces by a brigade of cuirassiers who covered their left. Bijlandt's unfortunate brigade, pounded beyond endurance and having lost all its senior officers, fled, leaving a gaping hole in the front. Picton brought up Kempt's brigade of veterans and was shot through his round-brimmed civilian hat as he did so. Kempt's brigade lined a straggling hedge and started a series of deadly volleys. The French went down in swathes before them but still they came on, firing back and causing heavy casualties. Even Highlanders cannot stand forever and there was some wavering. Wellington, who had galloped across to the vital point as soon as D'Erlon advanced, saw 'a column of French firing across the road at one of our regiments. Our people could not get at them to charge because they would have been disordered by crossing the road. It was a nervous moment. One of the two forces must go about in a few moments – it was impossible to say which it might be. I saw about two hundred men of the Seventy-Ninth who seemed to have had more than they liked of it. I formed them myself about twenty yards from the flash of the French column, and ordered them to fire and, in a few minutes the French went about.' To the left of Kempt, Sir Dennis Pack's brigade was equally pressed. The Gordon Highlanders had been 'lying down under cover of the position, when they were immediately ordered to stand to their arms, General Pack calling out at the same time, "Ninety-Second, everything has given way on your right and left. You must charge this column," upon which he ordered four deep to be formed and closed in to the centre. The regiment, which was then within about twenty yards of the column, fired a volley into them. The enemy on reaching the hedge at the side of the road had ordered arms, and were in the act of shouldering them when they received the volley from the Ninety-Second.' In Kempt's brigade, the Twenty-Eighth was moved up to the hedge and 'found a French column attempting to deploy at probably thirty or forty yards on the other side. We then poured in our fire, sprang over the hedge, and charged.'

The battle was in the balance. So strong and so determined were the French that 4,000 British infantry, veterans though they were, could not withstand them for ever. The deadlock was broken by the British heavy cavalry. They had been lying dismounted beside their horses during the bombardment when they were summoned to mount and advance. The Household brigade, led by Lord Uxbridge, charged obliquely across the Brussels road, parting in the centre to pass La Haye Sainte. The flank of the French infantry was covered on this side by cavalry. 'The brigade and the cuirassiers came to the shock like two walls, in the most perfect lines. A short struggle enabled us to break through them, notwithstanding the great disadvantage arising from our swords which were full six inches shorter than those of the cuirassiers. Having once penetrated their line, we rode over everything opposed to us.'

On the left, the Union brigade, regiments of English, Scottish and Irish dragoons, had no cavalry against them. They rode straight into the massed and unsuspecting infantry. 'Our colonel shouted out: "Now then, Scots Greys, Charge!" and waving his sword in the air he rode straight at the hedges in front, which he took in grand style. At once a great cheer rose from our ranks and we waved our swords and followed him. I drove my spurs into my brave old Rattler and we were off like the wind. It was a grand sight to see the long line of grey horses dashing along with manes flowing and heads down, tearing the turf about them as they went. The men in their red coats and tall bearskins were cheering wildly and the trumpets were sounding the charge. We heard the pipes of the Ninety-Second playing in the smoke, and I plainly saw my old friend Pipe Major Cameron standing apart on a hillock coolly playing "Hey Johnny Cope, are ye waulking yet?" in all the din. All of us were greatly excited and began crying out, "Hurrah, Ninety-Second! Scotland for ever!" Many of the Highlanders grasped our stirrups, and in the fiercest excitement dashed with us into the fight.' A sergeant of the Gordons wrote that, 'it was fearful to see the carnage that took place. The dragoons were lopping off heads at every stroke, while the French were calling for quarter. We were also among them busy with the bayonet and what the cavalry did not execute we completed.'

Sergeant Ewart of the Greys captured the eagle of the French 45me regiment and Captain Kennedy Clark of the Royals took that of the 105me. 'I did not see the eagle until we had been probably five or six minutes engaged. When I first saw it, it was perhaps about forty yards to my left and a little in my front. I gave the order to my squadron, "Right shoulders forward; Attack the Colour", leading direct on the point myself. On reaching it, I ran my sword into the officer's right side a little above the hip joint. He was a little on my left side, and he fell to that side with the eagle across my horse's head. I tried to catch it with my left hand, but could only touch the fringe of the flag, and it would probably have fallen to the ground, had it not been prevented by the neck of Corporal Styles' horse, who came up close on my left at the instant and against which it fell. On running the officer through the body I called out twice together, "Secure the colour, secure the colour, it belongs to me." On taking up the eagle, I endeavoured to break the eagle from off the pole with the intention of putting it into the breast of my coat; but I could not break it. Corporal Styles said, "Pray, sir, do not break it," on which I replied, "Very well, carry it to the rear, as fast as you can, it belongs to me."' An officer of the Gordons saw 'one of the Scots Grey, who either broke or lost his sword in an attack with one of the cuirassiers, obliged to retreat along the line pursued by his assailant and when enabled to gain some distance from him, secure a sword and return to the attack, cutting down his pursuer.'

The cavalry had broken up D'Erlon's attack but, since six of the seven regiments taking part had not been involved in a cavalry melée since the turn of the century, they had not the experience to stop in time to avoid disaster. Colonel Hamilton of the Scots Greys rode up to a group of his regiment 'crying, "Charge! Charge the guns!" and went off like the wind up the hill, towards the terrible battery that had made such deadly work among the infantry. It was the last we saw of him, poor fellow. His body was found the next morning with both his arms cut off. Then we got among the gunners, and we had our revenge. Such slaughtering! We sabred the gunners, lamed the horses and cut the traces and harness. I can yet hear the Frenchmen crying *"Diable!"* when I struck at them, and the long drawn out hiss through their teeth as my sword went home.'

An aide-de-camp who rode with the Union brigade, wrote 'The enemy fled as a flock of sheep across the valley, quite at our mercy. In fact, our men were *out of hand*. The general of the brigade, his staff and every officer within hearing exerted themselves to the utmost to re-form the men; but the helplessness of the enemy offered too great a temptation to the dragoons, and our efforts were abortive. It was evident that the enemy's reserves of cavalry would soon take advantage of our disorder. If we could have formed a hundred men we could have made a respectable retreat, and saved many; but we could effect no formation, and were as helpless against their attack as their infantry had been against ours. Everyone saw what must happen. Those whose horses were best, or least blown, got away.

'You can imagine my astonishment when down below, on the very ground we had crossed, appeared at full gallop a couple of regiments of cuirassiers on the right, and away to the left a regiment of lancers. I shall never forget the sight. The cuirassiers, in their sparkling steel breastplates and helmets, mounted on strong black horses, with great blue rugs across the croups, were galloping towards me, tearing up the earth as they went, the trumpets blowing wild notes. Around me there was one continuous noise of clashing arms, shouting of men, neighing and moaning of horses. What were we to do? There being no officers about, we saw nothing for it but to go straight at them and trust to Providence to get through. There were half-a-dozen of us Greys and about a dozen of the Royals and Enniskillens on the ridge. We all shouted, "Come on lads, that's the road home!" and, dashing our spurs into our horses' sides, set off straight for the lancers. The crash when we met was terrible; the horses began to rear and bite and neigh loudly, and then some of our men got down among their feet, and I saw them trying to ward off lances with their hands. "Stick together, lads!" we cried, and went at it with a will, slashing about us right and left over our horses' necks. The ground was very soft and our horses could hardly drag their feet out of the clay. Here I again came to the ground for a lancer finished my new mount, and I thought I was done for. It was just then that I caught sight of a squadron of British dragoons making straight for us. The Frenchmen at that instant seemed to give way, and in a moment we were safe. The dragoons, they were men of our 16th Light dragoons, gave us a cheer and rode on after the lancers.'

D'Erlon's attack had been broken just as it seemed to be breaking through to Mont St Jean. It had suffered shattering casualties and three of its four divisions* had been dispersed. Beside La Haye Sainte, 'the ground was literally covered with French killed and wounded, even to the astonishment of my oldest soldiers,

* The fourth division was on the extreme right and took Smohain. It was held by the Nassauers and retreated when the other divisions fell back.

49

who said they had never witnessed such a sight. The French wounded were calling out "*Vive l'Empereur*," and I saw a poor fellow, lying with both legs shattered, trying to destroy himself with his own sword, which I ordered my servant to take from him.' At least 2,000 prisoners were taken and more than twenty guns in the great battery were disabled. To set against that the Household and Union brigades were wrecked. More than half their horses and a third of their men were lost, due largely to Lord Uxbridge, whose tactical ability did not match his superb sense of timing. 'I committed a great mistake in having myself led the attack. The *carrière* once begun, the leader is no better placed than any other man; whereas, if I had placed myself at the head of the second line, there is no saying what great advantages might have accrued from it.' For the rest of the day Wellington was without a usable force of heavy cavalry.

As soon as D'Erlon could rally some of his battalions, he renewed the attack on Picton's division but, now reinforced with Lambert's brigade, they drove the French back easily. The French were badly shaken and needed an hour or two before they were ready to press their attack as they had done on the first occasion.

'Between three and four we were tolerably quiet, except for a thunderous cannonade. The enemy had, by that time, got the range so accurately that every shot brought a ticket for somebody's head. An occasional gun, far to our left, marked the approach of the Prussians.' Wellington had expected that his allies would be in action early in the afternoon. Their cavalry had been seen at eleven o'clock in the morning. Blücher was doing his best. Despite the delay inevitable from Gneisenau's decision to send forward the corps furthest from Waterloo and the fortuitous delay due to a fire breaking out in the main street of Wavre as Bülow's corps marched through, the two leading brigades were at Chapelle St Lambert, less than five miles from the edges of the battlefield, at noon. There they halted. In front of them was a muddy valley through which the Lasne stream flowed. To individuals it was more of a nuisance than an obstruction but it would have been awkward to have been astride the obstacle when counter-attacked. Blücher, as always, was for advancing regardless of the danger. Gneisenau, as always, was for caution*. He wanted to wait until the rest of Bülow's corps, delayed by the fire in Wavre, had come up. The Prussian head-quarters settled down to one of its customary wrangles. This time it took only two hours to persuade Gneisenau. The advance restarted at two. Getting the artillery across the Lasne was a herculean task for men who had already tramped ten miles over the ankles in mud. The gun teams could not move the guns. Infantry had to be put on the drag ropes to haul the 6 pounders, each weighing more than 2,000 lbs on their carriages through the stream or over the narrow bridge. Blücher was all the time with them, cheering them on,

---

* In justice to Gneisenau it must be added that when, on the afternoon of that day he received a plea from the commander of the Prussian rearguard who was in danger of being overwhelmed by Grouchy, he replied, 'Let him defend himself as best he may. It does not matter if he is crushed if we are successful here.'

begging for an extra effort, 'It must be done! I have given my word to my comrade Wellington. You would not have me break my word?' Fortunately their crossing of the valley was unopposed. By half past four, the head of the Prussian infantry was in order along the western edge of the Paris wood, ready to advance on Placenoit.

Between the French attacks there was a chance to collect some of the wounded. They lay everywhere and there had not been time or men to carry many of them back to the surgeons. Captain Napier of the Artillery had 'several wounds about the head, body and hands, and his thigh broken in two places.' Six years later it was written of him that 'He is still on crutches, has had upwards of fifty pieces of bone extracted from his thigh, two large pieces of shell, and there is supposed to be a ball now in the limb, and another in the right shoulder. He has had part of his skull taken away, a severe wound in the cheek, his right leg fractured in two places, three fingers of the right hand destroyed, and a wound in the left elbow; his sword saved the other leg, the steel scabbard of which was so beat in that the sword could not be sheathed.' Napier was one of the lucky ones who could be removed. Sergeant Morris saw an officer of the Thirtieth, 'lying with both legs broke, just below the knees, by a cannon ball. He requested me to cut off his legs, but I had not the heart to do it, though it would have been an act of mercy; for when I saw him next morning, he was in the same situation, having had no assistance.' McCulloch of the Rifles had had one of his arms shattered by seven sabre wounds in 1810. Now a ball 'had dreadfully broken the elbow of the sound arm, and had passed right through the fleshy part of his back.' The regimental surgeon immediately amputated his arm. 'When dressed, he lay upon the stump as this was less painful than the old exfoliating wound, and on his back he could not lie. He recovered, but was never afterwards able to feed himself or put on his hat.'

George Simmons had been a medical student before he got a commission. He was hit in the back while repelling D'Erlon's first attack. He was carried back to a farm house where, 'Sergeant Fairfoot, who had been wounded through the arm and through the hand, supported me while the surgeon cut into the breast and dislodged the ball, which being flat and terribly jagged required some time. The sergeant then went in search of a horse and returned with a Frenchman's and tried to put me on it, but I fainted and was carried back to my straw. When I came to myself, I heard the surgeons say, "What is the use of torturing him? He cannot live the night. He is better where he is than to die on horseback." But Fairfoot was very anxious to get me away as it was thought that the place we were in would shortly be between the fire of the parties and under such circumstances we should either be shot or burned. He got another horse and he and a Lifeguardsman put me on. I was held by the legs. I had to ride twelve miles. The motion of the horse made the blood pump out, and the bones cut the flesh to a jelly.'

The allied line, though it had suffered severely, was unbroken and Wellington busied himself bringing up units from the reserve on his right to fill gaps caused by casualties and the reinforcement of Hougoumont. Members of his staff constantly trained their telescopes to the left hoping for some sign of the Prussians. There was nothing but occasional groups of horsemen who bickered with the French cavalry guarding that flank.

Time was running out for Napoleon. Since 1 pm he had known that strong Prussian forces were threatening his left. The risk was growing that he would be crushed between the British and Prussian armies. His only hope was to break Wellington's line and pursue the allied army with his cavalry, leaving his infantry free to deal with Blücher. The problem of how to break Wellington's line remained. D'Erlon's corps was temporarily incapable of mounting a major attack. Reille's divisions were involved at Hougoumont. Lobau's corps was watching the Prussians. The only available infantry was the Guard, 12,000 incomparable soldiers who had never been beaten in battle. The Emperor could not bring himself to release them. He had given tactical control of the battle to Ney and, while Napoleon havered, Ney acted. Since there was no infantry, the cavalry would have to be used.

If Napoleon disapproved of Ney's decision to send the cavalry against the ridge, he did not lift a finger to restrain him. It is possible that he approved. He had said on the previous day, 'I shall bombard them with the great weight of my artillery, I shall charge them with my cavalry, so that they show themselves and, when I am quite sure where the English troops are, I shall march straight at them with my Guard.' There was a successful precedent for the use of massed cavalry in this way. At Borodino in 1812 Napoleon himself had used a mass of horsemen to capture the great Russian redoubt. If Russian infantry behind fortifications could be defeated in this way, why should not the same recipe serve for redcoats on an open ridge?

Ney intended nothing so grandiose. He started with the idea of an optimistic probing operation and, with a combination of hasty temper and the Emperor's encouragement, allowed it to grow into a vast, hopeless holocaust.

After the repulse of D'Erlon's second attack, Wellington had ridden along his line and ordered the battalions to fall back about a hundred yards so that the troops could shelter in the folds of the ground from the continuing bombardment. When they had made this short withdrawal the men were ordered to lie down in their ranks. From the French position they were invisible. Only the skirmishers and the guns could be seen on the ridge but watchers near La Belle Alliance could see a steady stream of wounded and stragglers making their way back to the Forest of Soignes. To Ney it seemed possible that Wellington had decided to retreat. Exploiting such a situation was the only chance the French had of the quick breakthrough they needed so badly. The chance, if it was a chance, must be exploited quickly. It was worth risking a single brigade even if the chance was a thin one. An aide-de-camp went to General Farine and ordered him to lead his two regiments of cuirassiers across the valley. Farine gave the order and the horsemen trotted forward. Immediately General Delort, commanding that cavalry division, galloped up and halted them. He was piqued at orders going directly to his subordinate. Troops under his command could, he asserted, only be employed on orders from Count Milhaud, who commanded 4th Cavalry Corps. It was the same kind of petty bickering which had kept D'Erlon's corps out of action two days earlier. Once again Ney lost his temper. The opportunity, if it was an opportunity, was slipping away. He ordered the whole of Milhaud's corps, eight cuirassier regiments, to advance. Milhaud queried his orders. It was, he said, suicide to use cavalry against unbroken, and notably staunch, infantry. Ney angrily over-ruled him. '*En avant*' he shouted, 'France depends upon this charge!' Milhaud could only obey but he asked Lefebvre-Desnoëttes, commanding the light cavalry of the Guard to support him. As the columns of cuirassiers trotted down the forward slope, the 'red' lancers and the *chasseurs à cheval* wheeled into position behind them. As the heavy horsemen inclined somewhat to their left to climb the slope between Hougoumont and La Haye Sainte, attacking in column of squadrons, echelloned from their left, the light cavalry came up on their right. 4,000 magnificent cavalry trotted steadily up the hill.

On the allied side the advance of this great mass of horsemen was welcomed with astonishment and relief. Astonishment that the French should hazard their cavalry in so hopeless a venture; relief that the French guns would have to stop playing on the allied position while the cavalry surged round it. The infantry was ordered to stand up and form square, the gunners were told to fire until the last moment and then dash for safety in the nearest square, bowling with them one wheel from each gun. The limbers and waggons were sent away to the rear. 'Bring the horses away,' said the Duke, 'never mind the guns.'

Up came the French. An ensign in the Guards thought that 'No man present could have forgotten in after life the awful grandeur of that charge. You perceived at a distance what appeared to be an overwhelming, long moving line, which, ever advancing, glittered like a stormy wave of the sea when it catches the sunlight. On came the mounted host until they got near enough, while the very earth seemed to vibrate beneath their thundering tramp. One might suppose that nothing could have resisted the shock of the terrible moving mass. Just before this charge the Duke entered by one of the angles of the square, accompanied by only one aide-de-camp. As far as I could judge, he appeared perfectly composed; but looked very thoughtful and pale. The word of command "Prepare to receive cavalry" had been given, every man in the front ranks knelt, and a wall bristling with steel, held by steady hands, presented itself to the infuriated cuirassiers.'

Before the horsemen could come within reach of the squares, they had to run the gauntlet of the guns. 'On they came in compact squadrons, one behind the other, so that those in the rear were still below the brow when the head of the column was at sixty or seventy yards from our guns. Their pace was a slow but steady trot and they moved in profound silence. I allowed them to advance unmolested until the head of the column might have been about fifty or sixty yards from us, and then gave the word "Fire!" The effect was terrible. Nearly the whole leading rank fell at once; and the round shot penetrating the column carried confusion throughout its length. The ground became almost impassable. Those who pushed forward over the heaps of carcasses gained but a few paces in advance, there to fall in their turn and add to the difficulties of those succeeding them. The discharge of every gun was followed by a fall of men like that of grass before a mower's scythe.'

The gunners could not alone stem this tide of cavalry. Hundreds of horsemen rode up to the squares of the infantry. 'Their appearance, as an enemy, was certainly enough to inspire a feeling of dread – none of them under six feet; defended by steel helmets and breastplates, made pigeon-breasted to throw off the balls. They came up rapidly, until within about ten or twelve paces of the square, when our rear ranks* poured into them a well-directed fire, which put them in confusion; as they retired the two front ranks, kneeling, then discharged their pieces at them. Some of the cuirassiers fell wounded, and several were killed: those of them that were dismounted by the death of their horses, immediately unclasped their armour to facilitate their escape.'

Napoleon's only comment on the charge of Milhaud's cuirassiers was that it was an hour too early, though he had made no suggestion as to how the hour should have been used and he could not afford to waste a minute. If he thought Ney had made one of the mistakes for which his headstrong nature had made him notorious, he made no effort to restrain him. Soult angrily remarked, 'Ney has compromised us as he did at Jena.' Napoleon replied, 'Since it has happened we must support him.' He ordered forward Kellermann's cavalry corps and the heavy cavalry of the Guard. If Ney had erred by committing Milhaud's twenty-four squadrons of cuirassiers, Napoleon compounded the error on the grandest scale by supporting him with thirty-seven squadrons, Horse Grenadiers, dragoons, cuirassiers and carabineers, the finest cavalry in the world.

This new wave of cavalry fared no better than their predecessors. Their task was more difficult, for the ground was already encumbered by the bodies of the cuirassiers and their horses. They came on with a bravery and discipline which earned them the admiration of their enemies. This time they were preceded by 'a cloud of skirmishers, who galled us terribly by a fire of carbines and pistols at scarcely forty yards from our front. We were obliged to stand with

---

* The squares were formed in four ranks at each face. Thus the two rear ranks fired in the first volley and the two front ranks remained loaded (in case of emergencies) while the rear ranks re-loaded. In most of the infantry this would take 15-20 seconds. This account is by a Rifleman of the Ninety-Fifth and with the Baker Rifle the difficulty of ramming the ball down the rifled barrel would mean that reloading could not be completed in less than half a minute.

port-fires lighted, so that it was not without a little difficulty that I succeeded in restraining the gunners from firing, for they grew impatient. Seeing some exertion beyond words necessary for this purpose, I leaped my horse up the little bank and began a promenade (by no means agreeable) up and down our front, without even drawing my sword, though the skirmishers were within speaking distance of me. This quieted my men. The column now once more mounted the plateau, and these popping gentry wheeled off right and left to clear the ground for their charge. The spectacle was imposing, and if ever the word sublime was appropriately applied, it might surely be to it. None of your furious galloping charge was this, but a deliberate advance at a deliberate pace, as of men resolved to carry their point. They moved in profound silence, and the only sound that could be heard from them was the low thunderlike reverberations of the ground below the simultaneous tread of so many horses. On our part was equal deliberation. Every man stood steadily at his post, the guns ready, loaded with round shot first and a case [shot] over it; the tubes were in the vents; the port-fires glared and spluttered behind the wheels.'

Again the guns blasted lanes through the columns; again the survivors struggled through to come face to face with the squares. 'They came within ten yards of us, and they found they could do no good with us; they fired with their carbines, and came to the right-about directly, and at that moment the man on my right hand was shot through the body, and the blood ran out of his belly and back like a pig stuck in the throat. He dropt on his side; I spoke to him; he just said, "Lewis, I am done!" and died directly. All this time we kept up a continual fire at the Imperial Guards as they retreated, but they often came to the right-about and fired; and as I was loading my rifle, one of their shots came and struck it, not two inches above my right hand, broke the stock and bent the barrel in such a manner that I could not get the ball down. Just at that moment, a nine-pounder shot came and cut a serjeant of our company in two; he was not above three file from me, so I threw down my rifle and went and took his, as it was not hurt at the time.'

'The charge of the French cavalry was gallantly executed; but our well-directed fire brought men and horses down, and ere long the utmost confusion arose in their ranks. The officers were exceedingly brave, and by their gestures and fearless bearing did all in their power to encourage their men to form again and renew the attack. The Duke sat unmoved, mounted on a favourite charger. I recollect his asking Colonel Stanhope what o'clock it was, upon which Stanhope took out his watch and said it was twenty minutes past four. The Duke replied, "The battle is mine; and if the Prussians arrive soon, there will be an end of the war."'

When this second wave of cavalry had exhausted itself and was in confusion, the remnants of the Household Brigade were sent to drive them away. 'We galloped at the cuirassiers and fairly rode them down; when they were unhorsed, we cracked them like lobsters in their shells, and by the coming up of the cannon afterwards many of them were squeezed as flat as pancakes.' 'It was a fair fight, and the French were fairly beaten and driven off. I noticed one of the Life Guards, who was attacked by two cuirassiers at the same time. He bravely maintained the unequal conflict for a minute or two, when he disposed of one of them by a deadly thrust in the throat. His combat with the other lasted about five minutes, when the guardsman struck his opponent a slashing back-handed stroke, and sent his helmet some distance, with the head inside it. The horse galloped away with the headless rider, sitting erect in the saddle, the blood spouting out of the arteries like so many fountains.'

Again and again the French renewed these cavalry attacks. 'I can compare it to nothing better than a heavy surf breaking on a coast beset with isolated rocks, against which the mountainous wave dashes with furious uproar, breaks, divides, and runs, hissing and boiling, far beyond up the adjacent beach. In a moment such shoals of lancers and others came sweeping down the slope that the whole interval between the lines was covered with them, a mixed and various multitude, all scattered and riding in different directions. Several minutes elapsed ere they succeeded in quitting the plateau, during which our fire was incessant, and the consequent carnage frightful, for each gun was loaded with a round and case shot; all of which, from the shortness of the distance *must* have taken effect. Many, instead of seeking safety in retreat, wisely dashed through the intervals between our guns and made their way round our rear; but the greater part, rendered desperate at finding themselves held in front of the battery, actually fought their way through their own ranks, and in the struggle we saw blows exchanged on all sides.'

★ ★ ★

After four separate attempts to sweep the ridge clear with cavalry alone, it occurred to Ney that some infantry could be spared from Reille's corps. One and a half divisions were formed beside the Hougoumont wood and Ney supported them with the wrecks of the heavy cavalry, mostly the carabineers who had been less engaged than the other brigades. The hope was that the horsemen would clear the gunners away from their pieces so that the 6,000 infantrymen could reach the crest in comparative safety. The attack was unfortunate since it aimed at a part of the position which Wellington had just reinforced with two brigades, one of the Legion, one of Hanoverians. It was also mistimed and, to the men struggling up the slope deeply poached by successive cavalry charges, the fact that some allied batteries had been overrun by the carabineers was scarcely apparent. General Foy, who led one of the brigades of his division up the hill, had his left flank on the hedge bordering the Hougoumont estate. In front he spread out a full battalion as skirmishers. 'Before coming up to the English we were met with a lively fire of grape and musketry. It was the hail of death. The enemy squares had their front ranks kneeling and showed us a hedge of bayonets. The division on my right broke first and their flight communicated itself to my columns. At that moment I was wounded. A ball entered the top of my right thigh and travelled down it from top to bottom without touching the bone. At the time I thought it no more than a bruise and did not go to the rear. Everyone was running for it; I re-formed the remnants of my division in the dip near Hougoumont wood. We were not followed.'

At long last, all the French cavalry who were still alive and mounted were swept off the ridge and there began, for the Allies, the grimmest part of the battle. By this time men were drawing deep on their stores of courage. Casualties were growing and every man was sickened by the carnage around him. Many, with or without an excuse, made their way to the rear. It was a time when only highly disciplined troops could hope to endure. An astonishing number did so. Even many of the untried German troops stood their ground like veterans. It was, wrote a British officer, 'a most trying time for the young Hanoverian levies; nevertheless they stood firm. I have since heard their own officers say that during the whole day they never evinced any disposition to give way but that, at first, when openings were made in their squares by the enemy's artillery, there was some hesitation before they were filled up, because the men fancied that the shot would always strike at the same spot; however, when the officers explained to them the absurdity of this notion, they readily closed the breach.' A gunner officer stationed next to a battalion of Brunswickers saw that 'the shot was every moment making great gaps in their squares, which the officers and sergeants were actively engaged in filling up by pushing their men together, and sometimes thumping them ere they could make them move. These were the very boys whom I had but yesterday seen throwing away their arms and fleeing panic-stricken from the very sound of our horses' hooves. Today they fled not bodily to be sure, but spiritually, for their senses seemed to have left them. They stood there with recovered arms, like so many logs. Every moment I feared they would flee; but their officers and sergeants behaved nobly, not only keeping them together, but managing to keep the square closed up in spite of the carnage made amongst them.'

A Rifleman admitted that, 'seeing we had lost so many men and all our commanding officers, my heart began to fail,' but after the cavalry had retreated and they were waiting in square in case the attack should be renewed, 'the Duke of Wellington came up to us in all the fire and saw we had lost all our officers. He, himself, gave the word of command; the words he said to our regiment were this: "Ninety-Fifth, unfix your swords, left face and extend yourselves once more. We shall soon have them over the hill." Then he rode away on our right, and how he escaped being shot God alone knows, for all that time the shot was flying like hailstones.' The Riflemen were fortunate in being able to fight in extended order except when the French cavalry actually charged. Their redcoated comrades had to stand shoulder to shoulder four deep in squares, a wonderful target for a gunner who had had hours to establish the range. 'Our square,' wrote a guardsman, was a perfect hospital, being full of dead, dying and mutilated soldiers . Inside we were nearly suffocated by the smoke and smell of burned cartridges. It was impossible to move a yard without treading on a wounded comrade or upon the bodies of the dead; and the loud cries of the wounded and dying were most appalling.'

Generals saw their commands shrinking to nothing. When Wellington rode up to Halkett's brigade, he said 'in his calm voice, "Well, Halkett, how do you get on?" The general replied, "My lord, we are dreadfully cut up; can you not relieve us for a little while?" "Impossible," said the Duke. "Very well, my lord," said the general, "we'll stand till the last man falls."' To another similar request Wellington sent to tell the commander, 'He and I, and every other Englishman on the field must stand and die on the spot which we occupy.'

When it was certain that the cavalry attacks had failed, Napoleon told Ney to take La Haye Sainte at all costs. The marshal, who had already had three horses shot under him, caught up the only formed troops immediately available and advanced. His force consisted of the weakened battalions of 13me Léger and the sapper company of D'Erlon's corps. With these few, perhaps a thousand men, he achieved what he had previously failed to do with sixteen times as many.

Good luck was on his side if at no other time in the campaign. The garrison was almost without ammunition. Twice the commander, Major Lewis Baring, had sent urgent requests for a fresh supply but none was forthcoming.* When Ney and 13me Léger, with some squadrons of cuirassiers covering their right, marched up to the farm there were only three or four rounds a man in the Light Infantry of the King's German Legion who held it. While this small supply lasted the French were kept at a distance but soon only straggling shots opposed them. Then, wrote Baring, 'the enemy, who soon observed our wants, boldly broke down one of the doors. However, as only a few men could come in at a time, these were instantly bayonetted, and the rest hesitated to follow. They now mounted the roof and walls from which my unfortunate men were certain marks. At the same time they pressed in through the open barn which could no longer be defended. Inexpressibly painful as the decision was to me, I gave the order to retire through the house into the garden. Fearing the bad impression which retiring would make upon the men, and wishing to see whether it was possible still to hold any part of the place, I left to three officers the honour of being the last.' One of these officers, Lieutenant Graeme, wrote, 'We had all to pass through a narrow passage. Ensign Frank of our company called to me,

* The reason for the failure of supply has never been clearly explained. The most probable reason is that the Light Battalion KGL was equipped with a rifle other than the Baker and that the only cart containing a reserve was overturned on the Brussels road.

"Take care", but I was too busy stopping the men and answered, "Never mind, let the blackguard fire." He was about five yards off, and levelling his piece at me, when Frank stabbed him in the mouth and out through the neck; he fell immediately. But now they rushed in. Frank got two shots and ran into a room where he lay behind a bed all the time they had possession of the house. An officer and four men came in first; the officer got me by the collar, and said to his men, "*C'est ce coquin.*" Immediately they had their bayonets down and made a dead stick at me which I parried with my sword, the officer always running about and then coming to me again and shaking me by the collar; but they all looked so frightened and pale as ashes. I thought, "You shan't keep me", and I bolted through the lobby. They fired two shots after me, and cried out "*Coquin*" but they did not follow me. I rejoined the remnant of the regiment.'

In an attempt to save La Haye Sainte, the Prince of Orange ordered the 5th Line Battalion KGL to deploy and advance. Colonel Ompteda respectfully asked, 'Would it not be advisable to advance in square, and not form line till close to the enemy's infantry?' The Prince, who was only twenty-three, and whose ardour and courage outran his judgment, angrily insisted that his orders be obeyed. The 5th went forward in line and were cut to pieces by the cuirassiers as were the 8th KGL whom the Prince sent in support of the 5th. The French managed to seize the colour of the 8th and sent it back in triumph to the Emperor.

The disaster to the two German battalions was not the only ill effect of the loss of La Haye Sainte. Ney brought forward every man of D'Erlon's corps who could be rushed to the spot, but there were only enough to form a thick chain of skirmishers. They reached the straggling hedge which marked the crest of the ridge but they could get no further. A battery of horse artillery was rushed to the farm and two guns opened on Kempt's brigade to the east of the main road. The range was less than three hundred yards but against them were the Rifles whose weapons could deal with them at that range. 'We destroyed all their artillerymen before they could give us a second round.' It was to the west of the farm that the cannonade was heaviest with the other four guns firing into the flanks of the squares on the crest. 'There was no variety for us, but one continued blaze of musketry. The smoke hung so thickly that, although no more than eighty yards asunder, we could only distinguish each other by the flash of the pieces.' Lewis Baring, having rallied his garrison on the ridge above the farm, was riding a dragoon horse, 'the third I had had in the course of the day, in front of whose saddle were large pistol holsters and a cloak, and the firing was so sharp that four balls entered here, and another the saddle, just as I had alighted to replace my hat which had been knocked off by a sixth ball.'

There was, at this time, a gaping hole in Wellington's centre. The KGL brigade stood firm but was reduced to less than the strength of a battalion. From their right Kielmansegge's Hanoverians were withdrawn behind the farm of Mont St Jean. In Halkett's brigade, next on the right, the colours of the regiments were sent to the rear for safety. So exposed were the brigade that Halkett ordered them to fall back about a hundred yards. During this move a panic developed in some of the battalions. An officer of the Thirtieth wrote that 'Though suffering sadly, and disordered by our poor wounded fellows clinging to their comrades thinking they were being abandoned, our little square retained its formation until a body of men (British) rushed in among us, turned us into a mere mob, and created a scene of frightful confusion. Fortunately the enemy took no advantage of it. Nothing could be more gratifying than the conduct of our people at this disastrous period. While men and officers were jammed together and carried along by the pressure without, many of the latter, some cursing, others literally crying with rage and shame, were seizing the soldiers and calling on them to halt, while these admirable fellows, good-humouredly laughing at their excitement, were struggling to get out of the *mêlée*, or exclaiming, "By God, I'll stop, sir, but I'm off my legs." I know nothing that remedied this terrible disorder but a shout which someone raised, and in which all joining the mass halted as if by a word of command. An officer was immediately desired by Major Chambers (who fell some minutes after) to take such men as he could get in addition to the light company, then reduced to fourteen rank and file, and push up the hill as far as he dare to cover the reformation. This was effected without difficulty, and all afterwards went right.'

Lord Uxbridge endeavoured to bring forward the brigade of Netherlands heavy cavalry but it refused to follow him. A regiment of Hanoverian hussars left the field in good order despite repeated orders to move forward. On the extreme left the French again drove the Nassauers out of Smohain. The situation was as serious as could be imagined but it had no effect on Wellington's habitual calm. The fall of La Haye Sainte caught him by surprise. It was the only major event of the battle which found him away from the critical point but when the news was brought him by Captain Shaw Kennedy, 'he received it with a degree of coolness and replied in an instant with such precision and energy as to prove the most complete self-possession. His Grace's reply to my representation was in the following words, or nearly so. "I shall order the Brunswick troops to the spot, and other troops besides; go and get all the German troops of the division to the spot that you can, and get all the guns you can find".'

If Wellington heard the news of the fall of La Haye Sainte with calm, Napoleon heard it with disinterest. Ney realised that he had not enough troops to exploit the breakthrough he had made and sent his ADC, Colonel Hèymes, to the Emperor to ask for some more infantry. 'Troops?' snorted Napoleon, 'Where do you expect me to find them? Do you think I can manufacture some?' He had fourteen battalions of the Guard in hand.

It was about six-thirty and Napoleon's attention was at last turned to his right. The Prussians, whom he had attempted to ignore, had at last erupted. At about five o'clock, when two brigades of Bülow's corps had struggled across the

Lasne valley, Gneisenau's caution could no longer restrain Blücher's ardour.* He ordered Bülow to advance on Placenoit. Lobau's two divisions and the light cavalry of Subervie and Domon checked them but more Prussians, the rest of Bülow's corps and the head of Pirch's, were close behind. Napoleon sent the Tirailleurs and Voltigeurs of the Young Guard to support Lobau. It was not enough. Irresistably Bülow's men forced their way into Placenoit. The Prussian artillery, stationed either side of the village and bombarding its retreating defenders, was sending its roundshot bounding and ricochetting on to the road south of La Belle Alliance, two thousand yards away. Some were pitching into the area of Napoleon's command post. The Emperor was forced to exert himself. All afternoon he had been gripped by a dreadful lethargy, content to leave control to Ney of whose limitations he was only too well aware. He sent two battalions of the Old Guard against the Prussians, supported by some of the guns from the great battery which had been bombarding Wellington's left. These two battalions, 1/2nd Chasseurs and 2/2nd Grenadiers, amounted to little more than a thousand bayonets but, just at the time that Ney's request for help reached the Emperor, they marched against Placenoit. It is little wonder that Napoleon could not wrench his attention from his right. Few sights in military history can have equalled the feat of these two magnificent battalions. Advancing to the beat of their drums they attacked Placenoit in two close columns, each with a front of thirty files. The Prussians fought stubbornly but they were forced steadily back. They could not withstand the superb discipline and implacable self-confidence of the French. Twenty minutes after they reached the first buildings of the village, Placenoit was re-captured. Not one of the guardsmen had fired a shot. It was seven o'clock.

⋆ * ⋆

Napoleon's pre-occupation with his right flank gave Wellington an hour's breathing space in which to re-construct his centre. The Brunswickers were brought up. Faced with an overwhelming fire they flinched and began to withdraw. Wellington and his staff rallied them. Again they came into line. Again they started to break and were brought up by the Duke who lost two of his ADCs at this time. The third time they stayed put and fought like old soldiers until the end of the day. Chassée's Netherlands division came up from the right rear and every British battalion that could be spared was brought across to fill up the line. The extreme right, so long Wellington's main preoccupation, was left in the charge of a single light infantry battalion. A battalion of First Guards advanced eastwards across the ridge to drive back Ney's skirmishers pushing out from La Haye Sainte. The Duke had merely

* Brigades in the Prussian army were equivalent in numbers to divisions in the armies of Napoleon and Wellington.

remarked to their colonel, 'Drive those fellows away,' and the Guards had completed their operation with as much steadiness as the Old Guard across the valley. Then they fell back to their old post above Hougoumont. All the time the rain of shell and roundshot continued to fall on the allied line. 'Hard pounding this, gentlemen,' said the Duke. 'Let us see who can pound the longest.'

Beyond the British left, a third Prussian corps was moving on Ohain. Its commander, Ziethen, had orders to keep in touch with Blücher's main body. Misled by the stream of wounded and stragglers pouring to the rear, one of his aides who had ridden ahead of the troops reported that Wellington's army was in full retreat. Ziethen swung his corps to the south, towards Bülow. Fortunately Wellington had sent Müffling to his flank to co-ordinate the junction of the two armies. 'General Ziethen's advanced guard, which I was expecting with the utmost impatience, suddenly turned round, and disappeared from the height. I galloped after them and saw them in full retreat.' Fortunately, Müffling soon overtook Ziethen himself and, remembering the gap that had been in the allied centre when he had left it, told him, 'The battle is lost if the 1st Corps does not go to the Duke's rescue!' Ziethen instantly turned about and marched on Papelotte. It was unfortunate that his leading troops were too impetuous. Not only did they drive the French from Smohain, they attacked the Nassauers, whose uniform made them indistinguishable from their enemies, in flank and rear and drove them from Papelotte and La Haye, something the French had not succeeded in doing in five hours fighting. Prince Bernhardt, their commander, reported that he 'rallied them a quarter of a league from the field of battle.' Nevertheless, Wellington's left was now impregnable and he withdrew his light cavalry from there to bolster his centre.

At seven o'clock, with his right temporarily secure, Napoleon made up his mind to make his last throw. He led twelve battalions of the Guard down the hill from La Belle Alliance. An onlooker recalled, 'I saw the Emperor at that moment. He went past me followed by his staff. As he passed the Guard he called *"Qu'on me suive!"* and went on down the road under the fire of a hundred guns. A hundred and fifty bandsmen led the Guard. They played the triumphant marches of the Carrousel. Behind them, platoon after platoon, marched the Guard. Grape and roundshot strewed the road with dead and dying.'

To rouse his troops for a final effort, Napoleon sent officers along the line to announce that Grouchy had arrived to complete the victory. Colonel Levasseur 'set off at a gallop, waving my hat on the point of my sabre, dashing along the line crying, *"Vive l'empereur! Soldats! Voilà Grouchy!"* My shout was taken up by a thousand voices. The men, exalted, cried *"En avant! En avant! Vive l'Empereur!"'* At the time Grouchy was disputing the approaches to Wavre with the Prussian rearguard. 'He might,' remarked Ney, 'have as usefully been a hundred miles away.'

For a short, crucial time the deception served its purpose. Men rejoined their battalions. The wounded staggered to their feet to join in a final effort. Those who could no longer stand propped themselves on their elbows to cheer their comrades forward. A veteran of Marengo, both legs shattered, sat with his back to the cutting on the road shouting, 'Never mind about me, comrades. *En avant! Vive l'Empereur!*' The frenetic enthusiam of Napoleon's last army swelled to its final astonishing climax.

At the foot of the slope Napoleon allowed himself to be dissuaded from leading the Guard in the culminating attack. He, however, supervised the tactical dispositions. They were disastrous. Five battalions, scarcely 4,000 men, of the Middle Guard formed the first wave. The Old Guard were to advance in second line. The remaining Middle Guard battalion, 2/3rd Grenadiers, stayed in the valley as a firm base. The five leading battalions advanced individually in columns*. Nothing more vicious could be contrived. A battalion column had neither the momentum of a brigade column nor the relative invulnerability of an advance in line. It was making the worst of both worlds. Further to decrease their chances the columns advanced in a ragged arrowhead so that their attacks came in succession and not as a single heavy blow. By accident or design, their advance led not to the allied centre, where they could have been supported by the fire from La Haye Sainte, but further to their left where they could be enfiladed by fire from Hougoumont. They advanced straight at the two British brigades most able to withstand them. Nevertheless, they were magnificent troops, full of self-confidence. Two horse guns advanced in the interval between each battalion. A general led each column and, in front of all, rode Ney, now on his fifth charger.

While this was preparing, Wellington rode along the threatened portion of his line in a tumult of French gun fire. The Brunswickers he exhorted to steadiness in 'an electrifying voice'. Seeing a gunner subaltern he told to him urge his battery commander to 'keep a look to his left for the French will soon be with him.' Where some of the British infantry were restive, longing to attack, he called, 'Wait a little longer, my lads. You shall have at them presently.' As he reached each unit there was a call of '"Silence – stand to your front – here's the Duke." As he crossed the rear face of our square, a shell fell amongst our grenadiers, and he checked his horse to see its effect. Some men were blown to pieces by the explosion, and he merely stirred the rein of his charger, apparently as little concerned at their fate as at his own danger. No leader ever possessed so fully the confidence of his soldiery.' At last he came to the 1st Brigade of Guards, reined up beside General Maitland, and 'desired me to form in line four files deep, his Grace expecting cavalry would take part in the affair. The formation of the brigade was scarcely complete before the advance of the enemy became apparent.'

* One battalion advanced in square.

As the Middle Guard made its way laboriously up the slope, every allied gun still in action opened on it with round shot, grape and cannister. 'They were seen ascending our position in as correct an order as at a review. As they rose step by step before us and crossed the ridge their red epaulettes and cross belts put on over their blue great-coats gave them a gigantic appearance which was increased by their high hairy caps.' The leading battalions, the 1st and 2nd battalions of the 3rd Chasseurs*, seem to have coalesced. Their march led them directly to the position of Maitland's brigade, two battalions of the First Guards. Apart from the sweating, exhausted gunners on either flank of Maitland's men, the French could see no enemy to their front. The British Guards were, nevertheless, awaiting them, despite the storm of fire which the French batteries sent over the heads of the columns. 'There ran along this part of the position a cart road, on one side of which was a ditch and a bank under which the [British] brigade sheltered during the cannonade. Without the protection of this bank, every creature must have perished. The Emperor probably calculated on this effect, for suddenly the firing ceased, and as the smoke cleared away a most superb sight opened on us. A close column of Grenadiers† (about seventies in front) was seen ascending the rise at the *pas de charge* shouting *"Vive l'Empereur!"* They continued to advance to within fifty or sixty paces of our front, when the brigade was ordered to stand up. Whether it was from the sudden and unexpected appearance of a corps so near them, which must have seemed as starting out of the ground, or the tremendous fire we threw at them, *La Garde*, who had never before failed in an attack, *suddenly* stopped. In less than a minute above 300 were down. They now wavered, and several in the rear divisions began to draw out as if to deploy, whilst some of the men in the rear beginning to fire over the heads of those in front was so evident a proof of their confusion, that Lord Saltoun, holloed out, *"Now's the time, my boys."* Immediately the brigade sprang forward. *La Garde* turned and gave us little opportunity of trying the steel.'

The Guards went forward until their right was near the corner of the Hougoumont orchard. This put their left in the air and Colin Halkett, commanding the much reduced brigade next to them, pushed forward two battalions to cover them. What happened at this stage is very difficult to determine. 'From the heaviness of the atmosphere we could see but little of what was going on. The fog and smoke lay so heavy on the ground that we could only ascertain the approach of the enemy by the noise and clashing of arms which the French usually make in their advance to attack.' What seems certain is that Halkett's two battalions saw the two battalions on the French right (1/3rd & 4th Grenadiers) looming out of the smoke. They fired a volley which stopped

* They were, respectively, the second and third battalions from the French left.
† Although they were Chasseurs they were wearing what, in the British Guards, were known as grenadier caps, i.e. bearskins.

the French dead in their tracks. A moment later the two battalions, Thirty-Third and Sixty-Ninth, were ravaged by grapeshot, partly from the guns at La Haye Sainte, partly from the guns accompanying the Guard. The battalions broke and dashed back on the rest of Halkett's brigade, causing utter confusion. Wellington despatched a staff officer to 'See what's wrong there'. Major Kelly rode across and 'addressed Sir Colin Halkett, who at the instant received a wound in the face, the ball passing through his mouth. Colonel Elphinstone [Thirty-Third] then ran up and asked if I had any orders. I replied none beyond inquiring the cause of the confusion. He stated that they were much pressed, and the men exhausted. The command of the brigade had devolved upon him and he added, "What is to be done? What would you do?"' Kelly managed to restore order, despite the colonel, before the French were able to resume their advance which was 'usual with the French very noisy and evidently reluctant, the officers being in advance some yards cheering their men on. They, however, kept up a running confused fire, which we did not reply to until they reached nearly on a level with us, when a well-directed volley put them into confusion from which they did not appear to recover, but after a short interval of musketry on both sides, they turned about to a man and fled.' To add to the discomfiture of the Grenadiers, Chassé led Ditmer's Netherlands brigade on to their flank and his field battery shattered them with grape.

It was not only in Halkett's brigade that there was a dash to the rear on the British side. Advancing in pursuit of the 3rd Chasseurs, the First Guards saw the 4th Chasseurs emerge from the smoke further to the French left. Although this was only a single battalion column, it struck all the British observers as being a most formidable formation. It seems probable that many from the rear ranks of the 3rd regiment attached themselves to it when their own column broke. To face this new menace, General Maitland shouted 'Brigade, *Halt!*' but his voice was distorted and drowned by the firing and the clamour of the French. Some thought he had ordered square to be formed, some believed the order to have been to retire. Some obeyed the order and halted. There was momentary chaos. Then both battalions streamed back to the bank where they had awaited the Guard's first attack. Here the order was given, 'Halt, front, form up.' This time there was no mistake. The guardsmen formed again four-deep with as much regularity as if they had been drilling in Hyde Park and they were ready to meet the last French column.

Wellington, seeing the confusion in the Guards, ordered the 2nd Rifles to skirmish against the Chasseurs, but before they could deploy, the Fifty-Second, the regiment on the right of the Rifles, had begun to wheel forward. Their colonel, John Colborne, the finest battalion commander in the army, had seen the problem and moved to solve it on his own initiative. 'I ordered our left hand company to wheel to their left, and formed the remaining companies on that company. This movement placed us nearly parallel to the flank of the Imperial **65**

Guard. I ordered a strong company to extend to our front, and at this moment Sir Frederick Adam [commanding the brigade] rode up and asked me what I was going to do. I think I said, "to make that column feel our fire." Sir F. Adam then ordered me to move on, and that the Seventy-First should follow. He rode away to the Seventy-First. I instantly ordered the extended company, about a hundred men under Lieutenant Anderson, to advance as quickly as possible and to fire into the French at any distance. Then the Fifty-Second formed in lines of half companies, the rear line at ten paces distance from the front – after giving three cheers, followed the extended company, passed along the front of the brigade of [British] Guards. I observed that as soon as the French column was attacked by our skirmishers, a considerable part of the column halted and formed a line facing towards the Fifty-Second and opened a *very* sharp fire. We suffered severely from this fire. Two officers of the skirmishing company were wounded. The right wing of the battalion lost nearly one hundred and fifty men during the advance; the officer carrying the colour was killed.' As one of the regiment's subalterns wrote, 'When the regiment was nearly parallel to the enemy's flank, Sir John Colborne gave the word, "Charge! Charge!" It was answered by a long steady cheer and a hurried dash to the front. In the next ten seconds the Imperial Guard, broken in the wildest confusion, and scarcely firing a shot to cover its retreat, was rushing towards the hollow road in the rear of La Haye Sainte.'

Wellington, seeing that the time had come, ordered forward his light cavalry. They had been waiting behind the ridge unable to see what was going forward on the crest and forward slope. One of the brigadiers recalled that 'We every instant were expecting through the smoke to see the enemy appearing under our noses, for the smoke was literally so thick that we could not see ten yards off. But we at last began to find that the shots did not come so thick and I received orders to advance.' A troop commander noted in his diary that, 'on our moving forward we were ignorant of our success, and not knowing whether we were going to charge a successful column of the enemy or pursue a beaten one and on our brigade getting to a point from which we overlooked them, they were seen running away on every side in the greatest haste and confusion. Being in a column of half squadrons, we were ordered to form line, descend into the plain and pursue the enemy. We did not feel inclined to lose any time.'

★ ★ ★

The Imperial Guard had never failed before. In the valley, the French, including the Emperor, had seen through the smoke the solid, magnificent columns reach the crest of the hill; they had seen the British guns standing abandoned and red coats dashing in disorder to the rear. Then clouds of smoke had closed over the scene. A wounded general on his way to the rear had reported that all was going well. Suddenly out of the smoke reeled the wreck of five battalions, with the

Fifty-Second sweeping from west to east behind them, while over the ridge came Vandeleur's light dragoons and Vivian's hussars. They formed line on the crest and came pouring down the slope. The three battalions of the Old Guard who had been in support halted and formed square beside the main road. Behind this screen their comrades could rally. There was still an outside chance that the army could withdraw in good order, fit to fight again when re-united with Grouchy. It was a hopeless dream. The greatest strength of this French army became its weakness. It was an army which had worked itself up, had been prepared to make amazing sacrifices, to achieve victory. No men could have done more but they had failed. Their morale collapsed as soon as the cry was heard *La Garde recule!*' The rout started on the extreme right. Here they had been sustained by the false news that Grouchy had arrived only to find that the Prussians drove in on Smohain in overwhelming numbers while, in the right rear of the defenders, von Bülow's guns were pounding their line of retreat. It was here that the cry *'Nous sommes trahis'* was raised but it spread along the whole line like a bush-fire. In a few minutes the army disintegrated. All that remained at their posts facing Wellington's army were the battalions of the Old Guard, a single battered brigade of D'Erlon's corps and some of the Guard cavalry. Napoleon took shelter in one of the Guard squares, ordering the remaining formed troops to retreat steadily and take up a position behind the crest. Slowly but in perfect order the three Guard battalions fell back, halting every fifty yards to close their ranks and beat off attacks from British dragoons. One square disintegrated under the pounding of allied batteries at short range, but another, stationed near La Belle Alliance, took over its task. The brigade of the line, declining Ney's invitation to 'see how a Marshal of the Empire can die,' broke and was cut to pieces by the British hussars. Officers of all ranks strove passionately to rally their units. General Cambronne, commanding the 2/1st Chasseurs, replied to a summons to surrender with the brusque defiance, *'Merde!'* Almost immediately he was struck on the forehead by a spent ball and fell, stunned, from his horse. Coming round a few minutes later, he was seen on his feet by Colonel Hew Halkett, who 'made a gallop at him. When about to cut him down, he called that he would surrender.' Halkett's horse being shot, Cambronne made a bolt for liberty but he was still shaken by the blow on the head and Halkett, 'instantly overtook him, laid hold of him by the aiguillette, and brought him in safety and gave him in charge to a sergeant of the Osnabruckers to deliver to the Duke.'

When the Old Guard reached Rossomme, the position was hopeless. Blücher and Bülow, by weight of numbers, had driven the Guard battalions from Placenoit and the right flank was wide open. The Emperor turned to Bertrand and said, *'A présent c'est fini – sauvons nous.'*

On the other side of the valley, the breaking of the Guard gave new life to the exhausted men who had stood all day under the rain of the French shot and **67** had beaten off all their attacks. 'Presently a cheer, which we knew to be British, commenced far to the right, and made everyone prick up his ears. It was Lord Wellington's long-wished-for order to advance. It gradually approached, growing louder as it grew near. We took it up by instinct, charged through the hedge, sending our adversaries flying at the point of the bayonet. Lord Wellington galloped up to us at the instant, and our men began to cheer him; but he called out, "No cheering, my lads, but forward and complete your victory."'

A sergeant of the Ninety-Second, now in command of two companies, remembered, 'Nothing was used now but the bayonet for, after the first volley we gave them, we set off at full speed and did not take time to load. All was now destruction and confusion. The French ran off throwing away knapsacks, firelocks and everything that was cumbersome, or that could impede their flight.'

The British infantry pushed on beyond La Belle Alliance. There they halted. The light cavalry were ahead, slashing at everyone who stood in their way. In Rossomme the Fifty-Second was drawn up beside the road with Ensign Leeke carrying the colour. A column of Prussians approached from the direction of Placenoit. 'They broke into slow time and their bands played "God save the King". A mounted officer asked me in French "if that was an English colour?" On my replying that it was, he let go of his bridle, and taking hold of the colour with both hands, pressed it to his bosom, and patted me on the back, exclaiming, *"Brave Anglais."'*

'It was now fine moonlight. The course of the fugitives could be discerned by the occasional fire of the Prussians pursuing, and shouts and clamour which gradually died away. A regiment of Prussian Uhlans advancing in pursuit passed us. After a little while we were ordered to bivouac, which we did in a wheatfield. We lay down under a hedge and, I believe, all slept soundly till daylight.' Ahead of them the Prussians pursued relentlessly. Behind them the dead lay sprawled and mutilated. The wounded bore their suffering with what fortitude they could muster and longed for water. In a space of about six square miles lay more than 52,000 dead and wounded. About 6,700 of these were Prussians; 15,000 were from Wellington's army. The rest were French. A gunner officer riding forward noted that 'In traversing the field it was hardly possible to clear with the guns the bodies of both armies which strewed the ground. It was with difficulty we could avoid crushing many of the wounded on the road near La Haye Sainte, that had crawled there in the hopes of more ready assistance.'

Wellington had been up with the forward troops to the end. As the Fifty-Second continued its triumphant advance against the last column of the Guard, their brigadier sent his ADC out to the right to see if any French were threatening their flank. 'Having gone some distance I met the Duke moving at a quick pace, followed by one individual to whom I spoke. His answer was, *"Monsieur, je ne parle pas un seul mot d'Anglais."* I told him in French the order I had received. He replied, *"Le Duc lui-même a été voir; il n'y a rien à craindre."'*

At the start of the battle Wellington had been attended by a notably numerous staff, including eight aides-de-camp. At the end he had only the Sardinian military attaché.

'Blücher and I met near La Belle Alliance; we were both on horseback; but he embraced me, exclaiming, "*Mein Liebe Kamerad*", and then "*quelle affaire!*" which was pretty much all he knew of French.'

EPILOGUE

Marshal Prince Blücher to his wife.

Genappe, 19 June, 1815

'My friend Wellington and I have put an end to Bonaparte's dancing. His army is in utter rout. All his artillery, his baggage, his waggons and his coaches are in my hands. The insignia of all the orders to which he belonged, which were found in his carriage, have just been brought to me in a casket. I had two horses killed under me yesterday. We shall be finished with Bonaparte shortly.'

Field Marshal the Duke of Wellington to Marshal Lord Beresford.

Gonesse, 2 July, 1815

'You will have heard of our battle on the 18th. Never did I see such a pounding match. Both were what the boxers call gluttons. Napoleon did not manoeuvre at all. He just moved forward in the old style, and was driven off in the old style. The only difference was that he mixed cavalry with his infantry, and supported both with an enormous quantity of artillery. I had the infantry for some time in squares, and we had the French cavalry walking about us as if they had been our own. I never saw the British infantry behave so well.
    'Boney is now off, I believe, to Rochefort.'

Napoleon I, Emperor of the French, to George, Prince Regent of the United Kingdom of Great Britain and Ireland.

Rochefort, 13 July, 1815

'Exposed to the factions which divide my people, and to the enmity of the greatest powers of Europe, I have terminated my political career; and I come, like Themistocles, to seat myself at the hearth of the people of Britain. I place myself under their laws, seeking this protection from Your Royal Highness as the most powerful, the most constant and the most generous of my enemies.'

Part 2
Arms, Tactics
and Uniforms

1. Arms

Battles between evenly matched bodies of trained troops depend on weapons and the skill with which they are used. All tactics, all training, even the way the troops are dressed, depend on the capabilities of the arms used by the contending armies.

Inefficient as it was, the musket was still the most important weapon on the battlefield in 1815. Napoleon, a gunner by training*, had greatly increased the role of artillery. The conception of 'softening-up' by an artillery preparation stems largely from his over-all endeavour to break or weaken the enemy's will to resist before the infantry came within musket range. At Waterloo this was not as effective as the Emperor had hoped. Apart from a number of not over-effective howitzers, cannon in 1815 had flat trajectories and could not reach troops drawn up behind a crest. The great barrage from eighty guns which heralded D'Erlon's first attack achieved little except against one Netherlands brigade which was on the forward slope. Later in the battle, when Wellington was forced by the French cavalry to keep his men in squares, Napoleon's guns did get within measurable distance of wearing the allied infantry down by continued attrition but, by that time, many of the guns had been disabled, ammunition was beginning to run short and the artillerymen were approaching exhaustion. The margin by which they failed was smaller than is generally admitted on the British side but, since they failed, it was muskets which decided the battle.

There was little to choose between the muskets used by the three armies. Those used by the British were better made and threw a larger ball than the French models. The British bore was 0.75″ and their balls were 14½ to the pound, whereas the French had a bore of 0.69″ and 20 balls to the pound. This

* Before the Revolution it was almost unthinkable to entrust a gunner with a force of all arms, such commands being reserved for officers from the more gentlemanly arms, the cavalry and infantry. No British artilleryman commanded an independent force until 1842 when Sir George Pollock relieved Jellalabad.

enabled the French to have a lighter weapon than the British musket which, with its bayonet, weighed eleven pounds. Against this French advantage in ease of handling, the British had greater stopping power and the ability to use, in emergencies, captured ammunition, whereas the British ball could not be rammed down the French barrel. The Prussian musket approximated to the British in size and to the French in roughness of manufacture.

The principal fault in manufacture was overboring the barrel, thus detracting from the accuracy which was, at best, minimal. Aimed fire was impossible, even for a marksman, at more than eighty or a hundred yards and a contemporary commented that 'a soldier must be very unfortunate indeed who shall be wounded by a common musket at 150 yards, provided that his adversary aims at him.' This limitation was so widely recognised that at Waterloo the only musket provided with a backsight was the somewhat more carefully made type issued to the British light infantry. For the rest it was enough to point the barrel, which had a rudimentary foresight, at the target.

Although the percussion cap had been made practicable eight years earlier by the Rev Alexander Forsyth, Minister of Belhelvie, Aberdeenshire, working under the auspices of the British Board of Ordnance, every firearm issued to the troops of all the armies was a flintlock. The principle of the flintlock was that a flint, mounted on a spring-loaded hammer, struck a steel surface above a priming pan thus (usually) causing a spark. This ignited a pinch of powder in the pan which, passing through the touch hole, set off the main charge in the barrel. The setting of the flint had frequently to be adjusted and a new flint had to be fitted after firing about thirty (or, if very fortunate, fifty) rounds. This presupposes fine weather. Even under dry conditions, the rate of misfires was two in thirteen and there would as often be a 'hangfire' when the charge would go off only after an appreciable interval and after the aim had been lost. In wet weather it was unlikely that any flintlock would fire at all and overnight dew would also be sufficient to make the charge unusable.

Being a muzzle loader, a properly loaded musket, with its charge, wadding and ball rammed tightly home, was difficult and tiresome to unload*. The easiest way to get damp powder out of the barrel was to reprime the flash-pan with dry powder and continue trying to fire until the main charge dried out. On the morning of Waterloo the Black Watch, 'stood to our useless arms for a few minutes, and then began to examine their contents. The powder was moistened in the piece and completely washed out of the pan.' That regiment went through the long process of 'drawing the shots' but most were not so painstaking. According to a hussar officer, 'the old soldiers of the infantry, who remembered well the Peninsula and foresaw what was before them, and knowing

---

* For this reason sentries usually loaded with 'running ball', ie a ball inserted without wadding. This greatly decreased the range and accuracy but it allowed the musket to be unloaded with more ease when the sentry was relieved. It also meant that the ball was likely to trickle out of the barrel if the muzzle was lowered.

that everything depended on their firelocks being in good order, commenced like old sportsmen squibbing their guns. This was continued along the line and the Duke rode up to Picton to know how he could have allowed it, who replied that he had done all in his power to prevent them, in vain. The fact was that old Picton, knew the value of Brown Bess being in good fighting condition as well as the men, but the Duke feared its bringing on an action before he was prepared.'

The Manual Exercise for loading and firing the musket prescribed twenty drill movements for each shot so that the rate of fire could not be high. Frederick the Great had trained the Prussian infantry to discharge five or even six rounds a minute but this had been achieved by a great sacrifice in accuracy. In the armies at Waterloo three rounds a minute was considered the practicable limit. Owing to the lenght of the barrel, loading could only be performed when standing or kneeling.

The only way to increase the range of the musket was to rifle the barrel. The French army had experimented with rifles around the turn of the century but their experience had discouraged them and in 1807 Napoleon had ordered all such weapons to be withdrawn. The British experience had been different. The sporting rifles used by the colonists in the American War had made a great impression on British military thinking, and, although it was clearly impracticable to arm the whole infantry in this way, it was generally agreed that there was a place for rifles in the hands of specially trained troops. A battalion of foreigners armed with German and American rifles had been raised in 1797*. Before a permanent British rifle regiment was established the Board of Ordnance went into the question of armament with quite uncharacteristic thoroughness. On 4 February, 1800 forty types of rifle, British, German and American, were subjected to tests at Woolwich. The most satisfactory model, that designed by Ezekiel Baker of London, was adopted for the Experimental Corps of Riflemen, which in 1803 became the Ninety-Fifth Regiment (Riflemen).

Baker's rifle was only thirty inches long in the barrel, nine inches shorter than the musket, and could be loaded while lying down. To minimise the difficulty of loading there was only a quarter of a turn on the seven rifling grooves in the barrel but even so loading was difficult and slow and it was a skilled Rifleman who could load, aim and fire two shots in a minute. When first issued the rifles were provided with a small wooden mallet to drive the ball down the barrel. These were soon found 'to be a serious incumbrance to the men and very soon dispensed with, as a man's strength is always found sufficient to make the ball enter, when it fits as it ought to do.' Wadding was not used in loading. Instead a 'greased patch of leather, calico or soft rag' (which was kept in a container built into the stock) was 'put on the end of the barrel, as near the centre as

---

* The 5th Battalion Sixtieth (Royal American) Foot, the first rifle-armed regiment, was raised from Hompesch's Chasseurs and Löwenstein's Jägers.

possible' and the ball placed upon it 'with the neck or castable, where it is cut off from the mould, downwards,' and then rammed home. The firing mechanism was the flintlock, identical to that used on the musket* and subject to the same troubles in wet weather. It was originally intended to make rifles of the same calibre as the musket to avoid the problems of a separate ammunition supply. When the musket-size rifles were issued they were disliked 'as requiring too much exertion, and harassing the men from their excessive weight.' Baker had always wished to use a smaller bore, pointing out that 'the smaller the ball, the less elevation is required,' and since the flat trajectory increased the accurate range, a bore of 0.615″ was adopted, standardising the ball with the carbines carried by the cavalry.

The rifle had its disadvantages. Its rate of fire was slow, the rifled barrel tended to foul so badly that the ball could not be rammed home and they were more costly to replace than muskets which, even at inflated war time prices, could be had for £2 a piece. Against that it had an accuracy unknown in military firearms. In the hands of a marksman the Baker could be used with effect at three hundred yards. At its trials it put twenty-four shots out of twenty-four into a man-sized target at two hundred yards. Major Hamlet Wade and Rifleman Spurrey of the Ninety-Fifth used to hold targets for each other at that range, one at which a musket would have hit the holder as often as the target and would have missed both nine times out of ten.

Rifles were carried at Waterloo by the fourteen companies of the Ninety-Fifth which were present, by more than half the men of the Light Battalions, King's German Legion†, and by the Jäger battalions in the Hanoverian, Netherlands and Prussian armies.

Since muskets and rifles were so slow to reload, both were useless as firearms for about forty-five seconds out of every minute. The infantryman, therefore, had to have some protection against his most fearsome enemy, the cavalryman. A galloping horse could cover the whole length of an infantryman's range in less time than it took him to reload. In the seventeenth century this danger had been countered by interspersing pikemen amongst the musketeers, but the pikeman was useless for all other functions and he was superseded by giving the infantryman a bayonet to attach to the muzzle of his musket, so that it became at once a firearm and a spear. Hand-to-hand fighting with the bayonet was then, as subsequently, very rare and the principal function of the bayonet was defence against cavalry. Consequently it was, by modern standards, very long. The British model was seventeen inches long and the French only fractionally shorter. Both were triangular in section. Riflemen had longer bayonets to

---

* The Baker was primed with a pinch of fine powder carried in a powder horn. This made it somewhat more reliable than the musket which was primed with part of the main charge.

† From a return dated 5 May 1814 it appears that the proportion of arms in both the Light Battalions KGL was Rifles 392; Muskets 253.

compensate for the comparative shortness of their weapons. Instead of a seventeen-inch blade on a thirty-nine inch barrel, they carried a twenty-five inch blade on their thirty-inch barrel, thus achieving rough equality in length and enabling Riflemen and musket-armed infantry to stand side by side in square and present a regular hedge of steel to an onslaught of cavalry. The original bayonet for the Rifles was also triangular in section but they hankered for the traditional short sword of light troops (probably because it could be used for cutting firewood). They were issued with a brass-hilted sword bayonet which, from the weight of its blade, made accurate firing impossible. Riflemen, therefore, 'fixed swords' only when forming square, while the rest of the infantry fought with their bayonets fixed. In the French army all Grenadiers, Chasseurs and Voltigeurs carried short swords *(sabre-briquet)* in addition to their bayonets, as did pioneers in all armies.

Infantry officers were supposed to carry swords although in practice many of them carried muskets or rifles in battle. In both the British and the French armies the regulation sword was not a formidable weapon. The British model was $32''$ long and $1\frac{1}{8}''$ wide in the blade. The French sword, a very poor thing, was four inches shorter and only $\frac{3}{4}''$ wide. Highland officers carried the far more formidable broadsword, although the regulations laid down that they should use the normal infantry officer's sword.

It is hard to know the extent to which infantry officers carried pistols. Some undoubtedly had them. Where they kept them when not in use is something of a mystery since holsters do not seem to have been worn. In the British army their existence was recognized by a regulation insisting that only pistols using the same sized ball as either the musket or the carbine should be carried. Wellington is reputed to have ordered an officer into arrest for displaying a pair of pistols with non-standard bore in battle. The reason for this uncharacteristic punctilio was that the pistols concerned were duelling weapons with the barrels notched with the number of the owner's victims. It may well be that the Duke discouraged the carrying of all pistols since their presence would lead to duelling which he considered amongst the worst of military crimes. The only infantry regiment in which the officers were instructed to carry pistols was the Ninety-Fifth Rifles, possibly to compensate for their regulation swords, or rather sabres, which were so curved as to be useless. Rifle officers were instructed to keep their pistols in the pouch on the back of their shoulder belt, the most inaccessible place in any uniform. It must, in any case, have been a very small weapon to fit into the pouch, and it is probable that the space was used for some more useful commodity, such as tea.

Sergeants of heavy infantry in the British, Hanoverian and Prussian armies carried a seven foot halberd (known officially as a pike). This had a certain utility when formed in square against cavalry but was an embarrassment in a rough and tumble. Halberds could, moreover, be dangerous to their owners.

A sergeant of the Guards was running in pursuit of a Frenchman when, 'the point of his pike ran into the earth and stuck fast, causing the butt-end to pass through his body.*' Sergeants also carried swords.

★ ★ ★

For all cavalry, except lancers, the sword was the principal weapon. Heavy cavalry sabres were straight or nearly so. Light regiments had more or less curved weapons. The British heavy horse had a detestable sabre. The blade was 35″ long and 1¼″ inches wide, the edges being parallel until about four inches from the tip where it was curved on one side to make a point. Being lightly hilted, it was very heavy in the point and was useful only as an unscientific chopper, dangerous if it connected with a vital part of an adversary, ideal for cutting at defenceless infantry, but unsuitable for sabre to sabre action, especially against the French equivalent, a beautifully balanced weapon, which was so functional that it was still used by the French cavalry in 1918, while a copy was used by the Prussians in the war of 1870.

The French heavy sabre was rather more curved than the British. In the light horse the British sabre was distinctly more curved than the French. Here the British had a much better weapon with a blade '32½ inches or 33 inches measured in a straight line from the hilt to the point but not to exceed the latter measurement.' It was a sword more calculated for the cut than the thrust and it was only sharpened for the six inches nearest the point because, said the drill book, 'not more than four of five inches should meet your adversary, and less still with a straight blade, whose construction is by no means so well calculated for extricating itself. No cut can be made with effect or security where the weapon does not at once free itself from the object to which it is applied; otherwise it must turn in the hand and give a contusion rather than a cut, for which reason those wounds are most severe which are made nearest the point.' The recommended aiming mark is the 'antagonist's left ear.' The drill book added, 'it should be remembered that little force is requisite to produce effect from the application of the edge, if conducted with skill.'

In Napoleon's army in the Waterloo campaign there were seven regiments of lancers. The Prussians had six regular Uhlan regiments and their fifteen regiments of landwehr cavalry were also armed with the lance. Under Wellington's command there was only a single squadron of Brunswick Uhlans. The reasons for the adoption of the lance in the French army are discussed later (see page 131). The British cavalry had met lancers in the Peninsula and had not been impressed by them. Writing after his first sword-against-lance action in 1811 an officer of the Sixteenth Light Dragoons said, 'The lancers looked well

78   * The sergeant recovered but was discharged because of his wound. He later kept a public house in London.

and formidable before they were broken and closed by our men, and then their lances were an encumbrance.' The British theory was that it was not too difficult to turn the point of a lance after which, in close combat, the swordsman had the lancer at his mercy. The survivors of Colborne's brigade at Albuera would have taken a less complaisant view of lancers than light dragoons could afford to do. Soon after Waterloo, four British light dragoon regiments (including the Sixteenth) were converted into lancers.

All cavalry carried pistols in saddle holsters. They were of little use in battle since the priming, if not the main charge, usually fell out in the holster but they were convenient if wounded horses had to be despatched in the absence of the farrier sergeant. Apart from cuirassiers and lancers, all other cavalry also had some longer firearm. The *Grenadiers à Cheval* carried full length infantry muskets, which must have been a severe handicap to them.

The British heavy cavalry had a rather cumbersome carbine with a 26″ barrel. The light cavalry carbine, ten inches shorter, was the most suitable weapon for mounted action in either army. Known as the 'Paget carbine', after Lord Uxbridge who secured its adoption, it was designed by Henry Nock. Its main feature was a flexible link which secured the ramrod to the barrel, making it impossible to drop the rod while loading. This invention was invaluable for cavalry since, like all muzzle loaders, a carbine without a ramrod was useless. In the Seventh and Tenth Hussars rifled carbines were used by at least some of the troopers.

While the carbine was useful to dismounted sentries its use on horseback, though not uncommon, was seldom effective.*

It is easy to overrate the effect, in terms of casualties, caused by artillery in the Napoleonic wars. It is equally easy to underrate its psychological effect. At Waterloo all the guns, except for the small proportion of howitzers, were in sight of their targets. Each gun was a scarifying monster, belching flame and black smoke. Those born towards the end of the eighteenth century were accustomed to a maximum noise level less than half that regarded as normal in the age of the jet aircraft and the motor cycle. To the young soldiers, who made up the bulk of the allied army, the noise of the bombardment was something unimaginable. Even the hardened veterans of the Peninsula must have been surprised by the thunder of Napoleon's *belles filles*. They would never have seen anything as large as a twelve pounder used as a field piece.†

---

* Accounts of wounds sustained from carbines are rare in the extreme. The most notable is that to Sir Stapleton Cotton, then commanding Wellington's cavalry, who was wounded by a Portuguese dragoon in error on the night after Salamanca.
† Bigger guns, 18 & 24 pounders, were used in siege operations.

Even by pre-atomic standards, the projectiles fired by these guns were not very dangerous. Most important was the round shot. As its name implies this was a solid sphere varying in diameter from 3.2″ for the French four pounder to 4.75″ for the twelve pounders. These were dangerous only to those in the direct line of fire. They did not explode. The maximum range, calculated to the point where the ball first touched the ground, varied from 1,800 yards for the twelve pounder, through 1,700 for the British nine pounder, down to 1,300 for the four pounders. The most effective range was, in every case, rather more than half the maximum. Beyond the point where the shot pitched it would, on dry ground, go bouncing on for a mile or more in a deceptively innocent way. A surgeon wrote, 'The ball appears to bound like a cricket ball; and we are only likely to establish its force by the manner in which it ploughs up the ground. A poor Irish lad of the Twenty-Seventh Regiment was silly enough to call out to his companions on seeing a shot of this kind, "Stop it, boys!"; and to endeavour to stop it with his foot, which was smashed to pieces so as to render amputation necessary.'

As long as the British were in two deep line, round shot was not likely to produce crippling casualties particularly since, on Wellington's orders, the men lay down whenever possible. The field officers, who were mounted, remained conspicuous targets but, given clear visibility, a ball could be seen in flight and the troops would call out to warn their officers of imminent danger. To troops in column or square, roundshot was a very different proposition. A ball would go through any close formation from end to end, smashing everyone in its path. An officer of the Fortieth wrote of Waterloo that 'towards evening, whilst the regiment was in open column, a round shot from the enemy took off the head of Captain Fisher near me, and striking his company on the left flank, put *hors de combat* more than twenty-five men. This was the most destructive shot I ever witnessed during a long period of service.'

Firing round shot could be a business of great accuracy. It is said that at the battle of Dresden Napoleon, laying a gun with his own hands, killed his old comrade and rival Moreau with his first shot. A better authenticated story is that of the Matagorda fort in Cadiz harbour which in 1810 had a British garrison. 'We had a flag staff of the usual size on which was hoisted the Spanish colours. The French cut it across with a cannon ball, it was repaired and replaced; but it was not five minutes up when another shot brought it down. This occurred four or five times.'

The other type of projectile used by field guns on both sides was case shot, also known as canister. This development of grape shot consisted of a thin tin cylinder, 'in diameter a little less than the calibre. It is filled with iron balls so as to make up the weight of the shot.' Musket or carbine balls were used for filling the cylinder so that a 9 pounder case filled with carbine balls, at 20 to the pound, would contain about 180 balls. Sprayed out of the muzzle, this blast of shot was a fearsome weapon against formed bodies of troops but 'from the very great divergency of the balls, little effect is to be expected from firing beyond 300 yards.' During the attacks of the French cavalry, the British gunners were loading with case over roundshot so that the musket balls would disable the front ranks while the round shot plunged the length of the column.

About one in six of the pieces used on both sides at Waterloo were howitzers. The British used a 5.5″ model, the French bore being about an inch larger. Howitzers were unwieldy and less reliable than field guns but they could be used for searching behind a crest. They could fire case shot, but their principal projectile was 'common shell'. This was a hollow metal sphere containing powder which was fired by a fuse cut to length and ignited by the gunner. Their effective range was between 750 and 1,300 yards but reliable fuses were hard to come by, especially on the French side. Sometimes they went out in the air, sometimes they exploded soon after leaving the barrel. Occasionally the fuse burned so slowly that a brave man could kick the smouldering fuse out of the shell as it lay on the ground. Waterloo was not a good day for common shell. The ground was so soft that they buried themselves and their explosion was muffled by a cushion of mud.

Considering that Napoleon was a gunner, it is remarkable that all the major technical advances in gunnery were made on the British side. The British blockade probably accounted for the fact that the French powder was always inferior but the British certainly pioneered two significant inventions. The more useful was Major Henry Shrapnell's 'spherical case shot', better known, after its inventor, as shrapnel. It combined the advantages of case shot and common shell. A metal sphere filled with small shot was exploded by one of a number of timed fuses which the gunner could select and was intended to 'airburst' over the enemy's heads. For their time they were remarkably reliable.

The British artillery brought shrapnel into service in 1803 and no continental artillery succeeded in copying them for more than twenty-five years. Wellington first used them in 1808 and, after the Vimeiro campaign, wrote to the inventor, assuring him that 'the spherical case shot had the best effect in producing the defeat of the enemy.' Later he had doubts about them. After Busaco in 1810 he saw the captured General Simon, 'who was wounded by the balls of Shrapnell's shells, of which he had several in his face and head; but they were picked out of his face as duck shot would be out of the face of a person who had been hit by accident while out shooting, and he was not much more materially injured.' Wellington was led to believe that 'the wounds they inflict do not disable the person who receives them, even for the action in which they are received.' He continued to experiment with them, however, and found that if the cases were filled with musket balls they had 'great effect'.

Whatever projectile was used, the discharge of artillery was a cumbersome business. A French twelve pounder complete with its carriage weighed a ton and a half (without the considerable weight of its ammunition chest). It needed twelve horses to move it when the ground was dry. The British nine pounder weighed almost as much (29 cwt) and although it was intended that six horses should draw it, eight horses were usually needed. The British Foot Artillery six pounder, which weighed only $14\frac{1}{2}$ cwt, was moved by four horses, although the French four pounder, which weighed a hundredweight less, required eight.* Once the horses had put the gun in its approximate position all subsequent movements had to be made by hand, using drag ropes and handling levers. The twelve pounder needed a crew of fifteen of whom eight were trained gunners, the remainder, whose main task was hauling on the drag ropes and bringing up ammunition, being seconded infantrymen.† The four pounder crew consisted of five gunners and three others.

The gun had first to be trained by swinging the trail until the sight bore on the target. Then it was adjusted for range by means of the elevating screw under the rear of the barrel. To load, the vent, or touchhole, had first to be stopped. The barrel was then sponged out to clear the detritus of earlier firings and to cool the barrel so that powder inserted in it was not ingited by the heat. Next, a pre-measured charge of powder was inserted, varying from $1\frac{1}{2}$ pounds for a British six pounder to $4\frac{1}{4}$ pounds for the twelve pounder. A wad of felt or grass was then rammed home and after that the projectile. At this stage, the vent was opened and cleaned with a picker. A reed filled with powder or impregnated cotton was put in the vent and, finally, the gun was fired by touching the reed with a linstock or slow match.

This, however, was not the end of the gunners' troubles. There was no mechanism for absorbing the recoil so that, every time a shot was fired, the gun ran back and had to be hauled back into position. A Horse Artillery officer wrote that at the end of Waterloo, 'the depth of the ground and the exhausted state of the few men remaining at the guns had latterly prevented the possibility of running them up after each round, so that when the action ceased their recoils had brought them together in a confused heap.' It is scarcely surprising that twelve pounders were not expected to fire more than one round a minute. Lighter guns could fire every thirty seconds.

The other British contribution to the science of artillery was the explosive rocket, the brainchild of Sir William Congreve. Rockets were very erratic in their performance and Wellington detested them. He had experimented with them in the Peninsula and his verdict was 'I do not want to set fire to any town and I do not know any other use for rockets.' It was probably a fair verdict as a civilian who had watched trials early in 1814 commented, 'I think they would

* The French guns were mounted on a well-designed standardised range of carriages designed by Jean-Baptiste Gribeauval in 1776 and had no limber, only a pair of detachable wheels for the trail. This design had many advantages but it seems that it made the guns more cumbersome than the British models with limbers which could be manhandled separately.

† In the British artillery only artillerymen acted as gun numbers.

have hit Bayonne somewhere or other; but the part of the town you could not very well choose.'

For the Waterloo campaign one troop of Horse Artillery was equipped with rockets, but the Duke ordered them to be put into store and the troop armed conventionally. It was with difficulty that he was persuaded to change his mind and, in the event, Whinyates' troop took both rockets and nine pounders into action. They used their rockets first on the retreat on 17 June. Twelve pounder rockets were fired from a 'Bombarding frame', a triangle 'cocked up in the air at an angle of 45°'. The first shot was a lucky hit on a French gun and 'our rocketeers kept shooting off rockets, none of them ever followed the course of the first; most of them took a vertical direction, while some of them actually turned back upon ourselves.'

In the battle itself both six and twelve pounder rockets were used. After the repulse of D'Erlon's attack six pounders were taken forward by the gunners who carried them in special holsters. They were fired from a small trough carried on the saddle bag of every third mounted gunner. They were 'not laid at angles of elevation but ricocheted along the ground. There were crops of high standing in front of the rocket section which screened all objects in front, and the rockets were fired through them in the direction of the enemy's troops.' After two discharges the men were recalled to their guns. A lieutenant claimed that they had put a brigade of French cavalry in 'total disorder'. This claim does not seem to be substantiated by other evidence.

The twelve pounders and their bombarding frame were not ordered forward but 'the non-commissioned officer in charge of it brought it into action quite of his own accord. As to what he might have been firing at 'tis hard to say, but I should think those rockets must have gone a mile and a half, and Major Whinyates ordered him to cease firing, as there were some foreign cavalry of our side between him and the enemy.'

2.Tactics

The aim of a combatant in war is to impose his will on his opponent or to prevent one's opponent imposing his will on oneself. The means whereby this might be achieved have varied through the centuries. In late medieval Italy war was endemic but it was conducted largely by mercenaries. They had no moral commitment to their cause and no hatred for their enemies who were only their professional colleagues under contract to another paymaster. Consequently, battles were seldom fought and when they did occur casualties were kept to a civilised minimum, a consummation much assisted by the absence of effective firearms. War under these circumstances was not so much a bloodbath as a game of human chess played to accepted rules. A mercenary army which was out-manoeuvred would not seek to restore its fortunes by offering battle. It would give ground, yielding some town which the enemy could loot. Meanwhile it would make some counter-manoeuvre giving it possession of one of the opposition's towns and its riches. A high standard of tactical skill was essential. A mercenary general without talent would soon lose his job. His paymaster would cease paying his salary and his own men would turn against him if he did not lead them into enemy territory where they could practice plunder and rapine. From the soldier's point of view it was the ideal kind of war. His rewards were substantial and his life, barring the accidents and diseases inseparable from campaigning, reasonably safe. Only the civilians suffered.

Although by the eighteenth century firearms had become widespread and national armies were becoming the rule rather than the exception, war was still largely a matter of elaborate manoeuvre and battles were rare. The Duke of Marlborough campaigned in Europe, mostly in the Netherlands, from 1702 to 1711 but fought only five general actions. For much of the time his expressed intention was to advance on Paris but, despite three crushing victories near the French frontier, no serious advance into France was ever made. Inadequacies in weapons and organization made outright victory impossible in wars where the two sides were matched in manpower and commanded with common prudence. The main attention of both sides was concentrated on the acquisition of fortresses which could be used as bargaining counters at the eventual peace conference. Since the total destruction of the enemy's military and civilian power was regarded as being unattainable and, indeed, undesirable, eighteenth-century generals kept their eyes firmly fixed on objectives which would be useful when the bargaining began. Armies were small and mercenaries, although expensive, still had to be used to make up the numbers. There were Swiss, Swedish and Irish regiments in the French army. The Spaniards employed Swiss, Irish and Flemish troops. The British relied largely on Hessians and other Germans. Croats always made up the fighting heart of Austrian armies.

The French Revolution changed the military manpower situation drastically and permanently. Conscription, the *levée en masse*, made military service a national duty rather than a profession. The ranks could be filled without emptying the Treasury. Rates of pay need no longer be attractive. They could lag behind increases in civilian earnings since service was compulsory. There was a slump in the employment prospects for mercenaries.

The size of armies increased enormously. In 1704 the main Franco-Bavarian army had put 60,000 men into the field at Blenheim against an Anglo-Austrian army, with German contingents, of 56,000. A hundred and five years later, two hundred miles further down the Danube, Napoleon and his vassals, 175,000 strong, attacked 130,000 Austrians at Wagram. At Blenheim the French army had 90 guns, at Wagram 544.

The swollen size of armies forced the nature of war to change. Wars of position, the marches and counter-marches, the pre-eminence of sieges, the bloodless confrontations, could no longer be continued. It was impossible to feed an army which remained concentrated. The passage of one of Napoleon's armies, or those of his opponents, had the same effect on a fertile countryside as a plague of locusts. A quick military decision became essential.

Napoleon was the first to recognise this new condition. While the Austrians were conducting the kind of war which might have been successful against the generals of Louis XIV, while the British were busy filching sugar islands to use as bargaining counters at a peace conference which became ever more remote, Napoleon was aiming for the knock-out blow, for the destruction, rather than the mere defeat, of the enemy's army.*

His problem was that the military means available to him were insufficient to conduct a *blitzkrieg* against an enemy general of talent supported by an army of good quality. Brilliant generalship sufficed against mediocre commanders such as Beaulieu, Wurmser or Mack. Austerlitz, Napoleon's masterpiece, was

* Napoleon retained some of the eighteenth century's obsession with the capture of important towns. His concentration on Madrid in 1808 and 09 and on Moscow in 1812 contributed largely to his downfall. At times in the Waterloo campaign he seems to have been at least as intent on the occupation of Brussels as on the defeat of Wellington and Blücher.

won against an Austro-Russian army with a command structure riddled with dissension and compromise. The last of the knock-out blows, the Jena campaign of 1806, saw the destruction of a Prussian army commanded by an elderly consortium whose ideas derived from the Seven Years' War. Meanwhile the forces against Napoleon were growing in strength, determination and, above all, in the skill to ride a blow meant to be devastating. Bennigsen after Friedland, the Archduke Charles after Wagram, Kutúzov after Borodino, were all able to retreat with an 'army in being'. Napoleon himself, after his shattering defeat at Leipzig, was able to withdraw enough troops to continue the war until he was reduced by attrition. The day of the knock-out blow was over. Only one more remained to be dealt – at Waterloo. It was dealt by Wellington only after Napoleon had used up his own army in repeated attempts to achieve more than was possible. The next knock-out in Europe was not to be achieved until Sadowa in 1866. By that time a new factor had entered the field. The victorious army was incomparably better armed than its opponents. Technology had produced the breech-loading rifle.

Napoleon fought his wars against armies which were, in all essentials, armed in the same way as his own, but this was not the only factor which militated against the hammer blow. The slowness of movement and communication was equally hampering. The movement of all armies was conditioned by the pace of the marching infantryman. Twelve miles a day counted as rapid movement for an army. Forced marches could achieve more but only for limited periods and at the cost of exhausting the troops. Davout brought 25,000 men seventy miles in forty-eight hours for the battle of Austerlitz. Craufurd's brigade marched forty-two miles in twenty-six hours to reach Talavera. Both these feats deservedly became legendary. Normally troops moved at a steady plod. Even on the battlefield, when speed was vital, formations could hardly move at more than four miles an hour. When historians describing battles speak of a general's 'lightning stroke', the phrase is largely hyperbole. The pause between a commander deciding a course of action and the troops coming into action was always very considerable. At Salamanca in 1812 where '40,000 men were beaten in forty minutes', Wellington was eating a leg of chicken on the ridge above Los Arapiles when he saw the careless dispersion of Marmont's army. He had to gallop two miles before giving separate orders to Pakenham's infantry and D'Urban's cavalry. The infantry then had to advance two miles, meanwhile performing the complicated drill movement of deploying from column into line without halting. It cannot have been less than an hour between the moment when Wellington slammed his telescope shut and remarked, 'By God, that will do,' and the moment when Pakenham, after 'holding them back until they were within a few yards of the enemy and seeing that the proper moment had come, called to Wallace to "Let them loose!"' It was another hour before the main attack on the French flank got within musket shot.

At Salamanca Wellington was fortunate in being able to see that his opportunity had come. In the valley between his command post and the ridge along which the French were advancing there was only some half-hearted skirmishing. If serious fighting had been in progress the far side of the valley would have been invisible. Muskets and artillery alike fired black powder and in a battle the atmosphere was comparable only to an old fashioned 'pea-souper'. At Waterloo, a staff officer wrote that, 'the fog and smoke lay so heavy on the ground that we could only ascertain the approach of the enemy by the noise and clashing of arms which the French usually make in their advance to attack.'

Deprived of vision a commander was hard put to it to know the movements of his own troops or those of the enemy. His subordinates, closely involved with the enemy, could only occasionally spare the time to send a hasty scrawl, written in the saddle, by the hand of an ADC. Few men in battle were more vulnerable than the ADC*. He was constantly running the gauntlet of musketry, artillery and marauding cavalry, always in danger of losing his way in the smoke and riding into the enemy's lines. If a commander wished to know the situation in any part of his front, his only course was to ride over and see for himself. Nothing is more noticeable than the contrast between Napoleon and Wellington in this matter at Waterloo. Napoleon, who was past his physical best and was suffering from lethargy and piles, spent most of the battle sitting on a chair outside La Belle Alliance. Only once did he advance, when the Guard attacked. His move took him into dead ground from whence the vital clash was invisible. Wellington was everywhere when he was needed. He 'was seen at every point when his presence was most required.' His instinct for the place of danger was almost as miraculous as his escape from the fire.

Supplying an army was a constant struggle. The French system of ammunition supply and of evacuating wounded were excellent but their arrangements for the provision of rations for men and horses were sketchy. On 16, 17 and 18 June valuable hours were lost while the troops scavenged far and wide in an attempt to feed themselves and their mounts. Even in the Guard, which always received first cut at whatever supplies were available, the officers could not keep their men in the ranks until action was joined. On 17 June men (and some officers) left the columns to dig for vegetables in the fields and gardens every time they halted. Wellington's ammunition supply was just adequate but, thanks to parliamentary parsimony, his ambulance service was non-existent. No commander of his time took more care over his mens' rations than Wellington. 'How should he fight, poor fellow, if he has, besides risking his life, to struggle with unnecessary hardships.' Providing food was a constant uphill fight. Supply was a Treasury responsibility and the Treasury affected to believe that transport

* At Quatre Bras and Waterloo four ADCs to British generals were killed and fifteen wounded. Three British generals were killed and nine wounded apart from the Prince of Orange and the Duke of Brunswick, both of whom held the rank of general in the British army.

was a matter that could be dealt with by local contract. For a British army in the Waterloo campaign of 30,000 men, only 162 men of the Royal Waggon Train were directly concerned with moving supplies. For the rest the army had to rely on Belgian civilians who brought their own carts*. Not unnaturally many of them deserted when a panic-stricken cavalry brigade of their compatriots charged through them on their headlong flight from Quatre Bras. Nevertheless, most, if not all, Wellington's army had breakfast on the morning of 18 June. Their enemies fought on an empty stomach.

★ ★ ★

With the power of an autocrat and a brilliant military instinct, Napoleon did all that was possible to improve the capability of his army. Under Alexandre Berthier the staff was developed to a level of efficiency unknown in any previous army. No other staff of the time could have organized the passing of 150,000 men, with their horse and artillery, across the Danube on improvised bridges on a single night before Wagram. Even after this amazing feat, Napoleon bitterly criticised the staff-work. Maps were provided on an unprecedented scale,† another contribution of Berthier, whose father had been a topographer. Napoleon was no innovator in artillery but under his inspiration the Gribeauval series of guns was extended to include the 12-pounder field gun, a weapon which, when first used in 1809, gave the French a marked advantage in range and weight of bombardment.

These and other improvements put the French army ahead of all its opponents but the advantages were insufficient to make overwhelming victory, the knock-out blow, certain or even probable. The basic weakness of all offensive tactics lay in the infantry musket. With its capability of firing three rounds a minute at an aimed range of little more than eighty yards it was, taken singly, a puny weapon. It could only be made effective if it was used in large numbers. A properly loaded musket ball could be lethal up to two hundred yards. Although the 'cone of fire' of a musket spread widely for the last five-eighths of this range, the inaccuracy could be compensated if sufficient balls were fired. A proportion of a large volley was certain to find a substantial target. Thus infantry had to be used in close formations and the more they were massed the more of them came into the cone of fire. To allow the maximum fire power to be deployed, the drill books of both France and Britain laid down that troops should fight in line three ranks deep. In theory all ranks could fire but it was rare for the rear rank to do so since their fire was inevitably inaccurate and the risks to the front rank were considerable. Fighting in line obtained the greatest possible fire

* This belief lasted until the end of the Nineteenth Century. Reporting the Grand Manoeuvres of 1898, *The Times* commented that among the second line transport 'the name of Lipton was particularly prominent'.
† In contrast, Wellington's engineers had to produce a map of the approaches to Brussels in the month before the battle.

power while presenting a minimum target to solid shot. On the other hand, it had serious disadvantages. To manoeuvre in line, even over smooth country, called for a very high standard of foot drill. A battalion at full strength stretched three hundred and fifty yards when three deep. A brigade covered more than a thousand yards. It was a formation quite unsuitable for even a moderate approach march and deployment from column of march to line was a manoeuvre of some complexity usually performed at the halt. The whole operation could fall into chaos if words of command were mistimed or if, as was only too likely in the noise of battle, they were unheard or misunderstood. As the drill book said, 'The justness of the formation depends altogether on officers judging their distances and timing their commands. The officer who leads his division* up into line must take great care that it does not overshoot its ground. Each division, when opposite to its ground will be most advantageously fronted, or at least corrected, by a mounted officer, in case its leader should not be critical in his commands, or that he should not be heard, or that his files should be too open.' All this is difficult enough to perform properly on a well rehearsed ceremonial parade. To execute it on uneven ground under fire calls for a remarkable standard of drill and discipline.

Although fighting in line made a unit very formidable to the front, it left it defenceless to flanks and rear. Cavalry coming on the rear of a battalion in line had the infantrymen at its mercy.† On the approach of horsemen, units had to go through another complicated manoeuvre, forming square so as to present an unbroken hedge of bayonets to the sabres and lances of the enemy. The flank companies had to be wheeled back to form the rear side of the new formation while others fell back through a right angle to fill up the sides. This could only be done at a steady pace. Doubling, or any symptom of panic would be fatal. Squares were very seldom square. In the British infantry, where there were ten companies to a battalion, the formation would be three companies on the front and rear of the 'square', and two companies on each flank. Where numbers were small, as happened towards the end of Waterloo, two battalions would form a single square, a manoeuvre requiring close liaison between the two commanders so that the companies would know where to station themselves when the order was given. A square of one or two battalions was an admirable target for artillery and commanders made every effort to deploy their men at the earliest possible moment. The temptation to delay forming square, or to deploy too soon, was great and sometimes led to disastrous results.

Two evenly matched lines of infantry blazing at each other at a range of a hundred yards or less would inflict frightful casualties on each other but, unless

---

* In this sense a division was half a company of infantry commanded by a subaltern. Apart from its use for a formation consisting of several brigades of infantry or cavalry, the word division was also used to denote a sub-unit of a brigade (6 guns) of artillery.

† The feat of the Twenty-Eighth at Alexandria where they turned their rear rank about to drive French cavalry off by fire was all but unique.

the discipline of one side gave way, no decisive result would be reached. To avoid this kind of bloody impasse both the British and the French resorted to modifications of the doctrine enshrined in their drill books. The British cut the depth of their line from three ranks to two. This enhanced both the advantages and the disadvantages of the line. The line became even more difficult to manoeuvre since it was greatly lengthened. A battalion at full strength was more than a quarter of a mile in length. It was even more vulnerable to cavalry and, from its thinness, placed a greater psychological strain on the soldier. At the same time it increased the effective firepower by a third and gave the opportunity of swinging the outer companies forward to fire into the flanks of the assailant's formation. Two-deep-line, a technique no other army adopted, was very suitable to the British. It made full use of the dogged steadiness in defence which was the British infantry's chief virtue over the centuries. It demanded a very high standard of training and discipline, a standard which could only be achieved by a professional army and Britain alone of the European powers did not raise her army by conscription, retaining a comparatively small force but one drilled to a perfection unknown on the continent.

The French have always excelled in the attack, a characteristic well suited to Napoleon's requirement for overwhelming victory. Their solution to the tactical problem went to the opposite extreme to that chosen by the British. In the wars immediately following the Revolution the *levée en masse* gave them huge numbers of soldiers but they had neither the officers nor the time to train them to the old professional standard. To deal with immediate urgencies the troops were employed as missiles of massed humanity launched at the enemy lines in heavy, close packed columns. Such was their patriotic fervour and the fearsome appearance of their advance that frequently they broke through, splitting the line and opening a gap through which cavalry could exploit to destroy the enemy from the rear. In the decades that followed these early, desperate, expedients, the training of French troops improved immeasurably but the successes of the revolutionary columns remained in the minds of French generals as giving the best chance of totally disrupting the enemy's army. The technique was used triumphantly against Austrians, Italians, Prussians, Russians and Spaniards. Basically, it was unsound practice. Packing battalions, brigades and even divisions into columns sacrificed firepower. Only those in the front two or three ranks could bring their muskets to bear on the enemy. The remainder, seven-ninths of the whole, could only add momentum and enthusiasm to the attack. A column was the perfect target for artillery; round shot, case shot, common shell and shrapnel could all be used with maximum effect. If the enemy stood his ground and was not overawed by the sight of this cheering, blazing, trotting mass of men hurling themselves at his line, musketry could inflict crippling casualties. Even muskets could not well miss such a target. Setting off for Portugal in 1808, Wellington remarked, 'If what I hear of their system of manoeuvre be true, I think it is a false one against steady troops. I suspect all the continental armies were more than half-beaten before the battle was begun.'

In his innermost thoughts, Napoleon agreed with him. The use of column was never prescribed for the French armies. Their drill books continued to lay down the three deep line. The furthest the Emperor was ready to recommend was a compromise. This was the *ordre mixte* in which a brigade was drawn up with one battalion in line with a battalion in column of each flank. 'In this order of battle,' he said before Austerlitz, 'you will be able to engage the enemy with the fire of the line and with close columns engage his.' Nevertheless, when a quick victory was essential, Napoleon fell back on the use of columns. At Waterloo, where everything depended on a breakthrough being gained before the Prussians could intervene, every French attack, by cavalry as well as by infantry, was made in column. Napoleon could claim, and it has often been claimed on his behalf, that Ney was in tactical control of the attacks but Napoleon and Ney were in constant communication and a word from the Emperor would have ensured that this vicious tactic was discarded.

★ ☆ ★

'I suspect,' Wellington had said, 'all the continental armies were more than half-beaten before the battle began.' With his usual perspicacity, he had identified the secret of Napoleon's success – psychological preparation. In August, 1808, the Emperor had remarked, '*À la guerre, les trois parts sont des affaires morales; la balance des forces réelles n'est que pour un autre part.*' He was speaking in bitterness. Three weeks earlier he had learned that General Dupont, a man whom he had recently chosen for rapid promotion, had surrendered 17,635 unwounded men to a Spanish army at Bailen. It was the first indisputable defeat that his empire had suffered. It was the first crack in the legend of invincibility that had been so brilliantly and gloriously acquired.

Invincibility was the chief asset of Napoleon's army. Belief in it was firmly held by every one who served in it and, subconsciously, by many of those who fought against it. With the passage of the years the aura had been transferred from the army as a whole to the Emperor and his Guard. Invincibility was a hard myth to sustain for those like Soult, D'Erlon, Reille and all those who had been repeatedly worsted in the Peninsula but few Frenchmen who fought at Waterloo doubted that, with Napoleon at their head, they must be victorious. It was supreme confidence in his leadership that allowed the French to renew their attacks again and again, even if it was desperation which drove Napoleon repeatedly to order them forward. Napoleon's invincibility was an article of faith in the French army. The disaster in Russia was ascribed to the weather, the collapse of 1813-14 to treason in high places.

Although 'to lie like a bulletin' became a French proverb, it was not only by propaganda, true or false, that the belief in imperial invincibility was communicated to friend and foe alike. The 'noise and clanging of arms,' the repeated shouts of *Vive l'Empereur* that heralded the approach of a French column of attack were all part of a concerted exercise in the destruction of the enemy's morale and the sustaining of French enthusiasm. The approach of such a column, shrouded in fast-moving skirmishers whose task was to gall the enemy and draw from them the first, best loaded, volley, was a fearsome spectacle. It had been preceded by a bombardment which caused at least as much loss of morale as casualties. The use of 12 pounders as field guns was largely an exercise in public relations. The damage done to a column of troops by an iron ball 4.75 inches in diameter was not notably greater than that done by a nine pounder ball half-an-inch smaller. The additional range they commanded was very small and was, in any case, seldom used. They were difficult and slow to move and the extra waggons they needed* encumbered the army on the march. But their detonation was more deafening, the clouds of smoke they belched forth were larger and thicker, the whistle of their shot was louder and more eerie. It was comforting to have them in support but unnerving to be facing their muzzles.

Everything that could be contrived, not least the provision of impressive uniforms, to give the French soldiers confidence was carefully undertaken. Few armies have ever had a higher belief in their own powers and in the genius of their leader. At Waterloo they met another army which had come to the same belief in themselves by a different road. The British army, as a whole, could not convince itself of its own invincibility. Too many officers and men remembered the disasters of the American War of Independence, of Flanders in 1794, of the Helder in 1799, of Egypt and Buenos Ayres in 1807. Many of the battalions at Waterloo had been defeated the previous year at Bergen-op-Zoom. The Inniskillings had been innocently involved in the disgrace of Tarragona. Lambert's brigade was just returned from the bloody fiasco at New Orleans. But, like the French, they had a talismanic belief in their commander. When Wellington was appointed to the command in the Netherlands, a sergeant of the Fifty-First could 'never remember anything that caused such joy, our men were almost frantic, every soldier you met told the joyful news. I had a bottle of gin thrust up to my mouth and twenty voices shouting, "Drink hearty to our old commander! We don't give a damn for the French, supposing every one of them was a Napoleon!"'

The British army had had its setbacks but of one thing every Peninsular infantryman was certain. Deployed in their two-deep line they could not be broken by any column. They had seen it all too often before. Alexandria, Maida, Vimeiro, Coruña, Talavera, Busaco, Fuentes de Oñora, Albuera, Sorauren, Nive,

* 12-pounders needed five *caissons*, 8-pounders three and 4-pounders two.

St Pierre. The battle honours on their colours, the clasps on the gold crosses worn by their generals all repeated the same story. They might be deserted by their allies, their cavalry might commit almost any folly, they might be destroyed by Napoleon's formidable artillery (although they knew the Duke would do his best to find them shelter from it) but the 'old Spanish infantry' knew that so long as there was a handful of them aligned on the colours, a supply of ammunition and 'Old Nosey' in command, the columns would not, could not, break through. Every continental general* believed them to be wrong but the redcoats and the greenjackets knew better. They were right.

A French officer described in graphic terms the contrast between the methods of the two sides, between the passionate enthusiasm of the French in their column and the silent stolidity of the British. 'As soon as we got about 1,000 metres from the English line our men would begin to get restless and excited. They exchanged ideas; the march began to get hurried. Meanwhile the English, silent and impassive, arms at the port, looked like a long red wall – most forbidding to our young soldiers. As we get closer shouts of *"Vive l'Empereur!" "En avant!" "À la baïonette!"* break from our ranks. Our march becomes a trot; men fire their muskets into the air. Three hundred yards in front the scarlet line stands motionless. They do not seem to be impressed by the storm which threatens to break over them. It is a striking contrast. Some of us begin to think that it will be devastating when, at last, they do fire. Their unshakeable calm is unnerving. Our enthusiasm begins to wane. We try to restore our confidence by redoubled shouting. Then, at last, the English muskets come down – they are making ready. Appalled, many of our men halt and open a scattered fire. Then comes the English volley, precise, deadly, thunderous. Decimated, our column staggers, half turns, tries to regain its balance. The enemy break their long-held silence with a cheer. Then a second volley, perhaps a third and, with the third, they are at us, chasing us in a disorderly retreat.'

* Except the Hanoverians who had learned in the same school.

3. Uniforms

Today when the armies of almost all nations dress for war in combinations of brown and green, it seems extraordinary that in 1815 soldiers should have gone to war wearing bright colours, trimmed with gold and silver, surmounted with long plumes. It was, of course, not the last time that they did so. In 1884 British infantry sweated across the Sudanese desert in scarlet serge on their abortive attempt to rescue General Gordon. French infantry in blue tunics and scarlet trousers charged German machine guns in 1914, a year in which their dragoons were still wearing classical helmets with long horsehair plumes.

As long as the musket, with its limited range, dominated the battlefield, camouflage clothing was useless. In daylight a man standing or kneeling is visible at a hundred yards whatever he is wearing. Only a few specialised troops, skirmishers, whose task required concealment, wore green or grey in the hope of merging into the summer landscape.

With the difficulties in communication and visibility mentioned in the last chapter, the first requirement in a uniform was recognizability. In one of Wellington's rare comments on uniforms, he wrote to London, 'I only beg that we may be as different as possible from the French in everything. It is impossible to form an idea of the inconvenience and injury which result from having anything like them either on horseback or on foot. Captain Lutyens and his piquet were taken in June,* because the 2nd Hussars had the same caps as the French *chasseurs à cheval* and some of their hussars; and I was near being taken on 25 September† for the same reason.' On the morning of Waterloo, a sergeant of the 12th Light Dragoons 'rode up to a party of French light cavalry, which he had mistaken for his own regiment, they were clothed so much alike; but the blow of a sabre, which wounded him slightly, soon convinced him of his error, and he owed his safety to the goodness of his horse.'

* Captain Benjamin Lutyens, 11th Light Dragoons, and 64 men were captured near Elvas on 22 June, 1811 by a French force which approached from the rear. The 2nd Hussars, King's German Legion, were on the immediate right of Lutyens' piquet.

† During the action at El Bodon, near Ciudad Rodrigo.

Such errors were not confined to one side. The crossing of the Douro in 1809 was assisted by the fact that French sentries assumed that the red-coated soldiers on their bank of the wide river came from one of their own Swiss regiments. They did not believe that the British would dare cross in broad daylight. The French also had a Hanoverian Legion dressed in red. This took part in the first attack on Fuentes de Oñoro (3 May, 1811) and 'was at first taken for a British regiment, and they had time to form and give us a volley before the mistake was discovered.' A few minutes later, however, the Hanoverians were heavily fired on by their own side, who also took them for British.

Red or 'Stroudwater scarlet' became the usual wear for British infantry soon after the Restoration of 1660, although it had been widely used in the rebel 'New Model Army'.

French uniforms also changed colour after their revolution. The old Bourbon infantry wore white or grey. Only the Household troops (except the *Cent Suisses du Roy*, who were in red) wore blue. Blue jackets faced with red were introduced by the revolutionary authorities. It would be wrong, however, to picture the French infantry fighting in blue. At Waterloo, and even in the height of a Spanish summer, they went into battle with a grey or beige greatcoat over their tunics. Blue greatcoats were the prized privilege of the Old and Middle Guards.

Prussians had worn blue for at least a hundred years and most of Wellington's allied troops wore a uniform derived, and at a distance indistinguishable, from the French. Many of the Germans and Netherlanders were, indeed, still wearing French uniforms, a legacy from their days of national vassalage. Most unfortunate of all were the Nassauers at Papelotte who, after a gallant stand, were driven from their post by Prussians who mistook them for Frenchmen.

For recognition at a distance, silhouette was quite as important as colour. Wellington continued the letter just quoted, 'At a distance, or in action, colours are nothing: the profile, and shape of the man's cap, and his general appearance, are what guide us. A *cock-tailed* horse* is a good mark for a dragoon, if you can get a side view of him; and there is no such mark as the English dragoon helmet†, and as far I as can judge, it is the best cover a dragoon can have. The narrow-topped caps [i.e. shakos] of our infantry, as opposed to the French broad top caps, are a great advantage to those who have to look at a long line of posts opposed to each other.' It will surprise no student of military history to know that, on receipt of this letter, the Horse Guards immediately put in hand a change in light dragoon headwear, adopting a shako identical in silhouette to that worn by the French.

Bright colours and elaborate accessories had uses other than recognition. They were designed to make the wearer more impressive. This is an idea as old as

---

* The French did not cut their horses' tails.
† At that time the light dragoons wore the combed helmet worn at Waterloo only by Horse Artillery (see Plates 91-93).

war itself and was valid so long as men fought at close quarters. Savages, who wore little else, sported feathered headdresses to increase their apparent height. Feathers continued to be worn, particularly by cavalrymen and Highlanders, but the most impressive addition to a man's actual height was the bearskin grenadier cap, a headdress of minimal utility and considerable inconvenience but one which is undeniably imposing. In 1812, when it was decided to cut down the weight (and consequently the height) of the shako worn by the British 'heavy' infantry, the new issue, copying an Austrian model, had a false front making it appear as tall as the old style. (Plate 119). Epaulettes increase the apparent width of the shoulders and brandenburgs, the elaborate braiding worn on the jackets of hussars, serve to make the chest appear broader.

Nor was all this finery intended to impress the enemy only. It was important to give the soldier a uniform of which he could be proud. It was not without significance that Britain, the only major army dependent on voluntary recruiting, dressed its infantry in the brightest colour. Many a man took King George's shilling in order to change his old and workworn clothes for a smart, new, splendid suit which he believed would have an irresistable effect on young women. Quite often he was right, whatever the incidental discomforts he incurred. It was not for nothing that recruiting sergeants were decked with ribbons at the public expense.

The proliferation of diverse details, the minute variation in the buttonhole lace, the shades of the facings, the design on the cross belt plate, were all essential properties with which to build pride in the various regiments, the fierce regimental pride which gave the British army so much of its strength. The white metal '28' on the back of the shakos of the North Glosters was not just something else to clean. It was a live reminder of the men in the rear rank at Alexandria who had turned about to drive off French cavalry. It was a pledge that those who wore it would not betray a tradition of bravery and discipline.

Faced with the twin demands of Recognizabilty and Impressiveness, Utility had to get along as best it could. Pipeclay is unsuitable for a battlefield, but white crossbelts greatly increase a man's apparent height. Even in the Rifles, where green was worn for camouflage, the buttons were of white metal and would have reflected the sun. The hussar-style pelisses, required wear for Rifle officers, would have proved an encumbrance when skirmishing through undergrowth. Nevertheless twenty-three years of almost continuous war had done something to increase the comfort and efficiency of British uniforms. The ridiculous and insanitary pigtail had been abolished. The infantryman's gaiters, which were knee length and took twenty minutes to button, had given way to a vestigial spat. The stiff leather stock, designed to keep the head upright, however difficult it made it to look along the barrel of a musket, was retained and the boots provided were still the same for both feet and continued so for thirty years after Waterloo.

James Laver has commented that 'All wars, especially long ones, affect military uniforms by jerking them back in the direction of utility.' 'Jerking' is perhaps too strong a word for the effect the Revolutionary and Napoleonic wars had on the British army but in France the process had gone the other way. At the beginning of the war the revolutionary government, largely for economic reasons, greatly simplified the dress of French soldiers. Napoleon had deliberately brought elaboration back as part of his policy of giving his soldiers a good opinion of themselves. Elaboration reached such a stage in the infantry of the line that a wholesale standardization had to be undertaken in 1812 but in the Imperial Guard there was no check in the process. The fantastic attire of the Mamelukes could be considered as a real life fantasy on an oriental dream, but the bearskins of the Old Guard, the *Grenadiers à Cheval* and the Foot Artillery of the Guard, the elaborate full dress of the hussars and the *Chasseurs à Cheval*, the pigtails and the gold earrings, were all designed to reflect glory on their imperial commander and to convince the Guardsmen that they were the finest soldiers in the world.

Cavalry in all armies had special elaborations. The fearsomeness of the approach of horsemen was greatly heightened by their high plumes and gleaming helmets. The fact that they had horses to keep them out of the mud and carry the weight made it easier to dress cavalrymen as theatrical figures. There was also an international consensus on how types of cavalry should be dressed. Even the Prussians, who had gone further in simplifying uniforms than any other army, dressed their hussars in a formalized version of the dress of Hungarian irregulars. Lancers almost always wore a variation of Polish fashions. With few exceptions heavy cavalry wore a helmet of Grecian inspiration.

All this finery cost money. A British ensign of infantry could not equip himself for less than £45, the equivalent of six months net pay. The uniform of a cornet of light dragoons was estimated to cost £169.10.0, more than he was paid in a year. A hussar officer would need twice as much. A trooper's pelisse for a hussar regiment cost £1.17.5d. as early as 1806.

It would be naïve to assume that troops appeared in battle with the impressive smartness shown in contemporary prints. In both the French and Netherlands armies, many articles were unobtainable before the campaign opened and men wore whatever substitutes, usually items discarded after some earlier reform, could be obtained from the quartermaster's stores. Many of the Prussian *landwehr* were in civilian clothes. The British troops should have been reasonably correct in their dress since the new war was only beginning and they were close to their home base and its large clothing industry. On 18 June one feature was common to men of all armies – a liberal coating of mud. A surgeon of the Life Guards said that the troopers were 'so covered in mud that their faces were scarcely distinguishable, and the colour of their scarlet uniforms invisible.'

Officers with long experience of campaigning paid little attention to the Dress Regulations in their search for comfort or self-expression. 'The consequence was that scarcely any two were dressed alike. Some with grey braided coats, others with brown; some again with blue.' 'Leather bottoms to the pantaloons' were widely favoured and a contemporary sketch shows a Rifle officer wearing sky blue trousers with his 'camouflaged' green jacket. Scruffiest of all was Lieutenant-General Sir Thomas Picton who, on the evening before the battle, was observed 'dressed in a shabby old greatcoat and a rusty round hat of no prepossessing appearance.'

A sprinkling of British officers were notably overdressed. A gunner marching up to Quatre Bras noticed that 'a cabriolet, driving at a smart pace, passed us. In it was seated an officer of the Guards, coat open, snuff box in hand – much in the same manner as he might drive to Epsom or Ascot Heath'. The Guardsman was on his way from the Duchess of Richmond's ball. So was an officer whom a commissary met sheltering from the thunderstorm. 'He was in full dress, with his gold epaulettes and white duck pantaloons, which from their brightness appeared to have been put on for the first time.'

Napoleon, who took a keen interest in uniform, fought the battle dressed for comfort rather than rank. As usual when on active service, he wore a gray greatcoat over the undress uniform of the colonel of the *Chasseurs à Cheval de la Garde*, a green coat faced with red, over white breeches. Wellington, on the other hand, had scarcely any feature of uniform in his dress. He admitted that 'there is no subject which I understand so little,' and, while insisting on cleanliness, had only one known prejudice about uniforms. He detested the carrying of umbrellas in battle. In 1813 he had protested crossly that 'the Guards may in uniform, when on duty at St James, carry them if they please, but in the field it is not only ridiculous but unmilitary.' He fought Waterloo in a blue frockcoat, with a white stock at the neck, white bucksin breeches, Hessian boots with gold tassels and his characteristic low-crowned cocked hat, decorated with the cockades (very small) of Britain, the Netherlands, Portugal and Spain, the countries of which he was a field marshal. His sword was that of a French officer captured in Spain and he wore the knotted gold sash of a Captain General of Spain. He was, however, equipped for all eventualities. One of the pistol holsters had been removed from his saddle and replaced by a small writing case,* while on the crupper was a small valise containing a change of clothes. It was not for nothing that he was known to his officers as 'The Beau'. He also had a short blue cape. 'I had it on and off fifty times because I never get wet if I can help it.'

Little is known about Blücher's dress for the battle. He certainly wore his service cap (*feldmütze*), his cloak and his decorations. This last suggests that he was wearing his general's uniform under the cloak. His most notable characteristic must have been his smell. After his fall at Ligny, he had dosed himself with gin and rhubarb and his limbs had been massaged with brandy. As he embraced his British liaison officer he remarked, '*Ich stinke etwas*'.

98   * Napoleon had to dictate all his letters since his handwriting was wholly illegible.

Strength returns of all armies are always confusing, frequently confused and, occasionally, deliberately distorted. They were generally made some time before any event of significance and different armies include or exclude different categories of men. Therefore the figures shown in this appendix are unlikely to be minutely accurate but almost certainly show an acceptable approximation of the strengths of the armies at the beginning of the campaign.

Appendix: Orders of Battle of the Armies

I FRANCE. (Army of the North)

Commander in Chief

The Emperor Napoleon I.

Chief of Staff.   Marshal Soult, Duke of Dalmatia.
Chief Staff Officer.   Lieut. Gen. Count Bailly de Monthyon.
Commander of the Artillery.   Lieut. Gen. Ruty.
Commander of the Engineers.   Lieut. Gen. Baron Rogniat.
Marshals Commanding Groups of Corps.
   Marshal Ney, Prince of the Moskowa (left)
   Marshal Count Grouchy (right)

Imperial Guard (Lieut. Gen. Count Druot, vice Marshal Mortier, Duke of
         Treviso, sick)   20,755 men

Infantry of the Guard   13,026 men
   Old Guard (Lieut. Gen. Count Friant)
      1st & 2nd Grenadiers (4 bns)
      1st & 2nd Chasseurs (4 bns)
   Middle Guard (Lieut. Gen. Count Morand)
      3rd & 4th Grenadiers (3 bns)
      3rd & 4th Chasseurs (4 bns)
   Young Guard (Lieut. Gen. Count Duhesme)
      1st & 2nd Tirailleurs (4 bns)
      1st & 2nd Voltigeurs (4 bns)

Cavalry of the Guard   4,100 men
    Light Cavalry (Lieut. Gen. Count de Lefebvre-Desnoëttes)
      1st Lancers (1 sqn)
      2nd Lancers.
      Chasseurs à Cheval.
    Heavy Cavalry (Lieut. Gen. Count Guyot)
      Grenadiers à Cheval.
      The Empress' Dragoons.
      Gendarmerie d'Élite

Note. The Carabineers were attached to 12th Cavalry Division.

Artillery of the Guard. (Lieut. Gen. Baron Desvaux de St Maurice)   122 guns
    13 foot btys.
    3 horse btys.
    Engineers of the Guard, 1 coy.
    Sailors of the Guard, 1 coy.

First Corps (Lieut. Gen. Drouet D'Erlon)   20,731 men

1st Division (Lieut. Gen. Allix, absent)
    1st Brigade (Maj. Gen. Quiot)
    54th & 55th Line (3 bns)
    2nd Brigade (Maj. Gen. Bourgeois)
    28th & 105th Line (4 bns)
2nd Division (Lieut. Gen. Baron Donzelot)   5,132 men
    1st Brigade (Maj. Gen. Schmitz)
    13th Light & 17th Line (5 bns)
    2nd Brigade (Maj. Gen. Baron Aulard)
    19th & 51st Line (4 bns)
3rd Division (Lieut. Gen. Baron Marcognet)   3,900 men
    1st Brigade (Maj. Gen. Noguez)
    21st & 46th Line (4 bns)
    2nd Brigade (Maj. Gen. Grenier)
    25th & 45th Line (4 bns)
4th Division (Lieut. Gen. Count Durutte)   3,853 men
    1st Brigade (Maj. Gen. Pegot)
    8th & 29th Line (4 bns)
    2nd Brigade (Maj. Gen. Brue)
    85th & 95th Line (4 Bns)
1st Cavalry Division (Lieut. Gen. Baron Jacquinot)   1,706 men
    1st Cavalry Brigade (Maj. Gen. Baron Bruno)
    7th Hussars
    3rd Chasseurs à Cheval.

2nd Cavalry Brigade (Maj. Gen. Gobrecht)
   3rd & 4th Lancers.
Artillery of 1st Corps (Col. de Salle)   46 guns
  5 Foot btys
  1 horse bty.
Engineers. 5 coys.

Second Corps (Lieut. Gen. Count Reille)   25,179 men

5th Division (Lieut. Gen. Baron Bachelu)   4,103 men
  1st Brigade (Maj. Gen. Husson)
    2nd Light & 61st Line (4 bns)
  2nd Brigade (Maj. Gen. Baron Campy)
    72nd & 108th Line (5 bns)
6th Division (Lieut. Gen. Prince Jerome Napoleon)   7,819 men
  1st Brigade (Maj. Gen. Baron Bauduin)
    1st & 3rd Light (7 bns)
  2nd Brigade (Maj. Gen. Soye)
    1st & 2nd Line (6 bns)
7th Division (Lieut. Gen. Girard)   3,925 men
  1st Brigade (Maj. Gen. Baron Desvilliers)
    11th Light & 82nd Line (3 bns)
  2nd Brigade (Maj. Gen. Baron Piat)
    12th Light & 40th Line (5 bns)
9th Division (Lieut. Gen. Count Foy)   4,788 men
  1st Brigade (Maj. Gen. Baron Gauthier)
    92nd & 93rd Line (4 bns)
  2nd Brigade (Maj. Gen. Baron Jamin)
    4th Light & 100th Line (6 bns)
2nd Cavalry Division (Lieut. Gen. Baron Piré)   2,064 men
  1st Cavalry Brigade (Maj. Gen. Baron Hubert)
    1st & 6th Chasseurs à Cheval
  2nd Cavalry Brigade (Maj. Gen. Vathiez)
    5th & 6th Lancers.
Artillery of 2nd Corps (Col. Pelletier)   46 guns
  5 foot btys.
  1 horse bty.
Engineers. 5 companies.

Third Corps (Lieut. Gen. Vandamme, Count of Unebourg) 18,105 men
8th Division (Lieut. Gen. Baron Lefol)   4,541 men
  1st Brigade (Maj. Gen. Billard)
    15th Light & 20th Line (6 bns)

2nd Brigade (Maj. Gen. Baron Corsin)
    37th & 64th Line (5 bns)

10th Division (Lieut. Gen. Baron Habert)   5,024 men
  1st Brigade (Maj. Gen. Baron Gengoux)
    34th & 88th Line (6 bns)
  2nd Brigade (Maj. Gen. Dupeyroux)
    22nd & 70th Line, 2nd Swiss. (6 bns)

11th Division (Lieut. Gen. Baron Berthezène)   5,565 men
  1st Brigade (Maj. Gen. Baron Dufour)
    12th & 56th Line (4 bns)
  2nd Brigade (Maj. Gen. Baron Lagarde)
    33rd & 86th Line (4 bns)

3rd Cavalry Division (Lieut. Gen. Baron Domon)   1,017 men
  1st Cavalry Brigade (Maj. Gen. Baron Dommanget)
    4th & 9th Chasseurs à Cheval.
  2nd Cavalry Brigade (Maj. Gen. Count Vinot)
    12th Chasseurs à Cheval.

Artillery of the 3rd Corps (Col. Dogereau)   38 guns
  4 foot btys.
  1 horse bty.
Engineers. 3 coys.

Fourth Corps (Lieut. Gen. Count Gérard)   16,219 men

12th Division (Lieut. Gen. Baron Pécheux)   4,719 men
  1st Brigade (Maj. Gen. Romme)
    30th & 96th Line (6 bns)
  2nd Brigade (Maj. Gen. Schöffer)
    6th Light & 63rd Line (4 bns)

13th Division (Lieut. Gen. Baron Vichery)   4,145 men
  1st Brigade (Maj. Gen. Le Capitaine)
    59th & 76th Line (5 bns)
  2nd Brigade (Maj. Gen. Deprez)
    48th & 60th Line (4 bns)

14th Division (Lieut. Gen. Count de Bourmont; deserted to Prussians on 15 June
    with his staff)   4,237 men
  1st Brigade (Maj. Gen. Hulot; succeeded to command of division)
    9th Light & 111th Line (4 bns)
  2nd Brigade (Maj. Gen. Toussaint)
    44th & 50th Line (4 bns)

Seventh Cavalry Division (Lieut. Gen. Maurin)   1,500 men
  1st Cavalry Brigade (Maj. Gen. Vallin)
    6th Hussars; 8th Chasseurs à Cheval.

2nd Cavalry Brigade (Maj. Gen. Berruyer)
    6th & 10th Dragoons.
Artillery of the Fourth Corps (Col. Balthus)   46 guns
    5 foot btys.
    1 horse bty.
Engineers. 3 coys.

Sixth Corps (Lieut. Gen. Count de Lobau)   10,821 men

19th Division (Lieut. Gen. Baron Simmer)   3,953 men
    1st Brigade (Maj. Gen. Baron de Bellair)
      5th & 11th Line (5 bns)
    2nd Brigade (Maj. Gen. Jamin)
      27th & 84th Line (4 bns)
20th Division (Lt. Gen. Baron Jeannin)   2,202 men
    1st Brigade (Maj. Gen. Bony)
      5th Light & 10th Line (4 bns)
    2nd Brigade (Maj. Gen. Tromelin)
      47th & 107th Line (3 bns)
21st Division (Lieut. Gen. Baron Teste)   2,418 men
    1st Brigade (Maj. Gen. Lafitte)
      8th Light & 45th Line (4 bns)
    2nd Brigade (Maj. Gen. Penne)
      65th & 75th Line (4 bns)
Artillery of the Sixth Corps (Col. Noury)   32 guns
    4 foot btys.

Reserve of Cavalry (initially commanded by Marshal Grouchy)

First Cavalry Corps (Lieut. Gen. Count Pajol)   2,536 men

4th Cavalry Division (Lieut. Gen. Baron (Pierre) Soult)
    1st Cavalry Brigade (Maj. Gen. St Laurent)
      1st & 4th Hussars
    2nd Cavalry Brigade (Maj. Gen. Baron Ameil)
      5th Hussars
    1 horse bty.   6 guns
5th Cavalry Division (Lieut. Gen. Baron Subervie)
    1st Cavalry Brigade (Maj. Gen. A. de Colbert)
      1st & 2nd Lancers
    2nd Cavalry Brigade (Maj. Gen. Merlin)
      5th Hussars
    1 horse bty   6 guns

Second Cavalry Corps (Lieut. Gen. Count Exelmans)   3,116 men

9th Cavalry Division (Lieut. Gen. Strolz)
  1st Cavalry Brigade (Maj. Baron Burthe)
    5th & 13th Dragoons
  2nd Cavalry Brigade (Maj. Gen. Baron Vincent)
    15th & 20th Dragoons
  1 horse bty.   6 guns
10th Cavalry Division (Lieut. Gen. Chastel)
  1st Cavalry Brigade (Maj. Gen. Bonnemains)
    4th & 12th Dragoons
  2nd Cavalry Brigade (Maj. Gen. Berton)
    14th & 17th Dragoons
  1 horse bty.   6 guns

Third Cavalry Corps (Lieut. Gen. Kellermann, Count of Valmy) 3,400 men

11th Cavalry Division (Lieut. Gen. Baron L'Heritier)
  1st Cavalry Brigade (Maj. Gen. Picquet)
    2nd & 7th Dragoons
  2nd Cavalry Brigade (Maj. Gen. Guiton)
    8th & 11th Cuirassiers
  1 horse bty.   6 guns
12th Cavalry Division (Lieut. Gen. Roussel d'Hurbal)
  1st Cavalry Brigade (Maj. Gen. Blancard)
    1st & 2nd Carabineers
  2nd Cavalry Brigade (Maj. Gen. Count Donop)
    2nd & 3rd Cuirassiers
  1 horse bty.   6 guns

Fourth Cavalry Corps (Lieut. Gen. Count Milhaud)   2,797 men

13th Cavalry Division (Lieut. Gen. Walthier)
  1st Cavalry Brigade (Maj. Gen. Dubois)
    1st & 4th Cuirassiers
  2nd Cavalry Brigade (Maj. Gen. Baron Travers)
    7th & 12th Cuirassiers
  1 horse bty.   6 guns
14th Cavalry Division (Lieut. Gen. Baron Delort)
  1st Brigade (Maj. Gen. Baron Farine)
    5th & 10th Cuirassiers
  2nd Cavalry Brigade (Maj. Gen. Baron Vial)
    6th & 9th Cuirassiers

  1 horse bty.   6 guns

Summary of the French Army in the dispositions of 18 June, 1815

	Infantry	Cavalry	Guns	Total (incl. arty & services)
Right Wing (Marshal Grouchy) (in pursuit of the Prussians)				
III Corps				
(less Domon's Div)	15,130		32	17,000
IV Corps	13,101	1,500	46	16,217
I Cav. Corps				
(Less Subervie's Div)		1,120	6	1,286
II Cav. Corps		2,900	12	3,116
Teste's Div.	2,418		8	2,550
	30,649	5,520	104	40,169
Left Wing (Marshal Ney) (opposing Anglo-Netherlands Army)				
I Corps	16,885	1,706	46	20,731
II Corps				
(less Girard's Div)	16,710	2,046	38	21,154
VI Corps				
(less Teste's Div)	6,155		24	8,271
III Cav. Corps		3,100	12	3,400
IV Cav. Corps		2,400	12	2,797
Domon's Div.		1,017	6	1,117
Subervie's Div.		1,120	6	1,286
	39,750	11,389	144	58,756
Reserve (in rear of La Belle Alliance)				
Imperial Guard	13,026	4,100	122	20,755
Joint Total of Left Wing and Reserve				
	52,776	15,489	266	79,511

Left out of Battle on 18 June (stationed at Quatre Bras)
Girard's Division, 3,925 men and 8 guns.

Grand Total of the Army of the North				
	80,350	13,049	286	123,665

Note. These are the totals at the outset of the campaign. Allowance must be made for about 13,000 casualties at Quatre Bras and Ligny and for sick and stragglers.

II. ANGLO-NETHERLANDS ARMY

Commander in Chief

Field Marshal the Duke of Wellington

Quartermaster General (acting)	Col. Sir William Delancey
Adjutant General	Maj. Gen. Sir Edward Barnes
Commander, Artillery	Col. Sir George Wood
Commander, Engineers	Col. Carmichael Smyth

Officers commanding corps:
    Gen. H. R. H. the Hereditary Prince of Orange
    Lieut. Gen. Lord Hill

Cavalry (Lieut. Gen. the Earl of Uxbridge)   14,480 men
Household Brigade (Maj. Gen. Lord Edward Somerset)
    1st & 2nd Life Guards, Royal Horse Guards (Blue)
    1st (King's) Dragoon Guards
2nd (Union) Brigade (Maj. Gen. Sir William Ponsonby)
    1st (Royal), 2nd (Royal North British), 6th (Inniskilling) Dragoons
3rd Brigade (Maj. Gen. Sir William Dörnberg)
    23rd Light Dragoons, 1st & 2nd Light Dragoons, King's German Legion
4th Brigade (Maj. Gen. Sir John Vandeleur)
    11th, 12th (Prince of Wales'), 16th (Queen's) Light Dragoons
5th Brigade (Maj. Gen. Sir Colquhuon Grant)
    7th (Queen's Own) & 15th (King's) Hussars
    2nd Hussars, King's German Legion *(detached)*
6th Brigade (Maj. Gen. Sir Vivian Hussey)
    10th (Prince of Wales' Own) & 18th Hussars
    1st Hussars, King's German Legion
7th Brigade (Col. von Arentschild)
    13th Light Dragoons, 3rd Hussars, King's German Legion
Hanoverian Cavalry Brigade (Col. von Estorff)
    Cumberland, Prince Regent's, Bremen & Vreden Hussars
Netherlands Heavy Cavalry Brigade (Maj. Gen. Baron Trip van Zoudtlant)
    1st & 3rd (Dutch), 2nd (Belgian) Carabineers
1st Netherlands Light Cavalry Brigade (Maj. Gen. Van Ghigny)
    4th (Dutch) Light Dragoons, 8th (Belgian) Hussars
2nd Netherlands Light Cavalry Brigade (Maj. Gen. Baron Van Merlen)
    5th (Belgian) Light Dragoons, 6th (Dutch) Hussars

Brunswick Cavalry
  2nd Hussars, 1 sqn Uhlans
Artillery attached to the cavalry (Lieut. Col. Sir Augustus Frazer)
  Royal Horse Artillery. Troops of Bull, Gardiner, Mercer, Ramsay,
      Webber-Smith & Whinyates
  Netherlands Horse Artillery. ½ troops of Petter & Gey   44 guns
Infantry Divisions
1st (British) Division (Maj. Gen. Cooke)   4,061 men
  1st (British) Brigade (Maj. Gen. Maitland)
    2nd & 3rd bns, 1st Guards
  2nd (British) Brigade (Maj. Gen. Sir John Byng)
    2nd bns, Coldstream & 3rd Guards
  Artillery: Sandham's Bty R. A. Kuhlmann's Bty KGL.   12 guns
2nd (Anglo-Hanoverian) Division (Lieut. Gen. Sir Henry Clinton) 6,833 men
  3rd (British) Brigade (Maj. Gen. Adam)
    1st bn, 52nd (Oxfordshire) & 71st (Highland) Light Infantry,
        2nd bn, (6 coys) & 3rd bn (2 coys) 95th Rifles
  1st (K.G.L.) Brigade (Col. du Platt)
    1st, 2nd, 3rd & 4th Line bns King's German Legion
  3rd (Hanoverian) Brigade (Col. Hew Halkett)
    Landwehr bns of Bremervörde, Osnabruck, Quackenbruck & Salzgitter.
  Artillery: Bolton's Bty, R.A. & Sympher's Bty KGL   12 guns
3rd (Anglo-Hanoverian) Division (Lieut. Gen. Sir Charles Alten) 6,970 men
  5th (British) Brigade (Maj. Gen. Sir Colin Halkett)
    2nd bn, 30th (Cambridgeshire); 33rd (1st West Riding),
        2nd bns, 69th (South Lincoln) & 73rd (Highland)
  2nd (K.G.L.) Brigade (Col. von Ompteda)
    1st & 2nd Light, 5th & 8th Line bns King's German Legion
  1st (Hanoverian) Brigade (Maj. Gen. Count von Kielmansegge)
    Field bns of Bremen, Verden, York, Luneberg & Grubenhagen. Jäger bn
  Artillery: Lloyd's Bty R.A. & Cleeve's Bty KGL   12 guns
4th (Anglo-Hanoverian) Division (Lieut. Gen. Sir Charles Colville) 7,217 men
  4th (British) Brigade (Col. Mitchell)
    3rd bn, 14th (Buckinghamshire), 1st bn, 23rd (Royal Welsh Fuzileers),
        51st (2nd West Riding) Light Infantry
  6th (British) Brigade (Maj. Gen. Johnstone) *Detached*
    2nd bn, 35th (Sussex), 1st bn, 54th (West Norfolk),
        59th (2nd Nottinghamshire), 1st bn, 91st
  6th (Hanoverian) Brigade (Maj. Gen. Sir James Lyon) *Detached*
    Field bn of Lauenberg & Calenberg
    Landwehr bns of Nienburg, Hoya & Bentheim
  (Artillery: Broome's Bty R.A. *(Detached)* & Rettberg's Bty KGL   12 guns   **107**

5th (Anglo-Hanoverian) Division (Lieut. Gen. Sir Thomas Picton)   7,158 men
  8th (British) Brigade (Maj. Gen. Sir James Kempt)
    1st bn., 28th (North Gloucester), 1st bn, 32nd (Cornwall), 1st bn, 79th
    (Cameron Highlanders), 1st bn, 95th Rifles (6 coys)
  9th (British) Brigade (Maj. Gen. Sir Denis Pack)
    3rd bn. 1st (Royal Scots), 1st bn. 42nd (Royal Highland)
    2nd bn. 44th (East Essex), 1st bn. 92nd (Gordon Highlanders)
  5th (Hanoverian) Brigade (Col. Von Vincke)
    Landwehr bns of Hameln, Gifhorn, Hildesheim & Peine
  Artillery: Roger's Bty R.A. & Braun's Hanoverian Bty   12 guns
6th (Anglo-Hanoverian) Division (no commander) Incomplete   5,149 men
  10th (British) Brigade (Maj. Gen. Sir John Lambert)
    1st bn. 4th (King's Own) 1st bn. 27th (Inniskilling),
    1st bn, 40th (Somerset), 2nd bn. 81 st *(Detached)*
  4th (Hanoverian) Brigade (Col. Best)
    Landwehr bns of Verden, Luneburg, Osterode & Munden
  Artillery: Unett's bty R.A. *(Detached)* & Sinclair's bty R.A.   12 guns
Reserve of British Artillery. RHA Troops of Ross & Bean   12 guns
1st (Netherlands) Division (Lt. Gen. Stedman) *(Detached)*   6,437 men
  1st Brigade (Maj. Gen. D'Hauw)
    4th (Belgian) Line, 26th (Dutch) Line, 16th (Dutch) Chasseurs,
    9th, 14th & 15th Militia bns.
  2nd Brigade (Maj. Gen. De Eerens)
    1st (Belgian) Line, 18th (Dutch) Chasseurs
    1st, 2nd & 18th Militia
  Artillery: Wijnand's bty   8 guns
2nd (Netherlands) Division (Lieut. Gen. Baron de Perponcher-Sedlnitzky)
                                      7,700 men
  1st Brigade (Maj. Gen. Van Bijlandt)
    7th (Belgian) Line, 27th (Dutch) Chasseurs
    5th, 7th & 8th Militia bns
  2nd Brigade (Maj. Gen. HSH Prince Bernard of Saxe-Weimar)
    2nd Regt. of Nassau (3 bns) Regt. of Orange-Nassau
    Coy. Nassau Jägers
  Artillery: Btys of Stievenart & Bijleveld   16 guns
3rd (Netherlands) Division (Lieut. Gen. Baron Chassé)   6,669 men
  1st Brigade (Maj. Gen. Detmer)
    2nd (Dutch) Line, 35th (Belgian) Chasseurs
    4th, 6th, 17th & 19th Militia bns
  2nd Brigade (Maj. Gen. D'Aubremé)
    3rd (Belgian), 12th (Dutch) & 13th (Belgian) Line, 36th (Belgian) Chasseurs,
    3rd & 10th Militia bns

Artillery: Btys of De Bichin & Lux   16 guns
Netherlands Indian Contingent (Lieut. Gen. Anthing) *(Detached)*   3,499 men
    5th East India Regt (3 bns) 10th & 11th West India Chasseurs,
      Flank Coys of 19th & 20th Line
  Artillery: Riesz' Bty   8 guns
Brunswick Contingent (HSH Frederick, Prince of
    Brunswick-Wolfenbuttel-Oels, Killed in Action, 16 June)   5,376 men
  Advanced Guard (Maj. von Rauschenplatt)
    Det. Uhlans. 2 coys Jägers; 2 coys light infantry
  1st Brigade (Lt. Col. Von Buttlar)
    Guard Bn, 1st, 2nd & 3rd Light Infantry
  2nd Brigade (Lt. Col. Von Specht)
    1st, 2nd & 3rd Line bns
  Artillery: Von Heinemann's Horse Bty
    Moll's Foot Bty   16 guns
Nassau Brigade (Maj. Gen. Von Kruse)
  1st (Duke of Nassau) Regt (3 bns)

Summary of the Anglo-Netherlands Field Army
Rank and File Only (except in Netherlands and Nassau formations)

	Infantry		Cavalry	Guns
British	17,077	Rank	5,911	72
K.G.L.	3,285	&	2,560	18
Hanoverians	11,748	File	1,682	12
Brunswick	5,376	only	922	16
Nassau	7,308	All	–	–
Netherlands	18,838	Ranks	3,405	56
	63,632		14,480	174

Note: An addition of 1/8th should be made to the numbers for British, KGL, Hanoverian and Brunswick troops to allow for officers, sergeants, drummers and trumpeters. This gives an overall total of 67,000 infantry and 15,300 cavalry before the campaign opened.

Casualties at Quatre Bras and on 17 June amounted to rather less than 5,000 all ranks. The detachment at Hal and Tubize consisted of 17,000 men and 2nd bn. 81st regt (470 all ranks) acted as garrison of Brussels.

Allowing for a small number of sick and stragglers, the force at Waterloo cannot have exceeded 60,000 infantry and cavalry with 154 guns.

III PRUSSIAN ARMY

Commander in Chief

Field Marshal Prince Gebhard Blücher von Wahlstädt

Chief of Staff	Lieut. Gen. Count von Gneisenau
Quartermaster General	Maj. Gen. von Grölman
Commander Artillery (acting)	Maj. Gen. von Holzendorff

First Corps (Lieut. Gen. von Zieten) — 31,308 men

  1st Brigade (Maj. Gen. Von Steinmetz) — 9,069 men
    12th & 24th Infantry, 1st (Silesian) Landwehr.
    Silesian Sharpshooters ($\frac{1}{2}$ bn)

  2nd Brigade (Maj. Gen. von Pirch II) — 8,018 men
    6th & 28th Infantry, 2nd (Westphalia) Landwehr

  3rd Brigade (Maj. Gen. von Jagow) — 7,146 men
    7th & 29th Infantry, 3rd (Westphalia) Landwehr
    Silesian Sharpshooters ($\frac{1}{2}$ bn)

  4th Brigade (Maj. Gen. Count Henckel) — 4,900 men
    19th Infantry, 4th (Westphalia) Landwehr

  First Corps Cavalry (Maj. Gen. Von Röder) — 2,175 men
    1st Cavalry Brigade (Maj. Gen. Von Treckow)
      5th (Brandenburg) & 2nd (1st West Prussian)
      Dragoons, 3rd (Brandenburg) Uhlans
    2nd Cavalry Brigade (Lt. Col. von Lutzow)
      4th (1st Silesian) Hussars, 6th (2nd West Prussian) Uhlans,
      1st & 2nd Kurmark & Westphalian Landwehr Cavalry

  Artillery of First Corps (Lt. Col. von Rentzel) — 88 guns
    8 Foot and 3 Horse btys
  1st Engineer coy

Second Corps (Lieut. Gen. von Pirch I) — 31,473 men

  5th Brigade (Maj. Gen. von Tippelskirch) — 7,153 men
    2nd & 25th Infantry 5th, (Westphalia) Landwehr

  6th Brigade (Maj. Gen. von Krafft) — 6,762 men
    9th & 26th Infantry, 1st (Elbe) Landwehr

  7th Brigade (Maj. Gen. von Bause) — 6,503 men
    14th & 22nd Infantry, 2nd (Elbe) Landwehr

  8th Brigade (Maj. Gen. von Böse) — 6,584 men
    21st & 23rd Infantry, 3rd (Elbe) Landwehr

  Second Corps Cavalry (Maj. Gen. von Wahlen-Jurgass) — 4,471 men
    1st Cavalry Brigade (Col. von Thumen)
      1st (Queen's) & 6th (Neumark) Dragoons
    2nd (Silesia) Uhlans

2nd Cavalry Brigade (Lt. Col. von Sohr)
    3rd (Brandenburg), 5th (Pomerania) & 11th (2nd Westphalia) Hussars
3rd Cavalry Brigade (Col. von der Schulenburg)
    4th & 5th (Kurmark) & Elbe Landwehr Cavalry
Second Corps Artillery (Maj. Lehmann)   72 guns
    7 Foot & 3 Horse btys.
7th Engineer Coy

Third Corps (Lieut. Gen. Baron von Thielmann)   24,256 men
9th Brigade (Maj. Gen. von Borche)   7,262 men
    8th (Lieb) & 30th Infantry, 1st (Kurmark) Landwehr
10th Brigade (Col. von Kemphen)   4,419 men
    27th Infantry, 2nd (Kurmark) Landwehr
11th Brigade (Col. von Luck)   3,980 men
    3rd & 4th (Kurmark) Landwehr
12th Brigade (Col. von Stülpnagel)   6,614 men
    31st Infantry, 5th & 6th Kurmark Landwehr
Third Corps Cavalry (Maj. Gen. von Hobe)   1,981 men
    1st Cavalry Brigade (Col. von der Marwitz)
        7th & 8th (1st & 2nd Rhineland) Uhlans
        9th (Rhineland) Hussars
    2nd Cavalry Brigade (Col. Count von Lottum)
        5th (1st Westphalia) Uhlans, 7th (Westphalia) Dragoons,
        3rd & 6th Kurmark Landwehr Cavalry
Third Corps Artillery (Maj. von Greventitz)   56 guns
    3 Foot & 3 Horse Btys
5th Engineer Company

Fourth Corps (General Count Bülow von Dennewitz)   30,585 men
13th Brigade (Lieut. Gen. von Hake)   6,560 men
    10th Infantry, 1st & 2nd (Neumark) Landwehr
14th Brigade (Maj. Gen. Count von Ryssel)   7,138 men
    11th Infantry, 1st & 2nd (Pomerania) Landwehr
15th Brigade (Maj. Gen. von Losthin)   7,143 men
    18th Infantry, 3rd & 4th (Silesian) Landwehr
16th Brigade (Col. von Hiller)   6,423 men
    15th Infantry, 1st & 2nd (Silesian) Landwehr
Fourth Corps Cavalry (Gen. HRH Prince William of Prussia) 3,321 men
    1st Cavalry Brigade (Col. Count von Schwerin)
        10th (1st Magdeburg) Hussars, 1st & 2nd Neumark,
        1st & 2nd Pomerania Landwehr Cavalry
    2nd Cavalry Brigade (Maj. Gen. von Sydow)
        1st (West Prussian) Uhlans, 6th (2nd Silesian) & 8th (1st Westphalian)
        Hussars

3rd Cavalry Brigade (Lt. Col. von Watzdorff)
1st, 2nd & 3rd Silesian Landwehr Cavalry
Fourth Corps Artillery (Maj. von Barbeleben)   80 guns
8 Foot & 3 Horse btys
4th Engineer Company

Summary of the Prussian Army

	Infantry	Cavalry	Guns	Total all arms
I Corps	27,817	2,175	88	31,308
II Corps	25,837	4,471	72	31,473
III Corps	20,611	1,981	56	24,256
IV Corps	25,381	3,321	80	30,585
	99,646	11,948	296	117,622

Note. Casualties on 15 and 16 June amounted to about 12,000 including deserters. This loss fell largely on I & II Corps. There must have been a substantial numbers of stragglers in the long and difficult marches of 17 and 18 June.

Napoleon's Army

1 Marshal of the Empire in Full Dress.

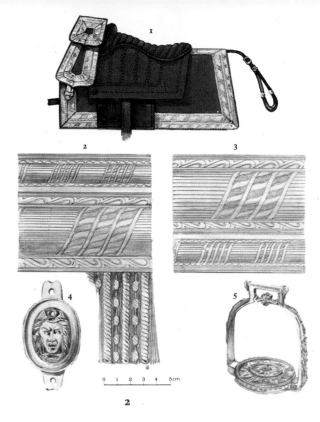

1 Generals' Saddle.
2 Saddle Lace for Marshals (with fringe).
3 Saddle Lace for Lieutenant-Generals and
   Major-Generals (without fringe).
4 Boss at either end of horse's bit (gilt
   for Marshals, silver for Generals).
5 Stirrup (gilt for Marshals, black
   for Generals).

3 Lieutenant-General *(Général de Division)*
   in greatcoat.

4 Major-General *(Général de Brigade)* in
   field uniform.

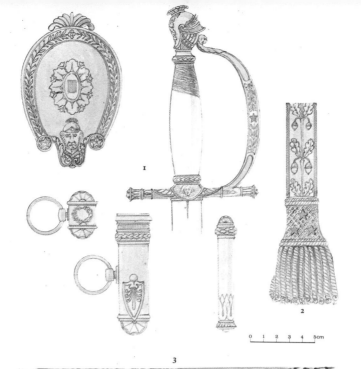

1 Details of the dress sword of a General.
2 Sword Knot of a Lieutenant-General.
   (Major-General's knot would have only
   two stars).
3 Buckle and detail of a Lieutenant-General's
   swordbelt. (The belt of a Marshal would
   have a white ground; that of a Major-General
   a blue ground).

6 Senior Staff officer (*Adjudant-Commandant*)
   in undress.

7 Aide-de-Camp to a Lieutenant-General.
   Undress.

8 *Grenadiers à Cheval.*
Officer.

9 *Grenadiers à Cheval.*
Trumpeter and Trooper.

10 *Chasseurs à Cheval*
Officer in Full dress.
Officer in Undress

11 *Chasseurs à Cheval.*
Trooper in Full Dress.
Trumpeter.

FRANCE
Imperial Guard

12 *Chasseurs à Cheval*. Saddlecloths.
　1 Officer's Saddlecloth.
　2 Trooper's Saddlecloth.
　3 and 4. Detail of Trooper's Saddlecloth.
　5 Detail of Trumpeter's Saddlecloth.

13 *Gendarmerie d'Élite*.
　Corporal.

14 The Empress's Dragoons.
　Officer and Trumpeter.

15 The Empress's Dragoons.
1 Helmet.
1a Helmet, frontal plate of crest.
2 Sabre.
3 Badge on Shoulder Belt Pouch.
4 Buckle of Sword Belt (officers).
5 Buckle of Sword Belt (other ranks).

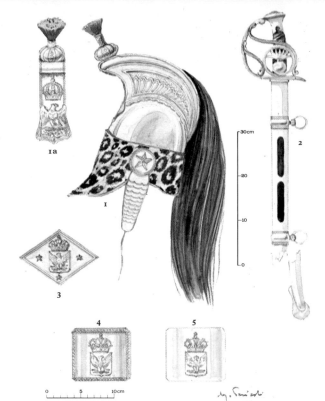

16 1st (Polish) Lancers.
(Chevaux-légers-lanciers) Trooper.

17 1st (Polish) Lancers.
(Chevaux-légers-lanciers) Officer.

18 1st (Polish) Lancers *(Chevaux-légers-lanciers)*.

   1   Officer's Jacket *(kurtka)*.
   1a Lace on officer's jacket.
   2   Trumpeter's jacket (worn with crimson overalls).
   3   Trooper's jacket.
   4   Trooper's jacket (rear view).
   5   Officer's sash.
   6   Overalls (officers).
   7   Button.
   8   Overalls (other ranks).

19 2nd Lancers *(Chevaux-légers-lanciers)* Trumpeter and Trooper.

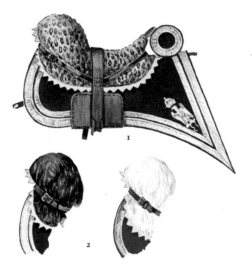

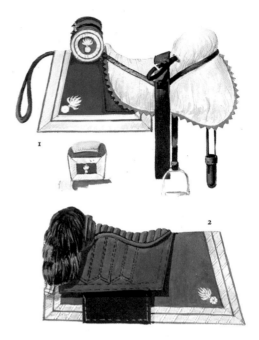

20 2nd Lancers *(Chevaux-légers-lanciers)*.
   1 Officer's Saddlecloth.
   2 Details of trooper's and trumpeter's saddlecloths.

21 Carabineers.
   1 Saddlecloth (other ranks).
   2 Saddlecloth (senior officer.

   The rank was shown by
   the width of the silver lace).

22 Carabineers. Corporal *(Brigadier)* and Major.

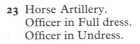

23 Horse Artillery.
Officer in Full dress.
Officer in Undress.

25 Foot Artillery, Major.

24 Horse Artillery.
Trumpeter in Full dress.
Gunner in Full dress with forage cap.
Sergeant in Undress.

26 Foot Artillery, Corporal in fatigue dress with long service chevron showing more than 7 years service.

27 Foot Artillery. Artificer of the
Bridging Company *(Ouvriers-Pontonniers)*
with forge waggon.

FRANCE
Imperial Guard

0 1 2 3 4 5cm

0   10   20   30cm

28 Foot Artillery.
  1 Officer's Epaulette.
  2 Officer's Gorget (detail).
  3 Button.
  4 Hilt of Officer's Sabre.
  5 Bearskin (other ranks).
  6 Bearskin (officers).

29 Grenadiers of the Old Guard.
Lieutenant-General in Uniform of
Colonel of Grenadiers.

30 Grenadiers of the Old Guard.
Officer.

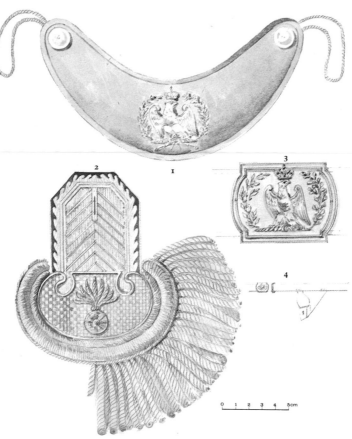

31 Grenadiers of the Old Gu
Officer's Distinctions.
1 Gorget.
2 Epaulette.
3 Belt Plate.
4 Design of Sword Belt.

32 Grenadiers of the Old
Guard
1, 2 and 3. Bearskin of
Corporals and Guards-
men. For officers the
lines would be of gold;
for sergeants-major of
gold (2/3) and red (1/3);
for sergeants of red
(2/3) and gold (1/3). The
same distinction was
used on the epaulette
(see Plate 32).

4 Cockade worn on the
left side of the bear-
skin concealing the
plume holder. For of-
ficers and sergeants-
major the eagle was
embroidered in gilt
wire.

5 Grenade on crown of
bearskin, which
would be in gilt
wire for officers.

6 Frontal Plate in cop-
per. Sergeants and
sergeants-major
wore the plate in
brass, officers in
gilt.

Grenadiers of the Old Guard.

33

rgeant-Major in Undress
th two 7-year service
evrons.

34

Guardsman in forage cap
and greatcoat (The bear-
skin is carried in a
cover on top of the
pack and the plume is
secured to the scabbard
of the short sword).

35

Guardsman in Marching Order.

36

Bandsman in Undress.

FRANCE
Imperial Guard

37 Chasseurs of the Old Guard.
Officer in greatcoat
and forage cap.

38 Chasseur of the Old Guard.
Guardsman wearing overalls.

39 Chasseurs of the Old Guard.
Corporal with more than
14 years service.

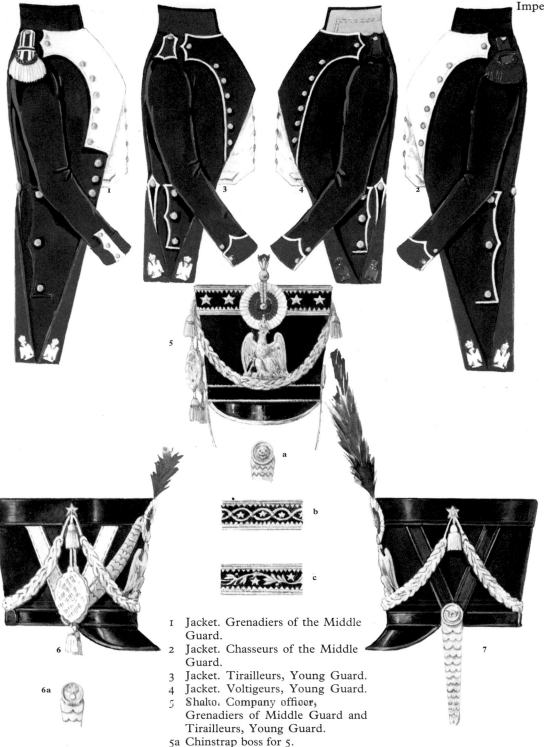

1 Jacket. Grenadiers of the Middle
   Guard.
2 Jacket. Chasseurs of the Middle
   Guard.
3 Jacket. Tirailleurs, Young Guard.
4 Jacket. Voltigeurs, Young Guard.
5 Shako. Company officer,
   Grenadiers of Middle Guard and
   Tirailleurs, Young Guard.
5a Chinstrap boss for 5.
5b Shako lace for field officers.
5c Shako lace for company officers,
   Chasseurs of Middle Guard and
   Voltigeurs, Young Guard.

40 Middle and Young Guards.

6 Shako for other ranks Grenadiers
   of Middle Guard and Tirailleurs,
   Young Guard.
6a Chinstrap boss for 6.

7 Shako for other ranks Chasseurs
   of Middle Guard and Voltigeurs,
   Young Guard.

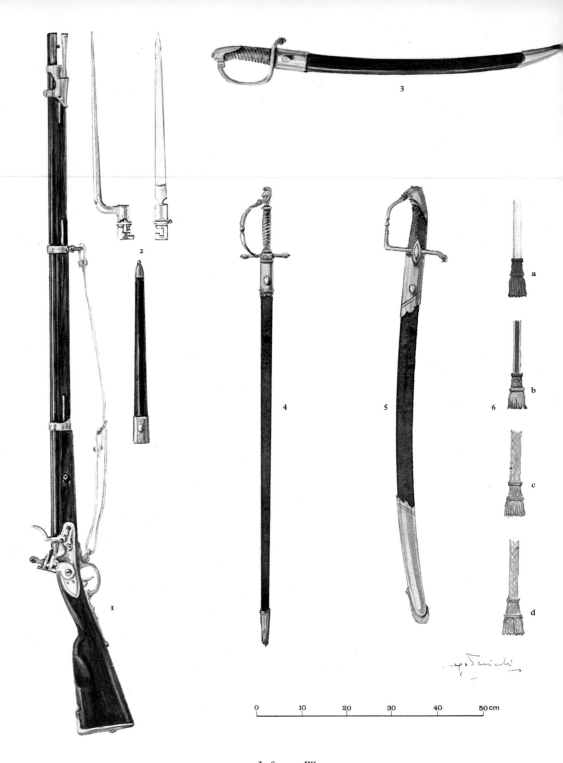

41 Infantry Weapons.

1 Musket of the Guard.
2 Bayonet and Scabbard.
3 Short sword *(sabre-briquet)* for other ranks.
4 Sword of company officers of the Grenadiers.

5 Sabre for mounted officers.
6 Sword Knots.
6a Grenadiers.
6b Sergeants of Grenadiers.
6c Company officers.
6d Field officers.

42 Cuirassiers.
Officer and Trumpeter, 6th Cuirassiers.

43 Dragoons.
Corporal 15th Regiment.

44 Cuirassiers.
1 Saddle Furniture (officers).
2 Saddle Furniture (other ranks).

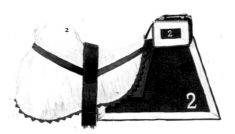

45 *Chasseurs à Cheval*, Corporal with more than 14 years service.

46 Lancers *(Chevaux-légers-lanciers)* Trooper and Officer, 1st Regiment.

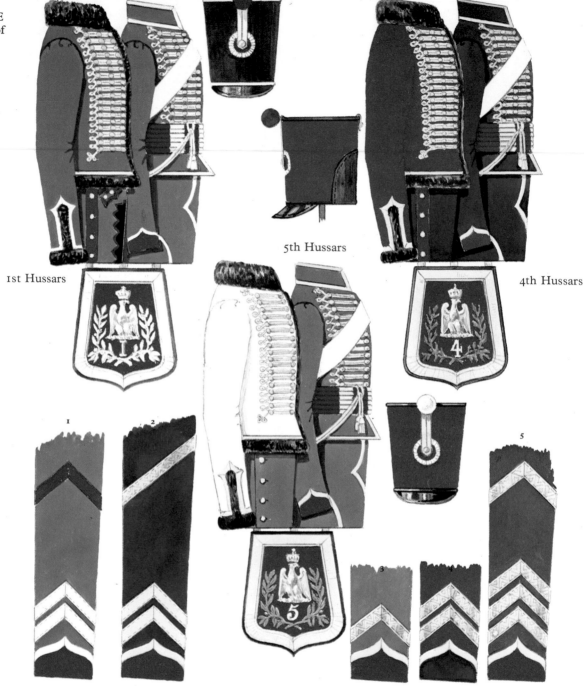

FRANCE
Cavalry of
the Line

1st Hussars

5th Hussars

4th Hussars

47 1st Hussars, 4th Hussars and 5th Hussars.
Pélisse and Overalls
Jacket and Breeches, Sash
Shako
Officer's Sabretache

1 Badge of Corporal with 1 seven-year service chevron
(the service chevron would have been yellow in 6th Hussars).
2 Badge of Quartermaster Corporal *(Brigadier Fourrier)*.
3 Badge of Sergeant *(Maréchal de Logis)*.
4 Badge of Sergeant-Major *(Maréchal de Logis Chef)*.
5 Badge of Regimental Sergeant-Major *(Adjudant)*.

These chevrons would be in gold or silver lace according to the colour of the regimental lace.
Note : These chevrons were those worn on the jacket. Those worn on the pelisse are shown on Plate 48.

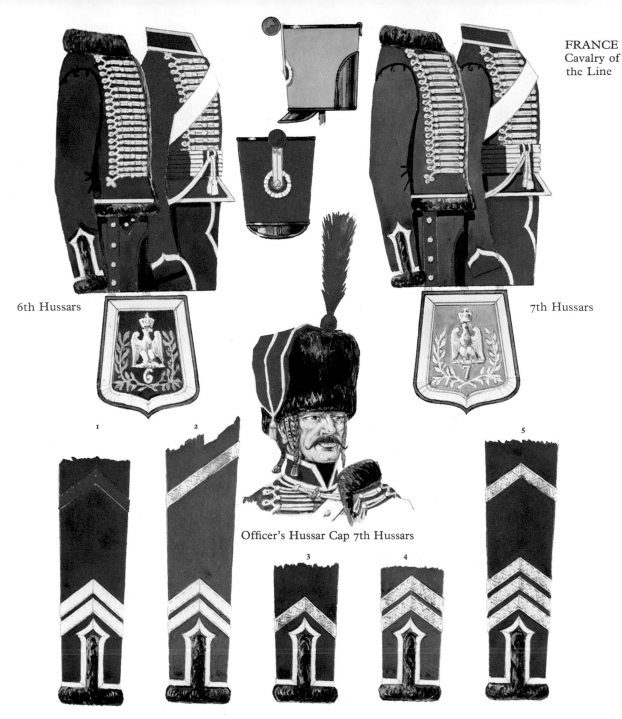

FRANCE
Cavalry of
the Line

6th Hussars

7th Hussars

Officer's Hussar Cap 7th Hussars

48 6th and 7th Hussars.
Pélisse and Overalls.
Jacket and Breeches, Sash.
Shako.
Officer's Sabretache.

The cap was the same in the 4th and 6th regiment and in
the 1st Regiment was varied only by silver piping and
tassel. In the 5th Hussars the busby bag was a rich sky
blue with gold piping and the red plume was tipped with
black.
The Badges of rank for warrant officers and sergeants are
those worn on the pelisse and correspond to those in Plate 47.

FRANCE
Cavalry of the Line

FRANCE
Artillery of the Line

49 Hussars.
Officer, 5th Hussars.
Corporal, 4th Hussars.

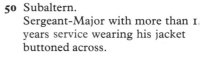

50 Subaltern.
Sergeant-Major with more than 1
years service wearing his jacket
buttoned across.

51 Gunner in forage cap.
Subaltern in greatcoat.
Ammunition chest which was carried
across the gun carriage on its carrying
handles when the gun was in motion.

52 Soldier, Voltigeur Company.

53 Colonel in Full Dress.

54 Subaltern in Field Service Order without greatcoat and wearing shako cover.

55 Officers' Shakos

1 Colonel and Lieutenant-Colonel (with two gold bands 35 mm and 15 mm wide).

2 Major (with one gold band 35 mm wide and one silver band 15 mm wide).

3 *Chef de Battalion* (with one gold band 35 mm wide).

4 Captain of Grenadier Company (red plume) and one gold band, 30 mm wide.

5 Lieutenant of Voltigeurs company (yellow, or occasionally green plume) and one gold band 25 mm wide.

6 2nd Lieutenant of 1st battalion company (with one gold band 20 mm wide).

6a Small plume for regimental officers employed on the general staff.

6b White disc for regimental officers employed on staff duties other than GHQ.

FRANCE
Infantry of the Line

57 Drum Major.

56 Corporal of Pioneers.

58 Corporal, Grenadier Company.

59 Bandsman.

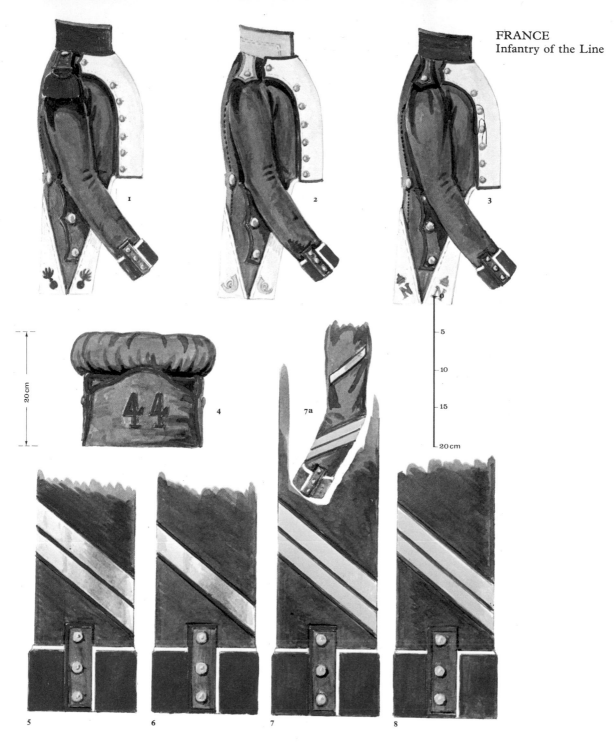

60 1 Jacket (other ranks) Grenadier Company.
    2 Jacket (other ranks) Voltigeur Company.
    3 Jacket (other ranks) Battalion (Fusilier) Company.
    4 Fatigue Cap *(Bonnet de Police)*.
    5 Badges of rank
    5 Sergeant-Major (gold lace).
    6 Sergeant (gold lace).
    7 and 7a. Quartermaster-Corporal (yellow wool stripes with
       gold stripe on left upper arm).
    8 Corporal (yellow wool stripes).

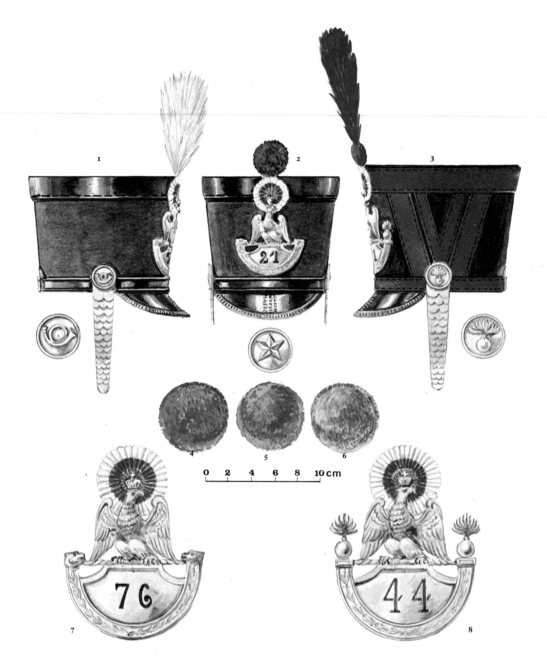

61 1 Shako (other ranks) Voltigeur Company and chinstrap boss.
   2 Shako (other ranks) 1st Fusilier Company and chinstrap boss.
   3 Shako (other ranks) Grenadier Company and chinstrap boss.
   4, 5 and 6 Woollen discs denoting 2nd, 3rd and 4th Fusilier Companies.
   7 Shako Plate, Voltigeur and Fusilier Companies.
   8 Shako Plate, Grenadier Company.

62

Chef de Battalion

63

Soldier, 1st Chasseur Company.

64

Sergeant Major, Carabineer Company
with more than 14 years service.

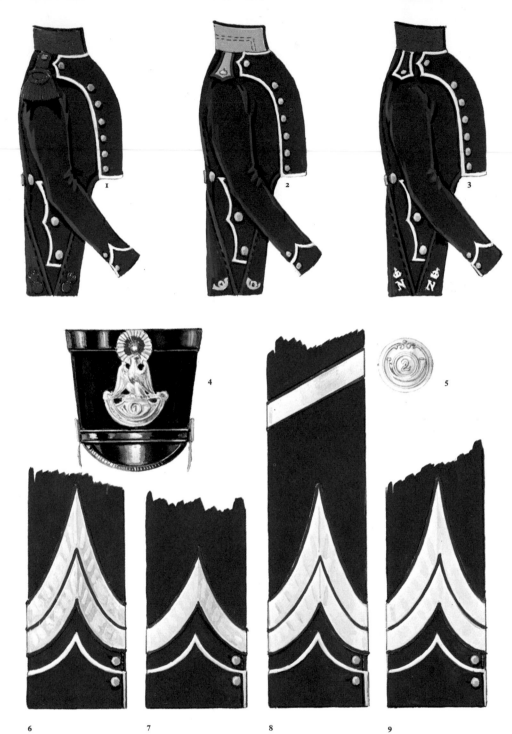

1 Jacket (other ranks) Carabineer Company.
2 Jacket (other ranks) Voltigeur Company.
3 Jacket (other ranks) Chasseur (Battalion) Company.
4 Shako, Voltigeur and Chasseur Companies.
  The officers' distinctions of rank were the same as for
  Infantry of the Line (See 55) but in silver lace.
5 Button.

6, 7, 8 and 9 Badges of rank for NCOs which were as fo
Infantry of the line (see also plate 60), except that the
senior ranks had silver lace rather than gold and the
junior ranks white wool braid.

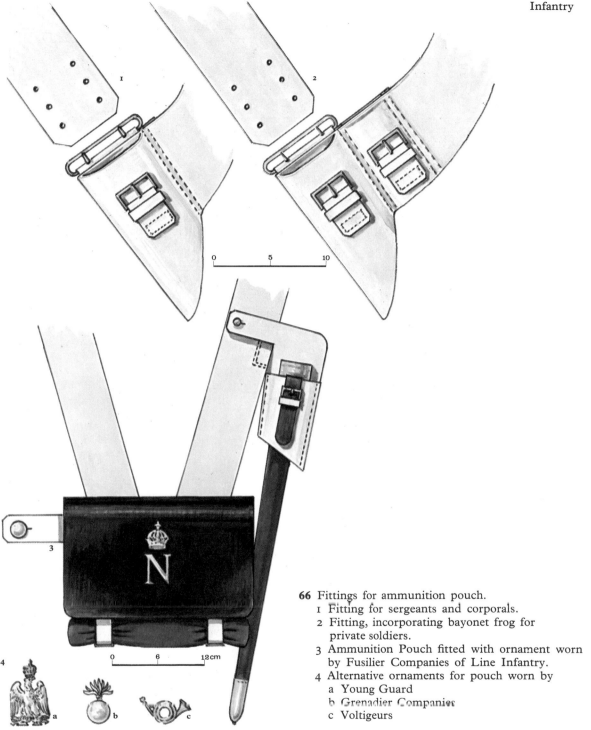

66 Fittings for ammunition pouch.
 1 Fitting for sergeants and corporals.
 2 Fitting, incorporating bayonet frog for
   private soldiers.
 3 Ammunition Pouch fitted with ornament worn
   by Fusilier Companies of Line Infantry.
 4 Alternative ornaments for pouch worn by
   a Young Guard
   b Grenadier Companies
   c Voltigeurs

67 Medical attendant *(Infirmier)*.
Stretcher Bearer.
Physician (2nd class) in undress with hat cover.

Wellington's Army

68 Major-General in Undress.

69 Distinctions of Rank: General Officers.
1 Field-Marshal.
2 Lieutenant-General.
3 Major-General.
4 Brigadier-General.

70 Adjutant-General or
Quartermaster-General.
Full Dress.

71 Aide-de-Camp to a General of Infantry.
Undress.

72 Aide-de-Camp to a General of Infantry.
Evening Dress.

73 1st Life Guards. Officer and Trooper.

74 Royal Horse Guards (Blue). Officer and Trooper.

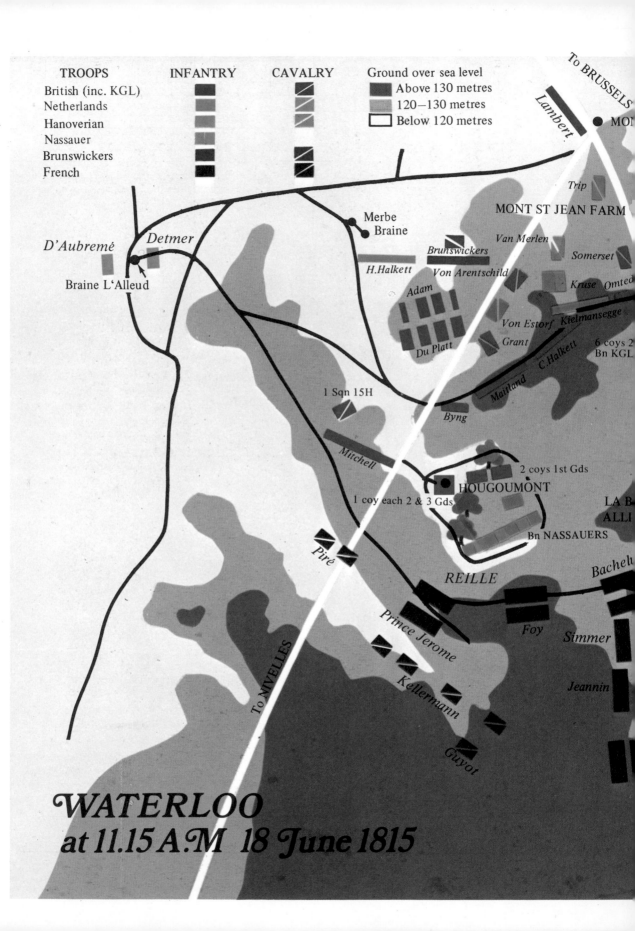

TROOPS

INFANTRY CAVALRY Ground over sea level

British (inc. KGL)
Netherlands
Hanoverian
Nassauer
Brunswickers
French

Above 130 metres
120—130 metres
Below 120 metres

To BRUSSELS

Lambert

MON

Trip

MONT ST JEAN FARM

Van Merlen

D'Aubremé

Detmer

Braine L'Alleud

Merbe Braine

Brunswickers

H.Halkett

Von Arentschild

Adam

Somerset

Kruse Omted

Von Estorf Kielmansegge

Du Platt

Grant

Maitland C.Halkett

6 coys 2
Bn KGL

1 Sqn 15H

Byng

Mitchell

2 coys 1st Gds

HOUGOUMONT

1 coy each 2 & 3 Gds

LA B
ALLI

Piré

Bn NASSAUERS

REILLE

Bachel

To NIVELLES

Prince Jerome

Foy

Simmer

Kellermann

Jeannin

Guyot

WATERLOO
at 11.15 A.M 18 June 1815

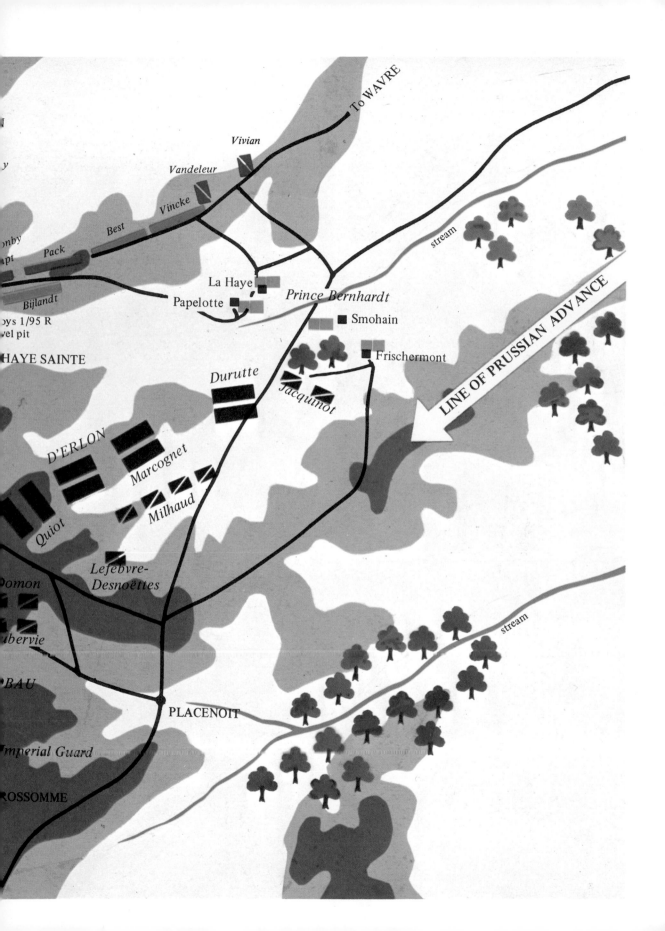

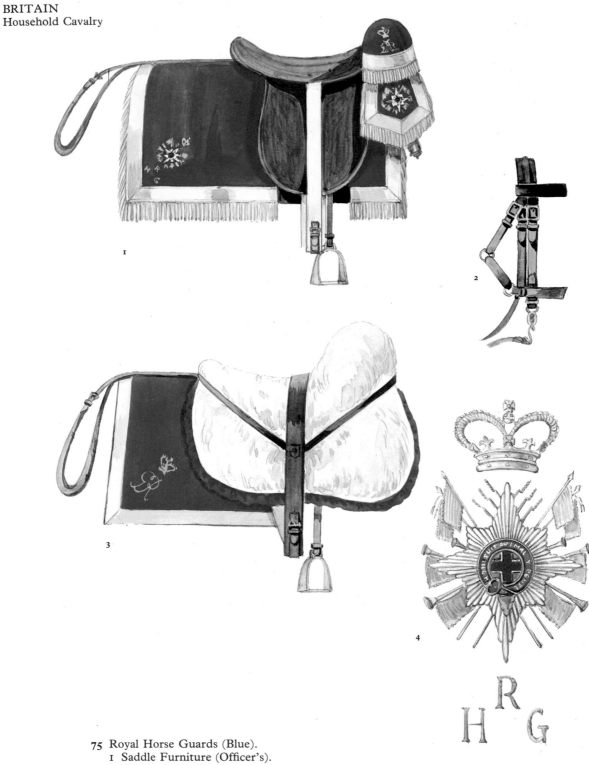

75 Royal Horse Guards (Blue).
   1 Saddle Furniture (Officer's).
   2 Harness (detail).
   3 Saddle Furniture (Other ranks).
   4 Garter Badge from officer's Saddlecloth.

76 1st (King's) Dragoon Guards. Officer and Trooper wearing overalls.

BRITAIN
Cavalry of the Line

77 1st (Royal) Dragoons. Corporal and Officer in cloak with helmet cover.

78 2nd (Royal North British) Dragoons (The Scots Greys). Trooper and Officer.

79 7th (Queen's Own) Light Dragoons (Hussars).
Officer and Troopers.

10th (Prince of Wales's Own Royal) Light Dragoons (Hussars)
Trooper and Officer.

81 11th Light Dragoons. Officer.
12th (Prince of Wales's) Light Dragoons. Corporal.

82 13th Light Dragoons. Other ranks' sash and Officer's Jacket.
16th (Queen's) Light Dragoons. Other ranks' shako and sash.
Officer's jacket.
Detail of Sleeve.
Gold lace epaulette for officers of Light Dragoons.
Detail of Light Dragoon button.
23rd Light Dragoons. Officer's jacket.
Other ranks' sash.
16th (Queen's) Light Dragoons. Officer's jacket (rear view).

83 1st (Dutch) Carabineers. Trooper.　　**84** 1st (Dutch) Carabineers. Officer.

85 8th (Belgian) Hussars. Officer.

86 8th (Belgian) Hussars. Sergeant.

87 5th (Belgian) Light Dragoons. Officer.   **88** 5th (Belgian) Light Dragoons. Trooper.

89 5th (Belgian) Light Dragoons. Trumpeter.

90 Brunswick Hussars. Trooper.

91 Royal Horse Artillery.
Officer.

92 Royal Horse Artillery.
Gunner, Rocket Troop.

93 Royal Horse Artillery.
Driver.

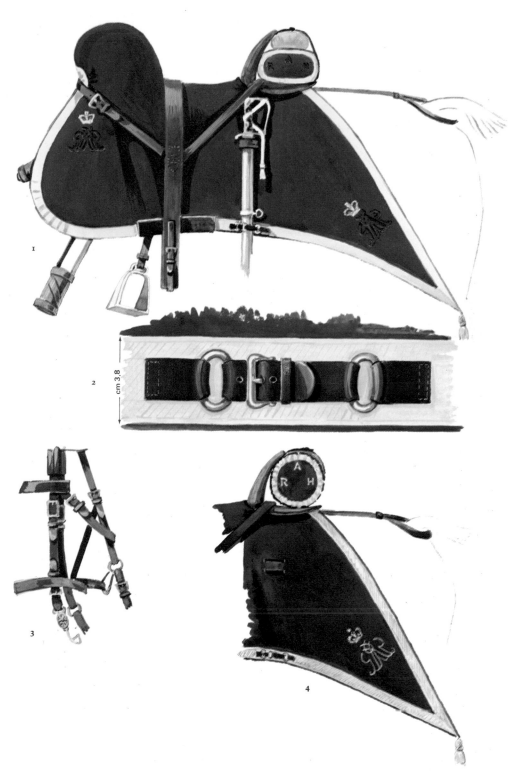

94 Royal Horse Artillery. Saddle Furniture.
1 Saddle Furniture Other Ranks.
2 Detail of strap to secure sabre.
3 Detail of Harness.
4 Detail of Officer's Saddlecloth.

95 Royal Artillery. Gunner, Sergeant and Officer with 6 pounder gun.

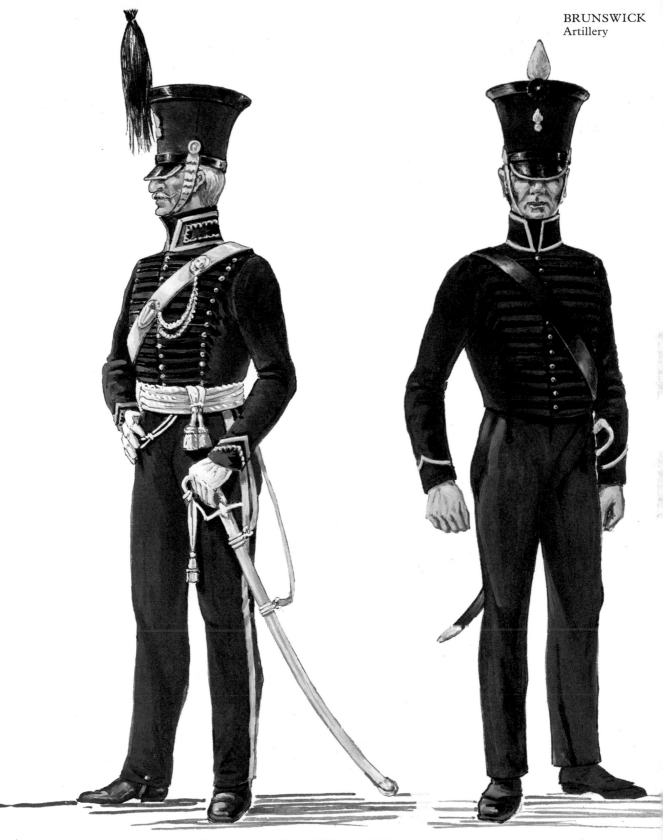

96 Brunswick Artillery. Officer and Gunner.

BRITAIN
Foot Guards

97 2nd (Coldstream).
Lieutenant and Captain in Ball Dress.

98 1 and 1a, 1st Guards. Subaltern and Guardsman,
Grenadier Company.

2 and 2a, 2nd (Coldstream) Guards. Subaltern and
Guardsman, Battalion Company.

3 and 3a, 3rd Guards. Subaltern and Guardsman,
Light Company.

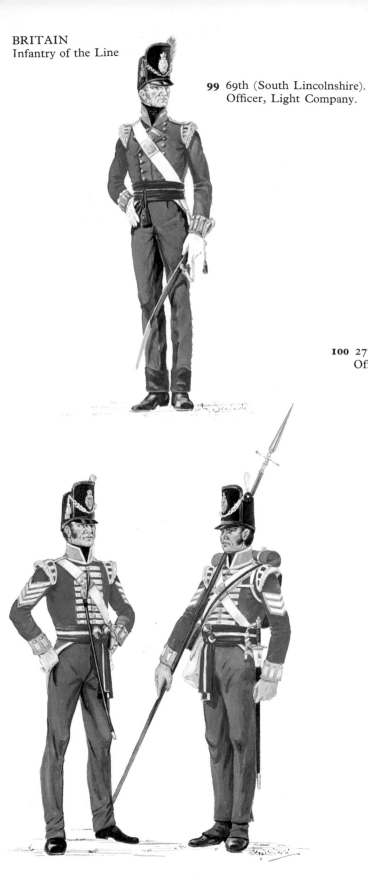

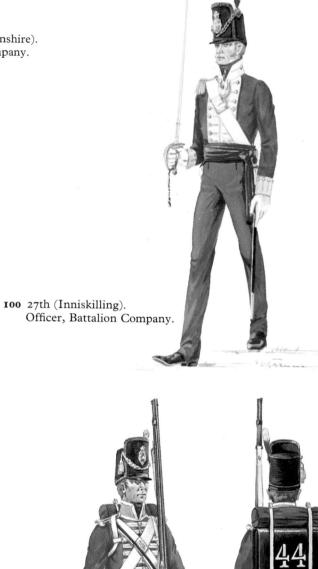

99 69th (South Lincolnshire).
Officer, Light Company.

100 27th (Inniskilling).
Officer, Battalion Company.

101 27th (Inniskilling). Sergeant-Major and Sergeant,
Grenadier Company.

102 44th (East Essex). Private Soldiers.

103 23rd (Royal Welsh Fuzileers).

1 Officer's jacket, Battalion Company.
2 Detail, Officer's jacket, Light Company.
3 Detail, other rank's jacket, Light Company.
4 Other rank's jacket, Battalion Company.
5 Drummer's jacket.
6 Detail of other ranks' buttonhole lace.
7 Cross Belt Plate.

104 28th (North Gloucestershire).
　1 Officer's jacket, Flank Company.
　2 Shako, Light Company.
　3 Other rank's jacket, Flank Company.
　4 Drummer's jacket.
　5 Detail of other rank's buttonhole lace.
　6 Cross Belt Plate.

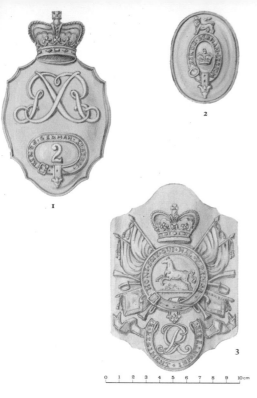

0 1 2 3 4 5 6 7 8 9 10 cm

105 King's German Legion.
1 Shako plate (2nd Battalion).
2 Cross Belt Plate.
Hanoverian Infantry.
3 Shako Plate.

106 King's German Legion.
Officer and Private Soldier,
Light Company,
2nd Line Battalion.

107 52nd (Oxfordshire) Light Infantry.
Subaltern and Private Soldier.

108 52nd (Oxfordshire) Light Infantry.
Officer in greatcoat.

109 51st (2nd Yorkshire, West Riding) Light Infantry.
1 Officer's jacket.
2 Shako.
3 Other rank's jacket.
4 Drummer's jacket.
5 Detail of other rank's buttonhole lace.

110 71st (Highland) Light Infantry.
   1 Officer's jacket.
   2 Shako.
   3 Other rank's jacket.
   4 Drummer's jacket.
   5 Detail of other rank's buttonhole lace.
   6 Cross Belt Plate.

111 42nd (Royal Highland),
The Black Watch.
Drum Major.

112 42nd (Royal Highland),
The Black Watch.
Officer in full dress.

113 42nd (Royal Highland
The Black Watch.
Private Soldier.

114 42nd (Royal Highland), The Black Watch.
1 Officer's jacket, Battalion Company.
2 Detail of Officer's jacket, Flank Company.
3 Detail of other rank's jacket, Flank Company.
4 Other rank's jacket, Battalion Company.
5 Drummer's jacket.
6 Detail of other rank's buttonhole lace.
7 Bonnet.
8 Cross Belt Plate.
9 Detail of Drummer's Lace.

BRITAIN
Highlanders

115 79th (Cameron Highlanders).
Sergeant, Battalion Company.

116 92nd (Gordon Highlanders).
Officer, Field Dress.

117 92nd (Gordon Highlanders).
Piper.

118 95th (Rifles). Officer and Private Rifleman.

119 Guards and "Heavy" Infantry.
  1 Officer's Shako.
  2 Other rank's Shako.
  a) Cockade and Plume, Battalion Company.
  b) Cockade and Plume, Grenadier Company.
  c) Cockade and Plume, Light Company.

120 Guards and "Heavy" Infantry.
Battalion Companies.
Officers' Badges of Rank.
In gold or silver lace and
bullion according to regiment
1 Colonel.
2 Lieutenant-Colonel
   (or Captain and Lieutenant-Colonel
   in Foot Guards).
3 Major.
4 Captain (Lieutenant
   and Captain in Foot Guards).
5 Lieutenant.
6 Ensign.
The difference between the epaulettes
of Captains and Subalterns lay in
the thickness of the strands of
the fringe. Both wore their single
epaulettes on the right shoulder.

121 Light Infantry, Rifles,
   and Flank Companies below.
1 Major of Light Infantry or
   Brevet Major commanding Light Company.
2. Captain (Lieutenant and Captain
   of Foot Guards), Grenadier Company.
3 Lieutenant, Light Infantry
   or Light Company.
4 Ensign of Flank Companies.
5 Adjutant.
Officers of the Guards wore a blue
backing instead of red. Rifle officers
wore their epaulettes in black on
a green backing.

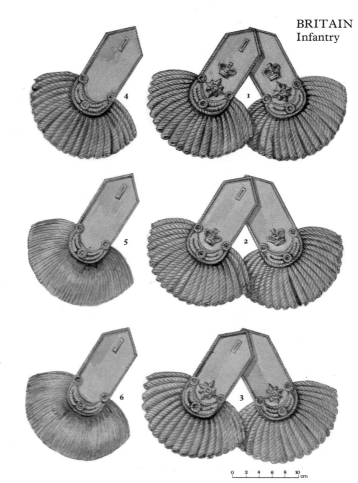

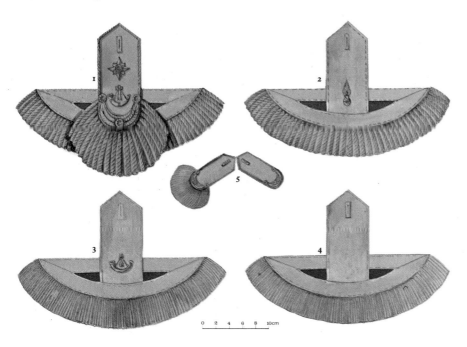

122 Badges of Rank, Non-Commissioned Officers.
1 Sergeant-Major of Foot Guards.
2 Sergeant-Major, Infantry of the line.
Chevrons were worn on both arms in Flank Companies (see A)
and on the right arm only in Battalion Companies (see B).
3 Sergeant.
4 Corporal.
5 Chosen Man.
6 Colour Sergeant. This was worn on the right arm with
Sergeant's chevrons on the left (see C). The duty of Colour
Sergeants was to escort the Ensigns carrying the King's
and Regimental Colours.

123 3rd (Belgian) Line Infantry.
Officer (in cocked hat for dress wear).
Drummer.

124 Corporal, 12th (Dutch) Line Infantry.
Private Soldier, 3rd (Belgian) Line Infantry.

NASSAU
Infantry

HANOVER
Landwehr Infantry

BRUNSWICK
Infantry

125

126

127

128

2nd Regiment of Nassau.
Private Soldier.

Private Soldier Light Company,
(for Shako see plate 106 (c).

Jägers.
Officer.

Infantry of the Line.
Private, 3rd Battalion.

Blücher's Army

129 General in Full Dress with Feldmütze.

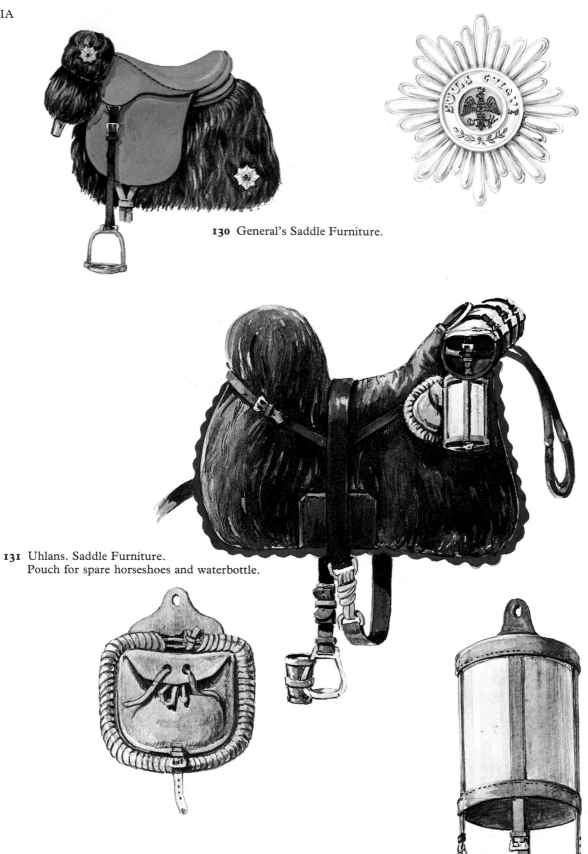

130 General's Saddle Furniture.

131 Uhlans. Saddle Furniture.
Pouch for spare horseshoes and waterbottle.

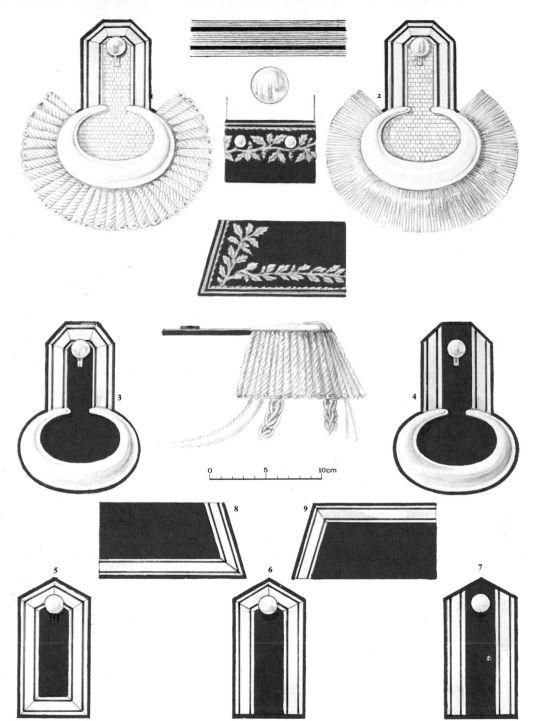

132 Badges of Rank. Officers.

1 General's epaulette (rigid bullion fringe).
1a General's cuff embroidery.
1b General's collar embroidery.
1c General's epaulette. Elevation.
2 Epaulette for Colonels, Lieutenant-Colonels and Majors.
3 Captain's epaulette (ground of facing).
4 Lieutenant's epaulette.
5 Counter-epaulette of Colonel, Lieutenant-Colonel and Major.
6 Captain's counter-epaulette.
7 Lieutenant's counter-epaulette.
8 Regimental officer's full-dress collar.
9 Warrant officer's collar.

Note: The centimetre scale applies only to the epaulettes and counter-epaulettes.

PRUSSIA
Cavalry

133 Dragoons. Captain,
2nd (1st West Prussian) Regiment.

134 Dragoons. Trumpeter, 1st (Queen's) Regiment.
Trooper, 7th (Rhineland) Regiment.
Sergeant, 6th (Neumark) Regiment.

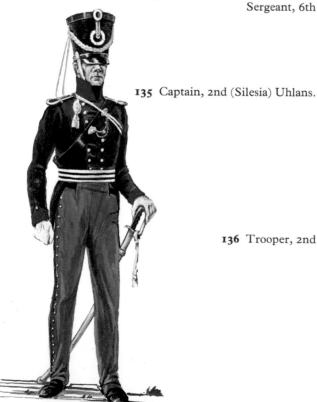

135 Captain, 2nd (Silesia) Uhlans.

136 Trooper, 2nd (Silesia) Uhlans.

137 Hussars. Captain, 1st Regiment *(Liebhusaren)*.

138 Hussars. Trooper, 2nd Regiment *(Liebhusaren)*.

139 Hussars. Trooper's Saddle furniture.
Detail of Officer's saddlecloth.

140 Landwehr Cavalry. Trooper Neumark Regiments.

141

Line Infantry.
Captain.
    6th (1st West Prussian) Regiment.

142

Line Infantry.
Drummer.

143

Line Infantry.
Private Soldiers
(front and rear view).

144 Landwehr Infantry.
Captain,
Silesian Regiment.

145 Landwehr Infantry.
Sergeant and Private Soldiers,
4th Silesian Regiment.

Notes on the Plates

FRENCH ARMY

Plates 1-7. **Staff.**

Marshals of the Empire. Plates 1 & 2.
There had been Marshals of France under the *Ancien Régime*, but it was an exceptional rank, reserved for generals of special distinction. When Napoleon declared himself Emperor in 1804 he created eighteen marshals at one stroke. He subsequently promoted eight more, the last of them, Grouchy, being gazetted at the beginning of the Hundred Days. All were designated Marshals of the Empire to distinguish them from those created by the Bourbons. Only four marshals set off on the Waterloo campaign and one of them, Mortier, fell out with acute sciatica before the frontier was crossed. The other three, Soult, Ney and Grouchy hardly enhanced their reputations during the four days fighting although some of the obloquy subsequently heaped on them has been the result of an inspired campaign to clear the Emperor's reputation. Ney, certainly, heightened his reputation for insensate bravery and Grouchy's extrication of his wing of the army after the news of Waterloo reached him at about 10.30 am on 19 June was a masterpiece.

The marshal's uniform, even in its service form, with embroidery only at the collar and cuffs, was so expensive and so heavy that it is unlikely that any of the three marshals wore it when campaigning. It seems likely that they followed the Emperor's example and wore the uniform of the regiments of which they were colonel. Soult, for example, probably wore the uniform of the *Chasseurs à Pied de la Garde*. They may, however, have carried their batons. These beautiful objects were nearly twenty inches long and had 32 gold eagles embroidered on blue velvet. At each end was a gold cap. On one end was inscribed the motto '*Terror belli. Decus Pacis*'. At the other end was engraved the marshal's name and the date of his promotion, for example, '*Michel Ney nommé par l'Empereur Napoléon, Maréchal de l'Empire, 19ᵐᵉ Mai 1804*'.

General Officers. Plates 2-5.
The nomenclature of French generals is confusing in modern terms. A *Général de Division* was the equivalent of a Lieutenant-General in the British army and a *Général de Brigade* of Major-General. It was then customary for divisions to be commanded by Lieutenant-Generals and

brigades by Major-Generals. To confuse the situation still further, *Généraux de Brigades* were, during the Hundred Days, occasionally known as *Maréchaux de Camp*, a pre-revolutionary rank which had been reintroduced at the Restoration.

The distinctions between the two ranks were many and intricate. The most obvious was that *généraux de division* had two rows of lace at collar and cuffs where *généraux de brigade* had only a single row. All general officers wore a gold embroidered sash, the net groundwork of which was white for Marshals, red for Lieutenant-Generals and sky blue for Major-Generals. The colours were also used on the reverse of the sword belt. Very small insignia of rank (crossed batons for Marshals, three stars for Lieutenant-Generals, two stars for Major-Generals) were worn on the sword knot, on the epaulettes, at each end of the cocked hat and on the two 'acorns' at the ends of the sash. Both grades of general had silvered spurs and black stirrups. Marshals had both spurs and stirrups gilded.

Staff Officers. Plates 6 & 7.
In 1812 the French and British armies both abandoned the cocked hat for fighting troops although it was retained for Generals, staff officers and non-combatants (e.g. surgeons). Although liable to fall off when riding and affording no protection against the weather, the two-ended cocked hat had some advantages for staff officers who spend much of their life indoors. In those days, an officer entering a house would remove his hat and place it under his arm. This was an inconvenient trick to perform with a bearskin or a shako. Its retention, therefore, was parallel to the adoption of the forage cap by the British army before the Second World War. Neither headdress has any virtues when worn but both were convenient to stow

away when not in use. In the French army, a cocked hat was known as *chapeau en bataille* (i.e. in line) when worn parallel to the shoulders and *chapeau en colonne* when worn fore and aft.

The uniform of staff officers had been greatly simplified in 1812 and at the time of Waterloo was one of the simplest in the army. Senior staff officers (*adjutant-commandant*) were distinguished by two gold epaulettes and by gold-laced button-holes at collar and cuffs. Junior staff officers (*adjoints à l'état major*) had a single epaulette and were without lace at collar and cuffs.

The reform of the uniform of *aides de camp* was long overdue. Until 1812 they had been dressed according to the whims of their generals. Some generals had been very whimsical. Marshal Murat when Grand Duke of Berg had arrayed his ADCs in white, gold and amaranthine purple. Under the new regulations they wore the simple staff uniform with a single epaulette and buff collars and cuffs. The rank of the general for whom they worked was indicated by a brassard and a feather in their cocked hats. The brassard was a miniature of the general's gold-embroidered sash and both the background to the gold and the hat-feather were in the distinguishing colour for the rank (see above) except that ADCs to Lieutenant-Generals had feathers of red over blue.

Since their duties required much riding, ADCs wore hussar boots, rather than the top boots worn by the rest of the staff.

Plates 8-41. **The Imperial Guard.**

The Imperial Guard combined the functions of personal bodyguard to the Emperor and of ultimate reserve to the whole army. It had representatives of all branches of the army and there was a naval section. It was an army within an army. At

Waterloo it was the second largest of the French army corps. It had set off on the Russian campaign of 1812 40,000 strong. Nearly 35,000 of these were killed, captured or incapacitated but it was immediately reconstituted. There was no difficulty in filling vacancies in the Guard. Most men in the line regiments were anxious to join an *élite* corps where the pay was better, the uniform was better cut and of better material, where there was every chance of being stationed in Paris between campaigns and where there was an *esprit de corps* unrivalled in the French army.

Although volunteers were plentiful there was a rigorous selection procedure and discipline was largely maintained by the threat of returning an unsatisfactory guardsman to the line. Even after the Russian disaster, Napoleon could still lay down that 'Officers and NCOs for the Old Guard must have twelve years service including several campaigns. Guardsmen for the 1st regiments of Grenadiers and Chasseurs must have ten years service including campaigns. For the second regiments eight years will suffice.' Apart from transfers from the line, the Guard had its own sources of recruits. Since 1804 the cream of each conscription had been skimmed off into *vélite* battalions where young men of talent (and preferably some private means) were trained to take their place in the Guard.

The Guard had its origin in the Consular Guard, hastily established from the *Garde du Corps Législatif* and the *Garde du Directoire Exécutif* after the Brumaire *coup d'état* in 1799. In its first form it was essentially a bodyguard for the persons of the three consuls and consisted of only 2,000 men under Joachim Murat. There was a battalion of Grenadiers, a company of Chasseurs (light infantry), three squadrons of light cavalry and a battery of artillery. The whole was sufficient for guard and escort duties, but this was not the role which the new First Consul, General Bonaparte, saw for them. The Guard was expanded as a model for the whole army and was composed of men who had distinguished themselves for bravery, steadiness and good conduct during the Revolutionary wars.

Soldiers with purely ceremonial duties cannot be a model in anything but drill and turn-out. If the Guard was to be a model of how to fight it had to be a fighting body. Thus the Guard was expanded until it was a body large enough to strike the deciding blow in a desperate, evenly balanced battle. Since they were the ultimate reserve the Guard was very seldom committed to battle. The infantry of the Old Guard frequently attended battles without firing a shot. This was the case at Austerlitz, at Jena, at Friedland and at Borodino. At Eylau only one Old Guard battalion was engaged. Nevertheless, their prestige was unrivalled. The sight of a mass of bearskinned soldiers standing in the rear of the French battle line lay as a permanent threat on the calculations of enemy commanders. To the rest of the French army, who, naturally, were passionately jealous of the Guard's privileges, they were the ultimate insurance. If they saw the Guard advancing they knew that the situation was serious but they knew equally that the Guard would break through. The Guard always broke through. When, at Waterloo, the Guard failed, the French army fled. The unimaginable had happened. There was an end to certainty.

The Guard was intended as a model not only to the infantry and cavalry but to the whole army. It therefore included representatives of all arms. The Guard had its own artillery, horse and foot, its own engineers, its bridging and waggon train, its pioneers *(ouvriers d'administra-*

tion), its military police. In 1803 a Guard unit of sailors was raised in an endeavour to improve the tarnished image of the navy in view of the scheduled invasion of England. This was a versatile body of men. Apart from their sea-faring abilities, they were useful craftsmen, served frequently as infantry or, as at Waterloo, assisted as gunners.

At times there had been some unusual Guard units. For a short time there was a Guard Scout Regiment of Lithuanian Tartars. Most exotic of all were the Mamelukes of the Guard, a legacy of Napoleon's Egyptian campaign. Clothed in an oriental fantasy, which had a great and lasting impact on the fashions of Paris, they were each armed with a carbine, two pairs of pistols, a sabre, a dagger, a mace, an axe and a bayonet. Originally they had also carried a blunderbuss but this had been found superfluous.

In 1814 a tiny force of the Guard had accompanied Napoleon to Elba. This was a composite battalion of Grenadiers and Chasseurs, two squadrons of Polish lancers, a hundred gunners and enough sailors to man the tiny Elban navy. Six battalions of infantry and four regiments of cavalry were included in the Bourbon Royal Guard. Their pay and privileges were reduced and they were affronted when Louis raised a bodyguard of ex-emigré nobles, *La Maison Militaire du Roi*, in which every private soldier had the pay and army rank of an officer. On Napoleon's return to Paris, the old Guardsmen rallied to a man to the Emperor and their numbers were swelled by former Guardsmen who had been put on half-pay or who had been prisoners of war.

At Waterloo the Guard was the epitome of Napoleon's army. The soldiers were experienced, self-confident, highly trained, passionately devoted to the Emperor's person and as rapacious as vultures.

Imperial Guard. Cavalry. Plates 8-22. Figures 1-3.
Grenadiers à Cheval. Plates 8 & 9.
The Horse Grenadiers were established in December, 1800, from two squadrons of light horse in the original Consular Guard. They were armed with the slightly curved heavy cavalry sabre, a pair of pistols and a full-length infantry musket. They did not carry grenades and the name *Grenadiers à Cheval* was a tribute to the distinguished service performed in the eighteenth century by the Horse Grenadiers of the Bourbon Household Cavalry. To perpetuate this memory they wore the tall bearskin grenadier cap, although unlike the *Grenadiers à Pied*, whose uniform theirs closely resembled in other particulars, they did not wear a brass plate in the front of it.

The grenadier cap dated back to the days when infantry and cavalry alike wore three-cornered cocked hats. This was unsuitable for those engaged in throwing grenades since the corners tended to obstruct the thrower's arm. Since the eighteenth-century grenade was as liable to damage the thrower as the enemy without the addition of gratuitous hazards, a special hat was designed for grenadiers. This was originally a mitre or sugar loaf of stiffened cloth which gave no protection against the weather and was apt to lose its shape when soaked with rain. The bearskin cap was therefore substituted at roughly the time at which all armies decided that grenades, in their existing state of development, were too erratic to be used in the field*. The tall cap was, however, retained as a mark of distinction for *élite* troops.

During the Restoration of 1814 the *Grenadiers à Cheval* survived as the Royal

---

* Grenades in the Napoleonic wars were used only in siege operations being dropped over the walls at assaulting troops. The protection of the walls made them safer to use for the thower.

Corps of Cuirassiers of France. In this guise they were ordered to wear chest armour and to adopt dragoon helmets instead of their bearskins. They succeeded in avoiding compliance with the latter part of the order and abandoned their armour without regret when the Emperor returned.

They took part in the second and subsequent attacks of the French cavalry at Waterloo. A gunner whose battery they approached described them as 'very fine troops. Broad, very broad buff belts and huge muff caps made them appear gigantic fellows.' Enough of them survived the cavalry holocaust for the *Grenadiers à Cheval* to advance in support of the Middle Guard in their final attack and to form part of the rearguard when the rest of the French army fled.

Chasseurs à Cheval de la Garde. Plates 10-12. Figures 1 & 2.

The *Chasseurs à Cheval* like the Horse Grenadiers derived from the cavalry regiment of the Consular Guard but they had a long-standing connection with Napoleon even at that time. They had originally been a squadron of Guides formed by General Bonaparte and used by him in the Italian and Egyptian campaigns. At that time their commander was Jean-Baptiste Bessières, who became a Marshal of the Empire and was killed at Lutzen. When they became a regiment of Chasseurs their commander was Eugène Beauharnais, the Emperor's step-son and later Viceroy of Italy.

Guides traditionally had green uniforms and, although the Chasseurs of the Guard adopted a hussar style of dress, their basic

Fig. 1 *Chasseurs à Cheval* of the Guard. Trumpet Banner.

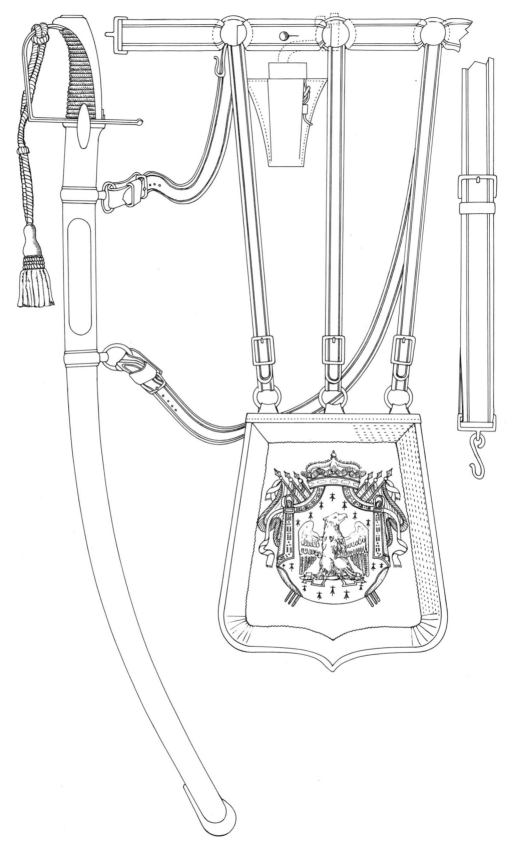

Fig. 2 *Chasseurs à Cheval* of the Guard. Swordbelt, Sabretache and Sabre.

colour remained green. Unlike most hussars, however, they tended to wear their pelisses as jackets rather than slung over one shoulder in the more usual fashion. Thus, when seen from a distance, they appeared to be wearing red jackets although their green saddlecloths remained distinctive.

In the Waterloo campaign the Chasseurs formed part of the brigade of Guard light cavalry commanded by Lefebvre-Desnoëttes. He had been their commanding officer. in Spain in 1808 when, at the head of the regiment, he had been captured by the hussars of the German Legion while attempting to force a crossing of the River Esla at Benavente. While in captivity he had established himself as a feature of the social life of Cheltenham until, with Napoleon's active encouragement, he broke his parole, returning to France and serving in the Russian campaign. Although not a man of honour he was a dashing and talented leader of light cavalry.

It was an officer of the Chasseurs, Captain Klein de Kleinenberg who captured the colour of the 8th battalion, King's German Legion, near La Haye Sainte.

They were known to the rest of the army as the Emperor's favourite regiment, his *'enfants chéris'*. It was their undress uniform he was wearing at Waterloo and in which he is shown in many of his best-known portraits. The version he wore was known as 'court undress'. Under the well-known green surtout he wore a white waistcoat, white breeches and silk stockings instead of the more normal undress of a scarlet waistcoat, frogged, with five rows of gilt buttons and green hussar style breeches and black boots.

A squadron of Chasseurs formed the Emperor's immediate body guard, *l'escadron de service*, at Waterloo and it was they who escorted him from the field, clearing a path for him through the struggling mass of fugitives with the flats of their swords.

Gendarmerie d'Élite. Plate 13.
The *Gendarmerie d'Élite* were the military police of the Guard. They were raised in 1802 from picked men from the gendarmeries of every department of France. Apart from normal military police functions, they undertook ceremonial duties within the Imperial palaces and were always on duty at Malmaison when Josephine was Empress.

Their uniform was very similar to that of the Horse Grenadiers except that their waistcoats, breeches and belts were buff rather than white. To the troops they were better known in their long blue cloaks faced with red.

Although armed with the heavy cavalry sabre and the carbine, they were not intended as fighting troops except in dire emergencies.

Dragoons of the Guard (The Empress's Dragoons) Plates 14 & 15.
Dragoons, as will be discussed later (p. 129) were supposed to be mounted infantry and it is remarkable that, at the beginning of the nineteenth century, the dragoons of most European nations took to wearing a helmet of Grecian design. It would be difficult to conceive a head-dress less convenient for dismounted men. The brass of the helmet would become intolerably hot in strong sunlight and the floating mane of horsehair which hung down behind would, if any wind was blowing, be a menace to accurate musketry.

The Dragoons of the Guard were raised in 1806 and seem never to have acted as infantry except on the retreat from Moscow when they lost all their horses. Only 120 members of the regiment survived the retreat.

Their uniform was modelled on that of

the Horse Grenadiers except that the Grenadiers' blue was replaced by green. As in the Horse Grenadiers the trumpeters wore sky blue jackets faced with red. When not on active service, a plume was worn on the helmet. This was white for colonel and trumpeters, red and white for the major and red for all other ranks. Officers had a plume of feathers; other ranks of horsehair.

Like other Guard units they were distinguished by white facings but they could also be recognised from the dragoons of the line by the leopard-skin turban (artificial for other ranks) worn round the helmet* and by wearing buttons of brass rather than white metal.

Lancers of the Guard (Chevaux-légers-lanciers) Plates 16-20.

During his campaign against the Russians in 1807, between the drawn battle of Eylau and the victory of Friedland, Napoleon authorized the raising of a Guard regiment of Polish light horse. His main object in so doing was political, a first token of his promise to establish an independent state. Whatever his motives, he obtained the services of some of the finest soldiers who ever served under him. Qualifications for enlisting were high. Applicants must be landowners or the sons of landowners. Some financial backing was certainly needed as those accepted had to provide their own uniforms, saddlery and horses.

The volunteers reached Paris, having established a considerable reputation for drunkenness and disorder on the way, and were given an intensive course in horsemastership and discipline. They soon

proved their value in action. In November, 1808, Napoleon was advancing on Madrid from Burgos. Across his road lay the Sierra de Guadarrama, crossed by the Somosierra pass which was garrisoned by 12,000 Spaniards. Marshal Victor, commanding the advanced guard, set about forcing the pass by conventional means, by sending infantry to the high ground on either side. Napoleon was impatient. He ordered a brigade of light cavalry to storm the pass. When their commander raised not unreasonable difficulties, the Emperor turned to the Poles who were acting as his escort and told them to charge. One hundred and fifty Polish horsemen charged uphill for a mile and a half, storming four successive batteries, two of them covered by earthworks. As they approached the crest the Spaniards fled. It was an incredible feat for light cavalry.

At that time they were armed only with light cavalry sabres and carbines. They were issued with lances in the following year. Their uniform had been consciously Polish from the start and was crossed with the square-topped lance cap, the *czapka*. When lances were issued they had pennants in the Polish colours, red over white.

A second regiment of Lancers of the Guard was raised in 1810. When Louis Napoleon abdicated the throne of Holland, the Dutch Royal Guard was incorporated into the Imperial Guard. The Dutch Grenadiers became the 2nd Regiment of Grenadiers and it was intended to convert the Dutch Guard Hussars into Cuirassiers. Owing to some administrative oversight the horses provided for the new Guard regiment were only 14 hands, too small to carry a cuirassier in his armour. They, therefore, became the 2nd Lancers of the Guard and were given a scarlet uniform. Although almost entirely Dutchmen they still had the Polish colours on their lance pennants but with the white over the red.

---

* A print by Vernet, commissioned by the Emperor and published in 1812, shows a colonel of the 1st Dragoons of the line wearing a leopard-skin turban. It is possible that he wore this because he had previous service in the Guard Dragoons.

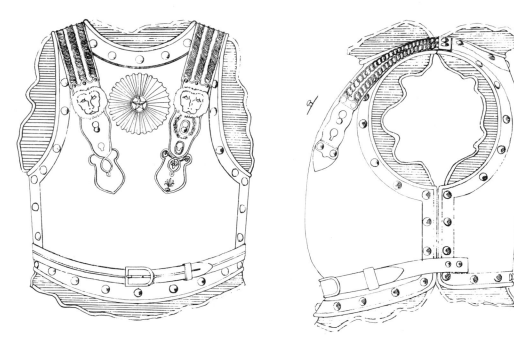

Fig. 3 Carabineers. Breastplates. Officers and Other ranks.

A squadron of the 1st (Polish) regiment accompanied Napoleon to Elba and, on his return, formed a supernumerary but senior squadron to the 2nd Regiment for the Waterloo campaign. Even in 1815 many of the Red Lancers were Dutchmen, but their old commander, General Van Merlen, died at the head of a Netherlands cavalry brigade, fighting on the other side.

Carabineers. Plates 21 & 22. Figure 3.
As the name implies, Carabineers were historically horsemen whose primary weapon was the short musket, the carbine. They were thus a sub-species of dragoon but had grown away further than dragoons from their dismounted role and had become a type of cuirassier. No one could seriously expect men wearing body armour to fight on their feet and at Waterloo the British noticed that, when an armoured horseman lost his horse, his first action was to disencumber himself from his breast- and back-plates.

The two regiments of Carabineers had an anomalous position in the French army. They thought of themselves as Guardsmen, they were paid the higher rate of Guardsmen but they seldom fought with the Guard. At Waterloo they formed a brigade in Kellermann's Cavalry Corps.

No regiment at Waterloo had a uniform as spectacular as the Carabineers. Their cuirasses, which were unusual since they were of copper for the officers and brass for the other ranks, were lined with blue cloth bordered with white which showed round the edge of the armour. Under it they wore a white jacket with sky blue facings. Taken together with their Grecian helmet, which like the cuirass was of copper or brass, and its red plume, they had a Wagnerian appearance, something from an exceptionally lavish production of Lohengrin.

This theatrical appearance was not deliberate. Until 1809 they had worn a blue jacket and bearskin cap. After the **121** losses they suffered that year in the Austrian campaign, the regiment had to be reformed and the Emperor took the opportunity to change their uniform. His intention was to clothe them in red but one of the unfortunate side-effects of the British blockade was a shortage of reliable dye-stuffs. Even the blue worn by the bulk of the French army varied greatly in colour. Red was known to be very unreliable with the dyes available and white was chosen instead. The distinction between the two regiments was shown only on the cuff, thus being invisible when, as was usual, gauntlets were worn.

Imperial Guard. Artillery. Plates 23-28. The artillery of the Guard was larger than that required to support the Guard considered solely as one of the army corps. None of the infantry corps of the army had more than 46 guns (including horse artillery batteries). The artillery of the Guard consisted at Waterloo of 122 guns. It had the additional task of acting as an

'Army Group' of artillery, to add weight to the artillery preparation which always preceded Napoleon's attacks. Consequently the artillery of the Guard had been actively engaged in many more actions than the infantry and cavalry. At Waterloo, it was one of the guns of the Guard which fired three shots to signal the opening of the bombardment. They participated throughout the battle in the cannonade and, at the end, they fired off the last of their ammunition covering the retreat of the Old Guard up the slope to La Belle Alliance.

Horse Artillery of the Guard. Plates 23 & 24. Figure 4.
In the Napoleonic wars, all artillery was horsedrawn but in the foot (or, as it would now be called, field) artillery the gunners marched beside their guns, while in the horse artillery they were mounted. Horse artillery was, therefore, suitable to accompany cavalry and, as a consequence, the personnel were dressed as light cavalry. The Horse Artillery of the Guard were wholeheartedly hussar in their uniforms, although they were restrained in an unhussarlike manner, keeping to the dark blue with red facing which was the uniform of gunners in most armies.

In full dress, pelisses were worn, those of the officers being trimmed with silver fur and those of the other ranks had black fur. Few, however, wore them after 1813 as a large store of pelisses was found to have been destroyed by moth while the Guard was absent on the Russian campaign. On active service the usual wear was undress which, while retaining the hussar busby, had a jacket similar to that of the *Chasseurs à Pied* piped with red and worn over a blue waistcoat. With this were worn blue overalls with a red stripe, reinforced with leather and fastened with eighteen buttons for each leg.

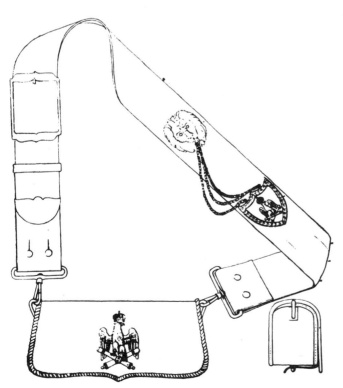

Fig. 4 Horse Artillery of the Guard. Shoulder Belt and Pouch.

All ranks wore aiguillettes even in undress, those of the officers being gold, of NCOs red and gold, of gunners red. In undress the officers wore shoulder belts of red leather edged with gold. Trumpeters followed a practice which in most of the French army had been abandoned. They wore the colours of the regimental jacket reversed, i.a. a red hussar jacket with blue facings. The trumpeter's pelisse was blue trimmed with grey fur.

Foot Artillery of the Guard. Plates 25-28.
The uniform of the Foot Artillery of the Guard closely resembled that of the Guard infantry, except that it was worn over a blue, rather than a white waistcoat. The piping also was red. They also had several distinctions normally reserved for *élite* troops. They wore the grenadier cap, although without the brass plate of the Grenadiers of the Guard and the private gunners wore the red epaulettes of grenadier companies. They also carried, in addition to muskets and bayonets, the short sword, *(sabre-briquet)*, usually an accoutrement of grenadiers and chasseurs. It was presumably intended for cutting away brushwood from in front of the gun position.

Plumes were worn in the bearskin except when in action. Commanding officers wore white, majors red over white and all other members of the battalion red. The gold aiguilette worn on the right shoulder by the major in Plate 25 denotes that he is serving on the staff.

In the French army the bridging of rivers was the responsibility of the artillery rather than the engineers. The *ouvriers pontoniers*, who performed this and other skilled mechanical tasks, wore the same uniform as the gunners but with red lapels.

The Engineers of the Guard played little part in the Waterloo campaign. In the early days of the Empire their chief concern had been with fire-fighting in the Imperial palaces. They wore a uniform similar to the artillery but with black lapels, collar and cuffs. Instead of the bearskin cap they wore the Grecian dragoon helmet with a black fur *chenille* or crest.

Imperial Guard. Infantry. Plates 29-41.
All units of the Guard were divided into Old, Middle and Young Guard. With cavalry and artillery this was merely a matter of prestige and did not affect their tactical deployment but with the infantry this is not the case and the categorization has often caused confusion. The Young Guard are easily identifiable as their regiments were known as Tirailleurs and Voltigeurs but the Grenadiers and Chasseurs are harder to categorize.

A regulation promulgated in 1812 laid down that all ranks of the 1st regiments* of *Grenadiers à Pied* and *Chasseurs à Pied*, together with the NCOs of the 2nd regiments of each, belonged to the Old Guard. Corporals and guardsmen of the 2nd regiments and NCOs and Guardsmen of the 3rd Grenadiers formed the Middle Guard. Officers of all five regiments belonged to the Old Guard.

In 1815 there were four regiments of Grenadiers and four of Chasseurs and, although no new regulation seems to have been issued, the first two regiments of each seem to have formed the Old Guard and the third and fourth regiments the Middle Guard.

In the Order of Battle for the Waterloo Campaign the four regiments of Grenadiers are listed as belonging to one brigade, under General Friant, and the four Chasseurs regiments into another under General Morand. The whole was described as the Old Guard. When committed to battle, however, the two senior regiments,

---

* Each regiment nominally consisted of two battalions.   **123**

1st Grenadiers and 1st Chasseurs, seem to have acted under General Morand, while the four junior regiments made the final attack under General Friant, who was wounded riding beside Ney. For all practical purposes all ranks of the 1st and 2nd Regiments of both Grenadiers and Chasseurs comprised the Old Guard and the 3rd & 4th Regiments were the Middle Guard.

Grenadiers and Chasseurs both stemmed from the Consular Guard which had a single company of light infantry which was expanded into the Chasseurs. By 1815 there was little, except details of dress, to distinguish between the two. Although the Chasseurs did not use the stiff-legged ceremonial march affected by the Grenadiers, they were no longer light troops in any but a titular sense. They were trained and used as 'heavy' infantry.

There is some doubt as to how the Guard was dressed at Waterloo. Most authorities have asserted that they fought in full dress and most artists have depicted them as doing so. On the other hand Sergeant Hippolyte de Mauduit of 2/1st Grenadiers wrote that 'We wore battle order, greatcoat, trousers and bearskin without ornaments, although it should have been an occasion for full dress.*' Certainly the Guard was not in undress, which would have entailed having the bearskin in a waterproof cover on top of the knapsack and wearing instead a cocked hat. They may have been wearing their full dress jackets, with white lapels, instead of the plainer blue jacket buttoning almost to the waist of undress, but whichever it was it was covered by their long blue greatcoats. They had their white breeches in their packs for the triumphal march into Brussels and their long plumes were dismounted, inserted into a cover of waxed canvas and strapped to the sheath of the *sabre-briquet*.

Grenadiers à Pied, Old Guard. Plates 29-36 & 41.

When, in the early eighteenth century, Grenadiers had been soldiers who threw grenades, they had been selected as the tallest and strongest men in the battalion. When the grenade passed into disuse, the picked men who threw them were kept together for use as assault troops, a role for which their size and strength made them specially suitable. In the armies of France and Britain, and many other armies, infantry battalions each had a grenadier company who always took the post of honour on the right of the line. In the eighteenth century it was customary to mass the grenadier companies of brigades or divisions into improvised battalions, a deplorable practice since it deprived the battalions of their strongest men. A logical consequence was to raise battalions of grenadiers on a permanent basis and when this was done in France such a body of picked men clearly belonged in the Guard.*

Apart from their magnificent professionalism, the Grenadiers of Napoleon's Guard must have been daunting opponents. They were required to be more than six feet tall (1.90 metres), an exceptional height in those days, and wore a bearskin cap fourteen inches (35 cms) high. They wore their hair long, powdered and in two plaits drawn tightly from their temples. The

* Mauduit was writing of Ligny but, in view of the torrential rain, it is inconcievable that the Guard would have changed into full dress in the interveing thirty six hours.

* In the British army the First Guards were not named Grenadier Guards until after Waterloo 'in commemoration of their having defeated the Grenadiers of the French Imperial Guard upon this memorable occasion'. In fact two of the three French Guard battalions who attacked the First Guards were Chasseurs. But since all wore grenadier caps the mistake was very natural.

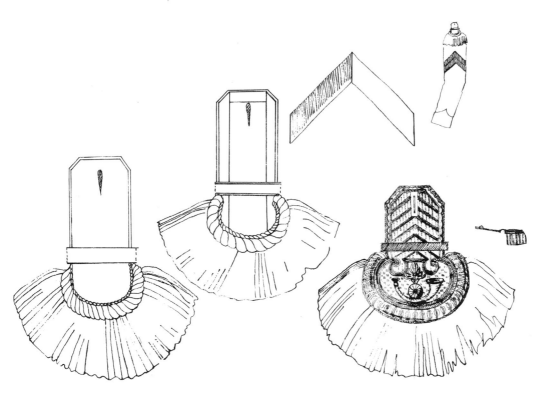

Fig. 5 *Chasseurs à Pied* of the Guard. Jacket (details).

plaits were tied with a black silk ribbon secured with a pin bearing a silver grenade. Moustaches and side-whiskers were obligatory and, supreme mark of the Old Guard, they all wore two gold earrings. Their pioneers, like all regimental pioneers, had beards and they, alone among the Grenadiers, did not wear the brass plaque (gilt for officers) in the front of their bearskins.

The jacket was blue with white lapels and red cuffs and lining. On each side of each of the two tails of the jacket the red lining was turned back and decorated with two grenades, embroidered in gilt on a white backing. As befitted Grenadiers, they wore red epaulettes, except for sergeants who had a mixture of red and gold. Officers' epaulettes were of gold. Their plumes were scarlet, except for the senior officers. Unusually their drummers were dressed much the same as the rank and file.

Chasseurs à Pied of the Old Guard. Plates 37-39 & 41. Figure 5.

The uniform of the Chasseurs differed from that of the Grenadiers as little as the fighting qualities of the two corps differed. Although nominally light infantry, they wore the bearskin grenadier cap but without the brass plaque in front. Their epaulettes were red in the fringe but green on the shoulder strap. Their plumes were red over green. On each coat tail, where the Grenadiers wore two gilt embroidered grenades, the Chasseurs sported one grenade and one hunting horn, the conventional sign of light infantry. On the jackets the white lapels came to a point at the bottom and, another conventional sign of light troops, their cuffs were pointed. It is scarcely surprising that the British assumed that all the bearskinned figures advancing against them were Grenadiers.

Middle and Young Guards. Plate 40 & 41. According to most authorities, bearskins were the cherished privilege of the Old Guard but it is quite certain that the Middle Guard were wearing them at Waterloo and they made a vivid impression on those they were attacking. It is generally held that they should have been wearing a shako similar to that worn by the infantry of the line but carrying more ornamentation. In fact there was a shortage of headress of all kinds during the Hundred Days and not a few of the Middle Guard were wearing the undress cocked hat or the fatigue cap *(bonnet de police)* during the battle.

Headwear apart, it required a close investigation to differentiate between the uniforms of the Old and Middle Guard. The shoulder strap of the epaulette had a coloured bar across it, red and white for the Grenadiers, red for the Chasseurs. On the turnbacks of the jacket tails the grenades and hunting horns were replaced by imperial eagles in white. These were small points to notice in the smoke of battle and the British were in no doubt that they were being assaulted by the Old Guard.

The Young Guard were more easily recognized. They were the apprentices of the Guard and the ambition of every man was to graduate first to the Middle Guard and eventually to the *Anciens*. It was a hard apprenticeship. Napoleon, who was justifiably jealous of the lives of the senior Guards, employed the Young Guard with the same disregard for lives that characterised his use of infantry of the line. Originally raised in 1809 and 1810 from picked conscripts they saw much action in Austria, Spain and Russia. Before the abdication of 1814 thirty-eight battalions of Young Guard had been raised. The names Grenadiers and Chasseurs were not used but those destined for the senior regiment were formed into battalions of Tirailleurs, while prospective Chasseurs were known as Voltigeurs.

The uniform of the Young Guard was midway between that of the senior Guards and that of the infantry of the line. They wore a heavily decorated shako and their lapels were blue, although piped with white to give a hint of the Old Guard's white lapels. There were no epaulettes. Instead they had counter-epaulettes ending in 'duck's feet'. Those of the Tirailleurs were red piped with white; those of the Voltigeurs were green piped with red. The former had red collars, the latter buff. The turnback ornaments were eagles, like those of the Middle Guard, but those of the Voltigeurs were green. Since the names of both corps suggested that they were light infantry, they wore pointed cuffs in the fashion of the Chasseurs.

Plates 42-49. **Cavalry of the Line.**

When Bonaparte became First Consul the French cavalry, apart from the Guard, consisted of 25 heavy regiments, 20 of dragoons and 35 of light cavalry, either *chasseurs à cheval* or hussars. In 1813, when his establishment of cavalry was at its greatest, he had 14 heavy regiments (exclusive of the Carabineers), 30 of dragoons and 35 of light horse. Although he cut down the number of heavy regiments Napoleon increased the weight of those which remained. In 1799 only one regiment wore the breastplate. After 1802 all French heavy regiments were armoured back and front. At the same date they were issued with steel helmets in the Grecian, dragoon style with long visor-like peaks bound with metal.

This well-protected body of heavy

horsemen, augmented by the Carabineers, was one of Napoleon's most formidable weapons in his constant search for a quick decision. Usually held in reserve with all the heavy regiments grouped together, their intended use was to exploit a break-through, or near breakthrough, made by the infantry. As soon as a weak point had been found in the enemy's line, the cuirassiers would be hurled at it. If they broke through they would turn against the enemy's rear and destroy his army totally. It was this kind of coup that Ney and Napoleon hoped to achieve when they made their prodigal cavalry attacks at Waterloo.

The heavy cavalry was always a force Napoleon kept under his own hand and its employment in the early days of the campaign of 1815 suggests that the emperor's view of the way the fighting would go underwent a rapid change during the morning of 17 June. Apart from the light cavalry divisions* attached to the five corps of line infantry, the French army contained four cavalry corps, one of light cavalry, one of dragoons and two, those of Kellermann and Milhaud, of heavy cavalry. In the original dispositions for dividing the advance into two columns, one of the two heavy corps was allocated to Ney on the left. It was not clear, before the campaign began, what opposition would be met with by the two columns and it was an obvious precaution to give Ney some horsemen heavier than the lancers, chasseurs and hussars of his corps cavalry divisions. The other three cavalry corps all fought at Ligny, the heavy corps, Milhaud's, forming part of the final victorious attack with the Guard. When the battle was won part of Pajol's light cavalry corps was entrusted with dis-

covering and reporting on the direction of the Prussian retreat, a task they performed with disastrous ineptitude.

It is generally supposed that on the morning after Ligny Napoleon assumed that he had knocked the Prussians out of the campaign for the time being and that his next task was to deal with Wellington. This does not seem to accord with the facts. It seems more probable that he believed that Wellington did not yet represent a serious menace and that the Prussians might need another beating before they could be temporarily disregarded. Such a belief would account for the first orders to Ney which took as a first premise that the Marshal had nothing in front of him that he could not drive away*. It would also explain the Emperor's remarkable unconcern on that morning while he waited to be assured of the Prussians line of retreat. There was no feeling of menace from Wellington's force at Quatre Bras, within five miles of the French left flank. Only a casual guard was kept on that side. Colonel Gordon, with a half squadron of hussars, was able to ride on to the previous day's battlefield without molestation or, apparently, attracting attention. The French army was still organized as two wings and a central reserve and was capable of striking either right at the Prussians or left at the British. Napoleon's first orders to Grouchy, issued at about 11.30 am, strongly suggest that his expectation was a move eastward against Blücher.

Grouchy was instructed to discover the Prussian intentions and to be ready to fall back if they attacked him. This could be taken to mean that the Marshal was only a covering force but it could equally well

---

* The cavalry division assigned to Gérard's corps included a brigade of dragoons. There was no cavalry with Lobau's small corps.

* 'His Majesty's intention is that you should take up a position at Quatre Bras; but, in the unlikely event of that not being possible, you must report the fact, giving details.'

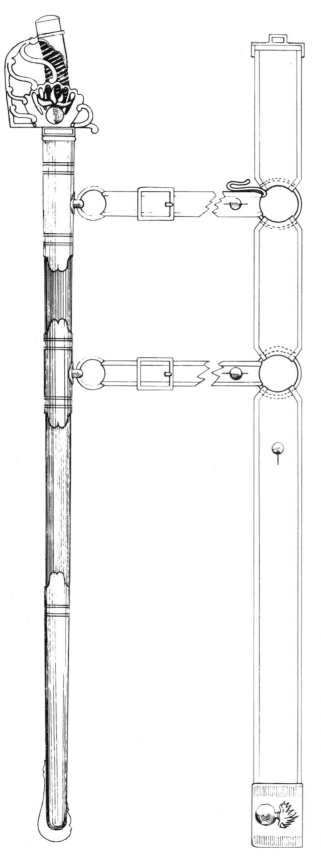

mean that Grouchy was the advanced guard of the main attack. The order to fall back if attacked could be a reflection of Napoleon's wish not to fight a partial action against Blücher. If Grouchy fell back before a Prussian advance he would fall back on the main French reserves, 28,000 men of the Guard and Lobau's corps. The troops allocated to Grouchy strongly suggest that this was the case. His two infantry corps were reinforced by Teste's division but he was allotted an overwhelming force of cavalry, three complete cavalry corps. With his two corps cavalry divisions this would give him 10,000 horsemen including ten dragoon and eight cuirassier regiments. If at this stage Napoleon was considering devoting his main strength to defeating Wellington, he was leaving himself only seven heavy and three dragoon regiments including the Guard.

Half an hour after issuing these orders, Napoleon changed his mind. Instead of making Grouchy far stronger in cavalry than could be needed for a covering force, he cut him down to an almost inadequate force. From having 8 heavy, 10 dragoon and 11 light regiments, he was reduced to 10 dragoon and 5 light regiments only. Soult was not a brilliant chief of staff but he was not likely to made a mistake of the magnitude of misallocating the equivalent of two complete cavalry corps without one of his many detractors subsequently calling attention to the fact and the only logical explanation is that until noon Napoleon was intending to strike another blow at Blücher since he did not consider Wellington to be in a position to do immediate harm. The return of a patrol from the direction of Quatre Bras, after Grouchy had received his orders, must have made the Emperor change his mind.

Fig. 6 Cuirassiers. Officer's swordbelt and sabre.

Cuirassiers. Plates 42 & 43. Figure 6.
The main strength of Napoleon's *Panzer-korps* consisted of the Cuirassiers regiments of which twelve took part in the battle of Waterloo. Their uniform was a more sober version of that worn by the Carabineers. While the latter were splendid in white jackets and sky-blue saddlecloths, the Cuirassiers had both in dark blue, set off with a red lining and red belt. While the Carabineers wore armour and helmet in brass and copper, the Cuirassiers had both in steel, although the heads of the rivets in the armour were of gold-coloured metal. On the helmet, where the Carabineers wore a scarlet crest, the Cuirassiers had a black horsehair tail in the dragoon style. Around their helmets was a turban of black fur. Their trumpeters had no armour and a white flowing tail to their helmets. They had jackets of the imperial livery, lavishly decorated with the imperial lace and red epaulettes. This was a style which the Emperor had made standard for trumpeters and drummers throughout the infantry and cavalry of the line.

It was difficult to distinguish between the cuirassier regiments unless one was close enough to see the buttons which were flat white metal and bore the regimental number. Facing colours were in groups of three. The senior regiment of each group wore the facing colour on both collar and cuffs, the second regiment on cuffs only and the third on the collar only. Where the collar or cuffs were not faced in the group colour, they were of blue, like the rest of the jacket, piped with the facing colour. The colours for the twelve regiments at Waterloo were: –

1st, 2nd & 3rd	Scarlet
4th, 5th & 6th	*Aurore* (pale gold touched with pink)
7th, 8th & 9th	Primrose
10th, 11th & 12th	Pink

This colour was also used to edge the saddlecloths.

Cuirassiers carried no firearm longer than a pistol. They relied for their undoubted effect on their sabres and the very considerable weight of their horses which, within France, could only be procured from Normandy.

Dragoons Plate 44. Figure 7.
Napoleon made a determined attempt to check the almost universal tendency whereby dragoons, who are ostensibly mounted infantry, become medium heavy cavalry. When the invasion of England was being planned in 1805 he ordered that twenty of his dragoon regiments should accompany the assault force and, since horse transports were unprocurable, they should go dismounted and acquire horses from the English countryside. While waiting for the invasion fleet to sail, the dragoons trained as infantrymen. Their knee boots were replaced by ankle boots and gaiters but their helmets with the flowing horsehair tails were retained. When the invasion camp at Boulogne was broken up so that the *Grande Armée* could take part in the Austrian campaign of 1805, a division of 5,000 dismounted dragoons marched from the Straits of Dover to the Danube. Eight regiments acted as baggage guard and, in the only Austrian success of the Ulm campaign, were overwhelmed by the Archduke Ferdinand. A court of enquiry came to the conclusion that the disaster was caused by the incompetence of the dragoons as infantrymen. The survivors were remounted on captured Austrian horses and their rôle was redefined by the Emperor. Henceforward **129**

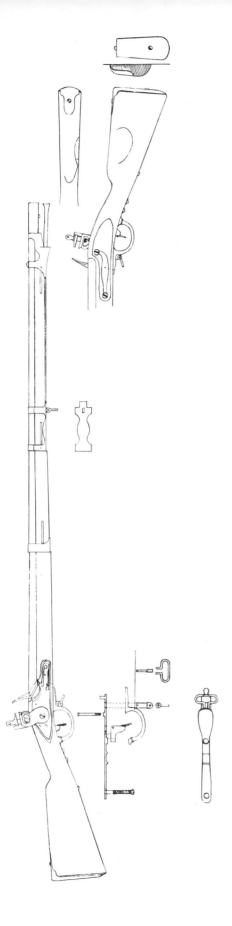

they would primarily be used as mounted troops but they were to retain the capacity to fight on foot for skirmishing and the garrisoning of villages captured by a cavalry advanced guard.

As mounted men they were equally unfortunate. At Burkersdorf in February 1807 six regiments under General Milhaud were routed by a single Russian hussar unit. Milhaud complained that the dragoons had been ruined by their infantry training and added '*Je ne veux pas commander de pareilles troupes.*'

It was on the dragoon regiments that the French had depended for their heavy cavalry in Spain. Wellington remarked that 'The Peninsula is the grave of horses' and it seems that Napoleon agreed with him. Cuirassiers were mounted on much more expensive horses and whereas twenty-four of the thirty dragoon units were allocated to the armies in Spain only two regular cuirassier regiments (3rd & 13th) were employed in Spain, one of them staying only a few months.

The infantry origins of dragoons were commemorated by the existence in each regiment of a pioneer section and the equivalent of a grenadier company, known as the *élite* squadron. Both the *élite* squadron and the pioneers wore the bearskin cap with a scarlet plume while the rest of the regiment wore the Grecian helmet in brass with a brown fur turban. Although the helmets were brass the buttons were white metal and the officers wore silver epaulettes, those of the other ranks being green, like the jackets, with a fringe of the facing colour.

The facing colours were arranged in groups of six regiments and, within the

Fig. 7 Dragoon. Carbine.

groups, were used in combinations on the collars, the cuffs and the cuff-slashes.

The facing colours were allocated as follows : –

1st-6th	Scarlet
7th-12th	Crimson
13th-18th	Pink
19th-24th	Primrose

Dragoons were armed with the heavy cavalry sabre, a pair of pistols, a carbine and a bayonet.

Chasseurs à Cheval. Plate 45.

The mounted Chasseurs of the French army were the equivalent of light dragoons in the British army and like the French dragoons they had, in each regiment, an *élite* squadron which wore the hussar busby and red epaulettes. The rest of the regiment wore the infantry style shako with, on ceremonial occasions, a tall plume. They undertook patrolling, scouting, manning the outposts and all the other basic light cavalry duties which hussars performed in fancy dress.

Their uniform was, by contemporary cavalry standards, sober and practicable. Even the officers' dress was not much more elaborate than that of their men, the most noticeable difference being a green saddlecloth with silver lace in place of the troopers' type which was of sheepskin edged with the regimental facing colour.

The facing colours for the seven Chasseur regiments present in the Waterloo campaign were; –

1st	Scarlet (with scarlet cuffs)
3rd	Scarlet (with green cuffs)
4th	Primrose (with primrose cuffs)
6th	Primrose (with green cuffs)
8th	Pink (with green collar)
9th	Pink (with green cuffs)
12th	Crimson (with green cuffs)

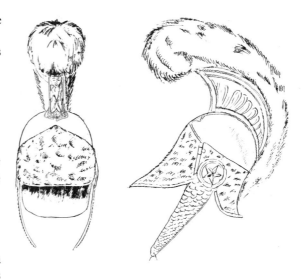

Fig. 8 Lancers. Officer's Helmet.

Green collars or cuffs were piped with the facing colour and collars or cuffs in the facing colour were piped with green.

Chasseurs à Cheval were armed with carbines and bayonets and the curved light cavalry sabre, but carried no horse-pistols.

Lancers. (Chevaux-légers-lanciers) Plate 46. Figure 8.

Although in medieval armies the lance had been the principal weapon of cavalry, it had fallen into disuse by 1600 in Europe except in Poland. The partition of that country brought lance-armed regiments, known by their Polish name of Uhlans, into the armies of Austria and Prussia. When, in 1807, Napoleon raised his Polish light horse regiment for the Guard he also acquired some line cavalry regiments of Poles, one of which, the Light Horse of the Vistula, carried the lance.

The value of this unit was dramatically demonstrated on 16 May, 1811, when they caught three battalions of Colborne's brigade in line and from the rear at Albuera. Of 1,650 infantry only 400 escaped being killed, captured or wounded. One battalion lost 643 out of 755. It was the only substantial success of French cavalry against British infantry in the six years of the Peninsular war.

Napoleon knew of this success by 17 June. Seventeen days later he gave orders to establish eight further lancer regiments. Two of these were created by re-arming two regiments of Polish *chevaux-légers*. The others, numbered from 1-6, were converted from French dragoon units. While the three Polish regiments, including the Light Horse of the Vistula, wore the square-topped *czapka*, the lance cap, the former dragoons kept their brass helmets but replaced the horsehair fringe with a black *chenille*. They wore a scarlet plume in full dress. They retained green dragoon jackets, although the lapels were made to approximate to the plastron of the Polish jacket. Their breeches, however, were cut and decorated in the Polish style with an inch wide yellow (gold for officers) lace down the outer seam ending in a bastion (or Austrian knot) on the thigh. All the lancer regiments carried the red and white Polish colours on their lance pennants.

There was much contemporary dispute about the merits of the lance in action. It was certainly an encumbrance in close action and its limitations were demonstrated in the clearest way a few minutes after its triumph over Colborne's brigade at Albuera. Exploiting their success, some of the Poles dashed at the British commander and his staff who were some way in rear of Colborne. Sir William Beresford had not drawn his sword and saw a lancer coming straight for him. With one hand he parried the lance point while with the other he seized the Pole by the collar and threw him from his horse. On the other hand, the lance was an excellent weapon against broken infantry. A horseman with a sword could not touch a foot soldier who threw himself flat on the ground but no such problem presented itself to a lancer. It was also valuable in heavy rain. Against cavalry armed with sabres, infantry in square was safe even if it was too wet for their muskets to fire but lances could overreach bayonets. At Dresden an Austrian square was broken in this way and the same fate overcame a Prussian square at the hands of the 6me *Chevaux-légers-lanciers* at Katzbach in 1813.

The three Polish regiments (Nos 7-9) could not be reformed during the Hundred Days but all six French regiments were present at Waterloo. The distinctions between them were clear. Lapels, collars, cuffs and turnbacks were all of the regimental facing colour. These colours were: —

1st	Scarlet
2nd	*Aurore*
3rd	Pink
4th	Crimson
5th	Blue
6th	Red

As a legacy of their dragoon past, lancer regiments had *élite* squadrons who wore red epaulettes. Troopers in the other squadrons wore counter-epaulettes piped with the facing colour. The *élite* squadron of the 6th regiment wore a red *chenille* on their helmets with, in full dress, a white plume.

Hussars. Plates 47-49. Figure 9.
The success of hussars in the wars against Frederick the Great decided the military

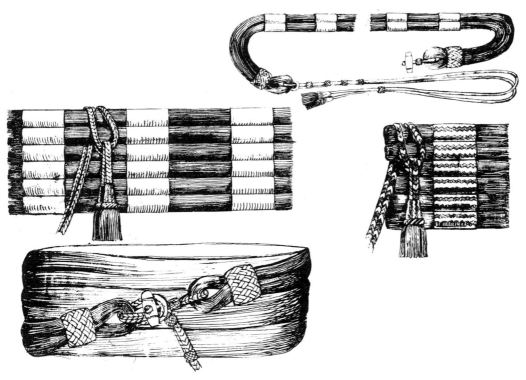

Fig. 9 Hussars. Sash.

authorities of Louis XV to incorporate hussar regiments in their own army which was, as were all western European armies, deficient in light cavalry. At that time France and Austria were allied and the original French hussar regiments were composed of a nucleus of Hungarians, hired from the Hapsburgs and brought up to strength by German mercenaries, so that the regiments were the mounted equivalent of the British 60th (Royal American) Foot. The elaborate Hussar uniform was a formalization of the dress of Hungarian irregular horse except that, as in the armies of Austria, Prussia and, eventually, Britain, the tunic worn in Hungary was abandoned in favour of the waist length dolman.

At the Revolution the six French regiments were still almost entirely composed of foreigners but that event caused the supply of mercenaries to dry up and the ranks were progressively filled with Frenchmen, although three hussar regiments of Dutchmen and Westphalians were added to the ten regiments existing in 1810-11.

The uniforms of all the hussar regiments were cut to the same fashion but there was no common colour for all hussar clothing as was the case with other types of French cavalry. Each hussar regiment had its own variation and these are illustrated in Plates 48 & 49. The fur hussar cap *(kolbak)* was worn only by officers and trumpeters. The busby bag for all the regiments at Waterloo was red, except for the 5th who had a light blue bag and their red plume was tipped with black. Troopers wore shakos.

Despite the fantastification of their dress, hussars performed the same duties

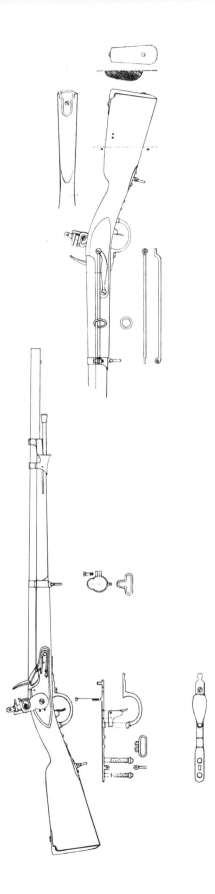

as *Chasseurs à cheval* and were trained and mounted in the same way. The uniform, doubtless, contributed to the social standing of the officers and the apparent virility of all ranks.

Plates 50 & 51. **Artillery of the Line.**

The French artillery started with great advantages over the artillery of all other armies. Not only was the Emperor a gunner himself, but the Revolution inherited a standardised range of guns and equipment designed as early as 1776 by Jean Baptiste de Gribeauval. Under Gribeauval's scheme items such as wheels and axles became interchangeable and carriages were, as far as possible, usable for several weights of gun. The characteristic Gribeauval carriage had a trail made with two parallel shafts, as compared with the single, central shaft used in the British and other armies. An ammunition chest with carrying handles was carried across this split trail, thus doing away with the need for a limber. The French limber was reduced to a vestigial form consisting of a pair of wheels with a pintle spike above, to fit into a corresponding hole in the rear of the trail, and a shaft in front for harnessing the draught horses. In the larger (8 and 12 pounder) guns the carriage had two resting places for the trunnions, one for travelling, one for firing. Thus before a large French gun could be fired its not inconsiderable weight (the barrel of a 12 pounder weighed 1,950 lbs) had to be shifted forward into the firing position.

It is difficult to decide on the comparative efficiency of the French and British guns. The British had nothing as formidable as the 12 pounder but soon after the Restoration of 1815 a nine pounder modelled on that used by the British Horse Artillery was introduced into the French army on the recommendation of

Fig. 10 Cavalry. Carbine.

Marshal Marmont, himself a horse gunner. It seems also that the British guns were more manoeuvrable than the French. There is no doubt that the French had difficulty in getting their pieces into position over the soft ground on the morning of 18 June. No British diarist notes this problem before the battle. The small difference in weight between the 12 pounder and the British long 9 pounder does not seem to be enough to account for this and it may be that the British retention of the conventional limber gave them an advantage over the Gribeauval guns.

In one point the French had a decided advantage. Their arrangements for the supply of reserve ammunition were much superior. Their Artillery Train handled the whole business of supply as far back as the depots. In the British service such transport as was out of the range of the waggons of the battery was the responsibility of the Ordnance Commissary who was not an officer of the army but an official of the Treasury.

Artillerie à Cheval de Ligne. Plate 50.
French Horse Artillery was unusual in that its uniform had been considerably simplified. Until 1810 they had worn a hussar type dress not unlike that of the Horse Artillery of the Guard although they seldom wore the pelisse. This was replaced in the first instance by the *habit kinsky*, a single breasted jacket with short tails. This was shortly succeeded by the *habit veste*, another short tailed jacket but one with the lapels buttoned back, like most French uniform jackets, and cut straight across the waist at the front. They continued to wear hussar breeches with bastions on the thigh, except on active service when they wore overalls. This revision of uniform made them resemble *Chasseurs à cheval* at a distance although,

like artillerymen of most nations, the cloth was blue and the facings red.

Since they were an *élite* corps the horse gunners wore red epaulettes and red chevrons on their shakos.

Artillerie à Pied de Ligne. Plate 51.
The jacket of the horse artillery was worn also by the foot branch, without the red epaulettes. Instead of hussar breeches, the foot artillery had plain blue breeches with black gaiters reaching to just below the knee. On service breeches and gaiters alike were covered by blue overallls strapped at the ankle. Occasionally these overalls had a broad red stripe intersected by blue piping. Foot artillery had worn red chevrons in their shakos until 1811 but then adopted a plainer shako.

Foot artillery were armed with the short sword *(sabre-briquet)* normally carried by light infantrymen and an infantry musket and bayonet. Horse gunners carried only the light cavalry sabre.

Plates 52-66. **Infantry of the Line.**

It was an axiom of Napoleon's army that promotion up to the highest ranks went by merit. As a slogan this was admirable for morale. Every soldier was, no doubt, encouraged to feel that he carried '*dans sa giberne le bâton de maréchal*' but, in practice, many factors other than merit weighed during the First Empire and where merit in the junior ranks was given its advertised weight the results were frequently unsatisfactory. It was, however, true that advancement of a somewhat horizontal kind was available to all worthy soldiers. Napoleon's army was organized as a pyramid of *élites*. In the line regiments the best men were creamed off into the *élite* grenadier com-

135

panies. Beyond that deserving men moved on to the Middle Guard and the best of all, provided that they survived, reached *Les Anciens*, the *élite* of *élites*.

In view of this continuous process of skimming the finest men from the line it is astonishing that the infantry regiments of the line continued, up to Waterloo, to be as excellent as they were. In that battle the superlatives of historians are usually reserved for the attacks of the Guard at Placenoit and beside Hougoumont. The greatest glory to the French infantry should surely go to the men of D'Erlon's corps. Although led forward in a formation which most of them must have recognized as being suicidal*, they attacked repeatedly and did not give up the attempt until the Middle Guard had been defeated and the Prussians were moving into their rear.

The French army was able to afford its *élitist* structure because of the conscription. This brought into the army a cross section of the whole male population of France so that there were enough good men left in the battalion companies of the line to keep them formidable and efficient even after the best had gone to the Guard. Wellington recognised this when he commented that, 'The French army is certainly a wonderful machine; but if we are to form such a one, we must compose our army of soldiers drawn from all classes of the population: from the good and middling, as well in rank as education, as from the bad, and not, as we in particular do, from the bad only.' In the British army, where the recruiting sergeant had to take what he could get, the regiments had, like Wellington, to do the best they could 'with the instruments which have been sent to assist me.' The British had no option but to place all their confidence in the regimental system. Regimental pride was the only effective appeal that could be made to the 'scum of the earth enlisted for drink' who comprised the vast majority of the private soldiers. Given this situation it was impossible to reward a man by promoting him to an *élite* corps. A private soldier of one of the crack line regiments would not regard tranfer to the Guards as promotion, however much he might admire the virtues of the Household Troops.

French line regiments proudly carried their battle honours on the *tricouleurs* attached to their eagles*, but the loyalty of the soldiers was primarily to France and the Emperor and every man could dream that one day he might become one of the Old Guard. One reason for this was the lack of continuity with pre-revolutionary regiments. The Bourbon regiments had been inclined to change their names and there had been some curious jockeying for seniority. When the *Regiment Le Roi* had been raised, its seniority had been forty-eighth. By a deal between the respective colonels it had changed places in the seniority list with the *Regiment Artois*, which had been twelfth. At the Revolution all regimental names had been swept away. The old regiments had been absorbed into numbered *demi-brigades* which in turn became numbered regiments. At the Restoration of 1814, names, although not necessarily those of the reign of Louis XVI, had been restored. Numbers were reintroduced for the Hundred days. It is not impossible that there may have been at Waterloo some old

---

* More than half the regiments in D'Erlon's corps had been engaged with British infantry in the Peninsula and must have recognized the difficulty, if not impossibility, of what they were attempting.

* 63me Ligne in Reille's corps wore the battle honour 'Chiclana'. The same battle was commemorated on the other side at Waterloo by the three regiments of British Guards, the 28th Foot, the 95th Rifles and 2nd Hussars KGL under the name 'Barossa'.

soldiers who had joined the *1er Ligne* when it was known as *Picardie* before it became *1er Demi-Brigade* or *1er Regiment*. Most would have known it in 1814 as the *Régiment du Roi*.

Nor were regimental distinctions made apparent in the uniforms. In the early days of the Empire colonels had introduced so many regimental peculiarities that a commission was set up in 1811 to standardize infantry uniforms. As a result only the regimental number on the shako plate was left as differentiation. At the same time the uniform of the drummers, on which much invention had been lavished, was changed throughout the infantry to the green imperial livery with a lace bearing alternately an eagle and an 'N'.

Infantry of the Line. Plates 52-61 & 66. Figure 11.

In 1815 the French infantry battalion, whether *Ligne* or *Léger*, was organized into six companies, compared to ten in the British army. The theoretical strength of each battalion was about 900 men though at Waterloo few had half that number. When formed in line the *élite* company, known in *Régiments de Ligne* as the Grenadier company, took post on the right. On the left was the light company, known as *Voltigeurs*. Between them, numbered from one to four, were the battalion companies, known as *Fusiliers*. Each company was divided into two sections and, when *colonne de bataille* was formed each company would be drawn up in three ranks with one section behind the other, giving a company at full strength a front of twenty-five men and a depth of six ranks. A battalion column would normally form on a two company front, with a width of fifty files and a depth of twelve, assuming that the *Voltigeurs* were performing their usual task of skirmishing

in front of the column. The *Grenadiers* might assist the *Voltigeurs* or form part of the column or be grouped, with the *Grenadiers* from other battalions into special *élite* units. At Waterloo, three of D'Erlon's four divisions attacked in columns with a four battalion front having, since all the units were far under strength, a front of about 150 men and a depth of 24 files.

Two of these massive columns, those formed by the divisions of Donzelot and Marcognet, came up against lines of highly trained British infantry who had scarcely been damaged by the preliminary bombardment. In each column only 300 or 450 Frenchmen could fire. Neither of the British brigades had more than 2,000 men in the ranks, less than half the number of their immediate assailants. Their fire power, however, was four times as great. Napoleon had remarked as early as 1811 that 'Columns will not break through lines of battle unless they are supported by a very superior artillery to prepare the attack.' Since the French artillery had failed to prepare the attack, Donzelot and Marcognet were inevitably checked. Having halted, their only course was to deploy into line so as to utilize their own fire power. They were in the middle of this complicated piece of foot drill, 'in the act of shouldering their arms,' under the steady British volleys when the British heavy cavalry broke in among them.

Napoleon had attempted in 1806 to reintroduce the white uniform of Bourbon days for the infantry of the line. He was induced to abandon the attempt and, from 1812 onwards, they wore the latest version of the uniform which emerged from the Revolution in the national colours of red, white and blue. The blue jacket had its tails considerably shortened and the front, with its turned back lapels ended at the waist. The white lining also showed where **137**

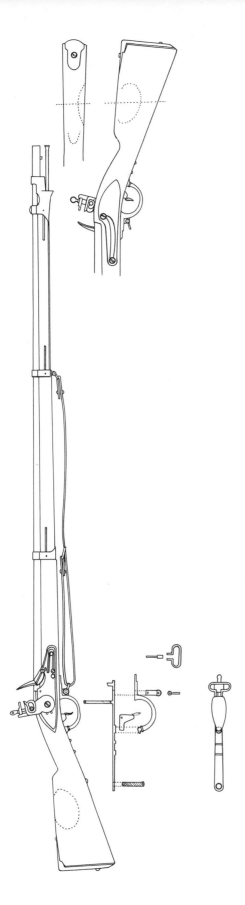

the tails were turned back. The piping of lapels and pockets was red. *Grenadier* and *Fusilier* companies wore red collars, piped with blue while the *Voltigeurs* had yellow collars, also blue-piped. *Grenadiers* had the usual red epaulettes of their kind but *Fusiliers* had blue counter-epaulettes. The *Voltigeurs'* counter-epaulettes seem to have varied from battalion to battalion, some having yellow, some green, some blue, some a combination of any two of those colours. Some even wore red. Turnback ornaments for the *Grenadiers* and *Voltigeurs* were the usual grenades and bugle horns and the *Fusiliers* wore the imperial monogram crowned.

The flank companies wore cross belts so as to support the *sabre-briquet* on the left. *Fusiliers* had only a shoulder belt which supported their ammunition pouch and bayonet which, like the flank companies, they wore on the right.

Grenadiers of the line did not wear the grenadier cap of bearskin, which was, however, worn by the pioneer sections, but had their shakos ornamented with red chevrons and, in full dress a long red plume. *Voltigeurs* wore a short yellow plume and the four *Fusilier* companies were distinguished by small coloured discs in company colours (see Plate 61). The rank of officers was shown by the width and number of bands of gold on the shako. (See Plate 61).

All the distinctions between the companies and battalions were, in action, obscured by the wearing of buff/grey greatcoats and, usually, of canvas shako covers. The cross- or shoulder-belts were worn outside the greatcoats and breeches were covered by blue (or occasionally white) overalls.

One French regiment was wholly distinct from the rest. This was the 2nd Swiss who wore a red uniform. They served with Grouchy's wing and were

Fig. 11 Infantry. Musket.

almost destroyed in taking the bridge at Wavre from the Prussians. The regiment was formed from volunteers from the three Swiss regiments hired by the cantons to Louis XVIII (and previously to Napoleon). The remainder dispersed to their homes when their paymaster was forced to fly from France.

Light Infantry. Plates 62-67. Figure 11. Although they were the lineal descendants of the Chasseurs of the old Royal army the *Régiments légers* of the Napoleonic army were indistinguishable from the *Régiments de ligne* in equipment, drill and training. The only differences were in nomenclature and uniform. In light battalions the battalion companies were known as *Chasseurs*, rather than *Fusiliers* and the *Grenadiers* became *Carabiniers*.

In uniform the only significant difference was that the lining to the jacket, which showed at the lapels and turnbacks, was blue instead of white and the piping was white instead of red. Buttons and shako plakes were white metal rather than brass and the officers' gorgettes were silver instead of gilt. The *Carabiniers* of some battalions still sported grenadier caps despite the regulations of 1812 which abolished them. The cuff piping of even the *Carabinier* company was pointed in light infantry style. All ranks wore the *sabre-briquet* but in other respects light regiments were armed in the same way as those of the line except that the officers carried curved swords.

Medical Services. Plate 67.
Thanks to Baron Larrey, Napoleon's Surgeon General, the medical service of the French army was better organized than any other in Europe and included, beside men with professional qualifications, personnel permanently allocated and trained for hospital and transport duties. Larrey succeeded in modifying standard artillery waggons so that they became the first custom-built military ambulances in Europe.

The stretcher-bearer's equipment is a tribute to Larrey's ingenuity and organizing powers. Attached to the knapsack is one of the wooden endpieces to the stretcher. The cloth 'bed' of the stretcher is worn by the bearer attached to the front of his belt and his spontoon (or pike) makes one of the carrying handles.

The officers of the *Service de Santé* wore a single-breasted jacket of a blue somewhat lighter than that of the fighting troops. Surgeons had scarlet facings, physicians black and pharmacists dark green. Medical officers of the Imperial Guard wore the aiguillette on the right shoulder. The uniform of the other ranks derived from an earlier uniform of the *Train d'Equipages*, which had been the source of supply of their ambulances. Hospital staff wore the brown jacket with scarlet facings; drivers had steel grey facings.

ANGLO-NETHERLANDS ARMY.

Plates 68-72. **Staff.**

The meaning of staff, in its military sense, has changed since the days of the Napoleonic wars. Then, in a strict sense, a staff officer was either a general who held some specific appointment (which more than half the generals in the Army List did not) or one of the small number of officers who, while on the active list, did not hold a regimental commission on which, through purchase or seniority*, their promotion depended. There were scarcely more than a hundred of these with the rank of lieutenant-colonel or below and half of them were either adjutants of recruiting districts or on secondment to the Portuguese army. The staff in its modern sense, the men who did the business of the army, consisted almost entirely of regimental officers, holding vacancies in their regiments, who drew a small staff allowance and were liable to be returned to their units at any time. It is likely therefore that very few of them went to the length of purchasing a special uniform for their temporary employment on the staff. Most of them would wear the uniform of their regiment.

General Officers. Plates 68-69.
It was only in 1814 that Britain started paying general officers as such. Up to that date they had received pay only if employed 'on the staff', that is to say in command of a brigade or division, of a fortress or district or in one of the few staff posts requiring an officer of high rank. Other generals had to manage for pay on what they received in their regimental rank, usually as a lieutenant colonel, sometimes as a major and, occasionally as a captain.

* Contrary to general belief, less than one commission in five went by purchase during the Peninsular War.

Any general officer who was employed would probably have to have the uniform of his rank to wear at reviews but he would naturally be averse to exposing so expensive a garment to the hazards of battle. Such information as is available suggests that few of the generals present at Waterloo were dressed as such. Wellington and Picton are known to have worn civilian clothes. Lord Uxbridge wore hussar costume, probably the uniform of colonel of the Seventh Hussars but possibly, since he was a great dandy, the special uniform for a general of hussars. The one man likely to have been dressed as a British general was the Prince of Orange. He had served as ADC to Wellington in Spain and had been created a full general as a compliment at the time of the peace. In Brussels he had been so attached to his British uniform that he had to be advised that he was causing offence to his fathers' subjects in the united Netherlands.

Plate 69 shows the distinctions between the various ranks of general officer. To distinguish between them it should be remembered that Field Marshals and full generals had the buttons on their sleeves and on the back panels of their jackets in groups of four while lieutenant-generals had two groups of three in those places (three groups of three on the lapels). Major-generals had these buttons arranged in pairs. Had there been a Brigadier* present at Waterloo, three buttons would have been arranged two and one. In undress the gold lace on the buttonholes would have been replaced by braid of a darker red than the uniform coat, very much as is worn on the red tabs of a brigadier today.

* The Army List referred to Brigadiers but in correspondence they were referred to as Brigadiers-General. The only officer of this rank in the Netherlands in June, 1815, was Alexander Bryce, RE, who was at Antwerp.

Staff Officers. Plate 70.

The staff (in the modern sense) of the British army was strangely arranged. It consisted of only two branches, the Quartermaster-General's Department, which dealt with the movement of troops and their quartering, and the Adjutant-General's, which was responsible for drill, discipline, the rendering of returns and, in a distant way, with clothing and medical services. The work of the non-existent Operations branch (G) was arbitrarily parcelled out between the QMG and the AG. Wellington gave the larger share of this work to his Quartermaster-General, who became a rough approximation of a chief-of-staff. Intelligence, however, remained the prerogative of the Adjutant-General since, among his duties, the AG was responsible for prisoners of war.

At brigade level the work of both departments was done by the Brigade Major, who was almost invariably a captain. He had no staff officers to assist him.

Members of both departments wore the same 'staff' uniform as generals except that their lace was silver instead of gold. The distinctions of the QMG and AG were those of a lieutenant-general and their deputies those of a major-general. Both these classes of senior staff officers wore two silver bullioned epaulettes with a red background to the shoulder strap. Assistants in both departments (DAQMGs and DAAGs) wore, in silver lace, the distinctions of brigadiers with a single epaulette. Brigade majors had the same distinctions but their single epaulette had a blue background and was worn on the left shoulder in the cavalry and on the right in the infantry. These distinguishing epaulettes would have been worn even by those officers, the great majority, who wore their regimental uniform while holding staff appointments.

Aides de Camp. Plates 71 & 72.

ADCs were not, strictly speaking, staff officers but were attached personally to their generals who were responsible for paying and feeding them, for which they received an allowance of 9/2d a day.

Their official dress was the 'staff' uniform with gold lace. Like Brigade Majors their epaulettes, although of gold bullion, had a blue background and were worn on the left or right shoulders according to whether their general commanded cavalry or infantry. ADCs to the Commander of the Forces wore epaulettes on both shoulders.

Wellington's had eight ADCs. They prided themselves on riding four miles across country in eighteen minutes. It is scarcely conceivable that they could have achieved this wearing a cocked hat.

Plates 73-82. **British Cavalry.**

The British cavalry did not fall into as many fragmentations as did the French. There were no Horse Grenadiers, no Carabineers*, no Cuirassiers and no Lancers. They can, therefore, be conveniently considered under three categories, Household Cavalry, Dragoons and Light Dragoons.

Household Cavalry. Plates 73-75. Figures 12-14.

Only two regiments, the 1st and 2nd Life Guards, were properly speaking Household Troops. They had their origins in two troops of Horse Guards which had been raised at the Restoration of 1660 and two troops of Horse Grenadier Guards of slightly later date. As befitted the Sover-

* The 6th Dragoon Guards were known as Carabineers (although they were not so named in the Army List of that date) but they were armed and trained as dragoons.

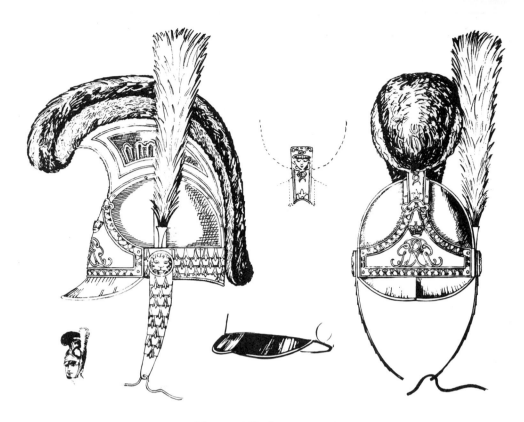

Fig. 12 Life Guards. Helmet.

eign's *Garde du Corps* they were the senior regiments of the army. With them were the Royal Horse Guards (Blue), previously the 1st Regiment of Horse. Although they did not technically become Household troops until 1820, the Blues had been doing duty around the king and his palaces since the middle of the eighteenth century and were Household troops in all but name. Since royal duties had to be carried on in war as in peace, each of the three regiments had left a squadron in England and a line regiment, the King's Dragoon Guards, was included in the Household Brigade to make it up to effective numbers.

The Household Cavalry did not campaign in all the finery they wore in London and at Windsor. Blue-grey overalls (pale blue in the Horse Guards) replaced the thigh boots and the white buckskin breech-es which, since they had to be put on wet to achieve a close fit, were so productive of rheumatism. Officers did not fight wearing their aiguillettes and wore a minimum of lace on their jackets. Their embroidered and sequinned sabretaches and pouches were also discarded as being too expensive to be risked in a *mêlée*. It is not clear why, in the British cavalry, sabretaches were issued to the troopers. The sabretache is intended as a portable writing desk with pen and paper stored inside. Since it is unlikely that (except perhaps in the Scots Greys) one trooper in twenty was literate, this article must have been more of an encumbrance than an asset.

Until 1812 both the Life Guards and Horse Guards had worn a large and cumbersome cocked hat. This was re-

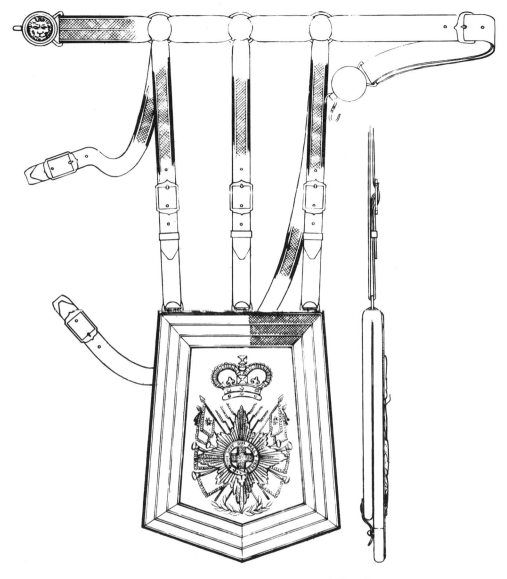

Fig. 13 Life Guards. Sabretache. (Officers).

placed by the elegant Grecian helmet which was at first ornamented with a flowing horsehair tail. This made it so easy to mistake them, at a distance, for French dragoons that it was changed to a crest of red and blue wool projecting well forward.

As today, the uniform of the Life Guards was red faced with blue, the colours being reversed for the Horse Guards. Where officers wore gold lace, other ranks had yellow braid and the Life Guards saddlecloth was blue-grey for troopers.

143

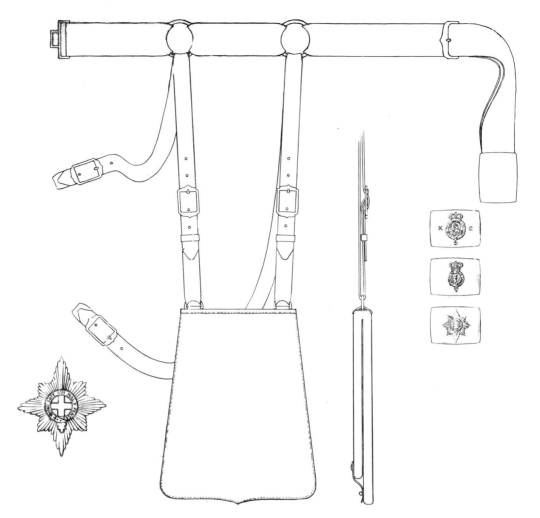

Fig. 13a Heavy Cavalry. Sabretache (Other ranks).

It was not possible to distinguish between the First and Second Regiments of Life Guards without a minute examination of the shabraque, the swords (which bore on the hilt the regimental cypher in the 1st and a grenade in the 2nd) or the spurs (which were steel in the 1st, brass in the 2nd). When wearing cloaks the 1st Life Guards had a blue collar and the 2nd was entirely red.

Fig. 14 Heavy Cavalry. Carbine.

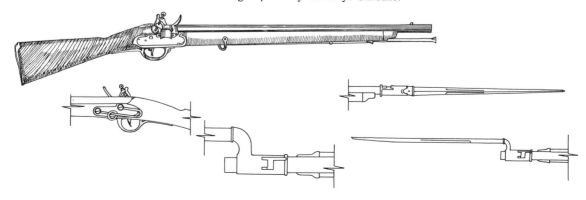

Fig. 15 1st (King's) Dragoon Guards. Helmet.

Dragoons. Plates 76-78. Figures 15-18 & 19.

The nomenclature of British dragoons is confusing since there is an arbitrary and meaningless distinction between dragoons and dragoon guards. The reasons for this lie in an unsuccessful attempt to achieve economy. In the early eighteenth century cavalry was divided into two categories, horse and dragoons. The former were intended to fulfill the heavy cavalry functions performed by Napoleon's cuirassiers, while the latter were, supposedly, mounted infantry. Dragoons were paid less, had less elaborate uniforms and rode horses costing a third less than those of regiments of Horse. Between 1746 and 1788 all but one of the British regiments of Horse were, in order to save on the Army Estimates, converted into dragoons. To salve their pride (and to avoid a complicated and invidious re numbering of dragoon regiments) they were designated dragoon guards, the 2nd to 8th regiments of Horse becoming the 1st to 7th Dragoon

Guards. The remaining regiment, the 1st (Royal) Horse became the Royal Horse Guards.

As an economy measure this was a failure. Not only did it deprive the army of all its heavy cavalry (except the Household regiments) but dragoon guards and dragoons alike detested their dismounted role, refused to regard themselves as anything but cavalrymen and, in the fullness of time, succeeded in getting themselves paid, dressed and mounted as regiments of horse. The army had to do without mounted infantry, except in an improvised form, until the Second World War*.

The only discernable difference between the uniforms of dragoons and dragoon guards was that the former had pointed cuffs and the latter square. Otherwise they

* The problem of providing mounted (by that time motorised) infantry was solved in the nineteen thirties by giving the task to the two Greenjacket regiments whose officers were so certain of their social standing that they would have regarded it as degrading to drift into becoming cavalrymen as all other mounted infantry had done.

145

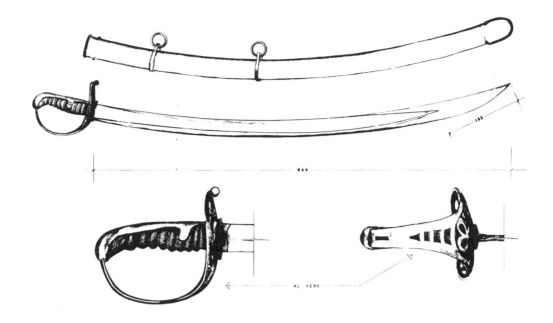

Fig. 16 2nd (RNB) Dragoons. Sabre and Scabbard.

were dressed and armed alike. Since their principal role was shock action, the formed charge, they were armed with the heavy cavalry sabre although they also carried pistols and an elderly and unhandy carbine with a 26″ barrel. Like the Household cavalry they had changed in 1812 from the cocked hat to the Grecian helmet but, despite the resemblance to the French, they had retained the hanging horsehair tail. According to the Dress Regulations they should have worn plush breeches but for active service these were replaced by grey-brown overalls worn over webbing breeches.

One regiment, the 2nd (Royal North British) Dragoons, better known as the Scots Greys, had several peculiarities of dress. Most noticeable was their grenadier cap. This item commemorated their triumph over the French infantry of the *Maison du Roi* whose colours they had captured at Ramillies in 1706. When

originally adopted as a battle honour this had been the mitre-shaped cloth erection worn by grenadiers but when grenadiers adopted the bearskin the Scots Greys followed suit. The regiment also had its own design of sabre, more curved than the chopper used by the rest of the heavy cavalry.

All dragoon and dragoon guard regiments wore scarlet jackets and, of those present at Waterloo, the King's Dragoon Guards, the Royals and the Scots Greys, being royal regiments, had blue facings and gold lace. The Inniskillings had yellow facings and silver lace.

British heavy cavalry has always suffered from serious defects. Most of these were due to inexperience. Living on an island, the British have always had difficulty in transporting their cavalry to the seat of war and it was always easier to use such horse transports as were available to move the smaller, less expensive horses of

146

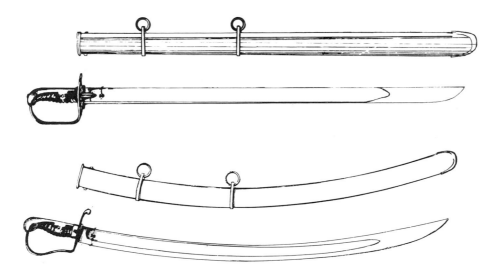

Fig. 17 Cavalry. Sabres, Heavy and Light.

light dragoons. The heavies, in consequence, seldom went to war and, at Waterloo, had all the faults of young troops. Of the four dragoon units present only the Royals had seen action since the turn of the century and even the Royals, who had had a distinguished career in the Peninsula, were more fitted by experience to act as light cavalry than heavy. The result was that, although they performed the one evolution they knew, the set-piece charge, perfectly, they could not be stopped or rallied when their object had been

achieved. As Wellington had acidly remarked three years earlier, 'Our cavalry officers have acquired the trick of galloping at everything and then galloping back as fast as they gallop at the enemy. One would think they cannot manoeuvre except on Wimbledon Common.'

Light Dragoons. Plates 79-82. Figure 18. While dragoons were trained (or partly trained) for shock action, light dragoons were intended for reconnaissance and outpost duties. For this they were mounted

Fig. 18 Light Cavalry Carbine (Paget carbine).

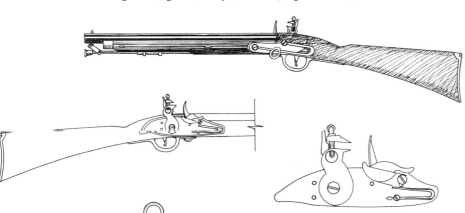

on lighter handier horses and were armed with the lighter, more curved, sabre and the shorter carbine with the 16″ barrel. They were also capable of the formed charge and, having learned through bitter and costly experience in Spain and Portugal, were better able to rally afterwards. In the later stage of Waterloo, they had to perform heavy cavalry duties since insufficient Householders and dragoons survived from Lord Uxbridge's classic charge to fulfill the requirements for heavy cavalry.

Fourteen regiments of light dragoons on the British Army List were in Flanders at the time of Waterloo and all except one, which was detached at Tubize, took part in the battle. These regiments fell into two categories, light dragoons and hussars. The latter, with three exceptions, were officially designated 'Light Dragoons (Hussars)'. There was no difference in duties and training of the two categories but hussars wore a much more extravagant uniform and hussar regiments were larger by two troops.

Five of these regiments, three of hussars* and two of light dragoons, were part of the King's German Legion. This body of all arms had been raised in England in 1803 from the escaped remnants of King George's Hanoverian army. It was on the strength of the British army and was dressed, drilled and armed on the British model. Cavalry, artillery, engineers and infantry of the Legion had taken part in every British expedition on the continent of Europe† during the Napoleonic war and the German light cavalry was recognized as being the best in the British service. In Spain and Portugal every British infantryman had slept the

* 2nd Hussars, KGL, were at Tubize during the battle.
† KGL troops were enlisted for service in Europe only.

sounder for knowing that Frederick von Arenschildt and the 1st Hussars of the Legion were in charge of the outposts. One officer wrote that 'If we saw a British dragoon at any time approaching at full speed, it excited no great curiosity among us, but whenever we saw one of the first hussars coming on at a gallop, it was high time to gird on our swords and bundle up.' The two KGL regiments of light dragoons had been 'heavy dragoons' until almost the end of the war but there had been a shortage of light cavalry and by an order of 25 December, 1813, they were converted into light horse. It is ironic that they should be chosen for this change since, in July 1812, they had performed the most memorable heavy cavalry feat of the Peninsular war when they broke two squares of French infantry at Garcia Hernandez.

Hussars. Plates 79 & 80.
The German Legion regiments were the first in the British army to be dressed as hussars. From 1803, the German light dragoon regiments wore hussar-type braided jackets (dolmans) and the furred pelisse. Only the first regiment wore the hussar fur cap *(kolbak)* from their formation, the other two originally wearing the shako. Soon afterwards the Prince of Wales dressed one troop of his regiment, the 10th Light Dragoons, as hussars at his own (or his creditors') expense. By 1807 the 7th, 10th and 15th were dressed as hussars and soon afterwards they were joined by the 18th. All four were officially permitted to describe themselves as Light Dragoons (Hussars). In 1815 only the three German regiments were known as Hussars *tout court* so as to distinguish them from the two light (formerly heavy) German regiments of dragoons.

The *kolbak* had been found unsatisfactory in the Peninsula since it was admirably

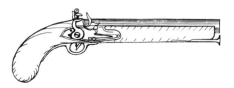

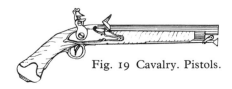

Fig. 19 Cavalry. Pistols.

designed to drip rain water into the eyes. It is not clear how many hussars wore it at Waterloo. The troopers of the Fifteenth had never adopted it and wore a black shako, their officers usually wearing the same in red. All ranks of the 3rd Hussars continued to wear the black shako, while the 2nd Regiment adopted a tall cylindrical fur cap (a mirliton), of a type discarded by the 7th some years earlier. The two senior German regiments had their fur caps fitted with small leather peaks, making it a more satisfactory headdress for wet weather. The kolbaks of the officers of the 10th Hussars were, uniquely, of grey fur. All the hussar regiments wore red busby bags except the 18th who had blue.

Blue jackets were worn by all seven regiments, the British regiments having silver lace and the Germans gold. Collars and cuffs were white for the 7th, the 18th and the 2nd Germans, red for the 10th and 1st Germans, scarlet for the 15th and yellow for the 3rd Germans.

Hussars, like light dragoons, were armed with the curved light cavalry sabre and the short Paget carbine. Officers were supposed to wear mameluke-hilted swords of the design carried by generals. Since this hilt gave minimal protection to the hand, most hussar officers preferred some less ornamental weapon for use in battle.

Light Dragoons. Plates 81 & 82.
The dress reform of 1812 had moved the dress of light dragoons in the direction of lancer fashions, the effect of a plastron being achieved by turning back the unusually shaped lapels. At the same time the old light dragoon helmet had, despite Wellington's plea (see p.   ), been replaced by a belltopped shako, indistinguishable from that of the French *chasseurs à cheval*. In the shako was worn a plume of red over white, the officers having feathers, the troopers worsted.

While hussars wore a sash with vertical stripes (known as a barrelled sash), light dragoons had horizontal stripes. Officers of all light dragoon regiments wore sashes of red and gold stripes, other ranks had stripes of the regimental facing colour on, usually, a blue background. An unusual feature of light dragoon clothing was a fringe, 5½ inches long and known as a waterfall, worn in the small of the back. It appears to have had no function of any kind.

The facing colours and lace of the regiments at Waterloo were as follows:

Regiment	Colour of lapels, cuffs and piping	Lace and Epaulettes
11th LD	Buff	Silver (or white)
12th LD	Yellow	Silver (or white)
13th LD	Buff	Gold (or yellow)
16th LD	Scarlet	Silver (or white)
23rd LD	Crimson	Silver (or white)
1st LD, KGL	Red	Gold (or yellow)
2nd LD, KGL	Red	Silver (or white)

Plates 83-89. **Netherlands Cavalry.**

Experience in India and the Peninsula had given Wellington a realistic opinion of the limitiations of allied cavalry serving under his orders. In 1811 he had remarked, 'Few troops will bear a general panic; at any event young cavalry are much more easily affected by these circumstances by such circumstances, and the effect on them is much more extensive and more sensibly felt by the whole army, than similar circumstances operating upon in-

Number & Nationality	Designation	Colour of Jacket	Facings Colour		Shako (where worn)
1st Dutch	Carabineers	Blue	Blue (red piping)		(helmet)
2nd Belgian	...do...	Blue	Red		(helmet)
3rd Dutch	...do...	Blue	Blue epaulettes (red piping) Yellow collar		(helmet)
4th Dutch	Light Dgns.	Blue	Red		Black
5th Belgian	...do...	Green	Yellow		Green
6th Dutch	Hussars	Light Blue	Light Blue	Gold Lace	Red (officers) Black (troopers)
8th Belgian	...do...	Light Blue	Red	Silver Lace	Red (officers) Black (troopers)

Note. The 7th Netherlands cavalry was a colonial regiment stationed in the East Indies.

fantry in the same state of discipline. Their horses afford them means of flight, and when once cavalry loses their order it is impossible to restore it. For this reason I am always inclined to keep the cavalry out of action as long as possible.'

Nor was there any opportunity of attending to the training of the Netherlands horse before the campaign opened. Although the King of the Netherlands had put his infantry and artillery under Wellington's command during May, he did not do the same with his cavalry until the eve of the battle. Uxbridge, who commanded the allied cavalry, remarked, 'I will do my best with them, but it is unfortunate that I should not have had an opportunity of making myself acquainted with any of the officers or their regiments.'

Waterloo was a battle which tried the discipline of the best troops and it is scarcely surprising that none of the three Netherlands cavalry brigades present earned themselves any credit. Worst was Van Merlen's light brigade. They were the only allied cavalry present early in the day at Quatre Bras. Van Merlen, who had made his reputation commanding the 2nd Lancers of the French Imperial Guard, led them to a charge but none of them closed the enemy and many, if not most, took to their heels and fled to Brussels and beyond. A civilian in Brussels recalled that on the morning of 17 June, 'between five and six we were roused by loud knocking at the door and cries of "*Les Français sont ici*." Starting up, the first sight we beheld was a troop of Belgic cavalry, covered not with glory, but with mud.' Van Merlen was killed at Waterloo trying to persuade the rest of the brigade to face the enemy.

The heavy brigade under Baron Trip did no better. Uxbridge tried to lead them forward but to no purpose. 'They promised to follow me and I led them beyond the ridge of the hill, a little to the left of Hougoumont. There they halted, and finding the impossibility of making them charge, I left them.' The remaining light brigade, Ghigny's, did manage to get a few men forward when the British light cavalry went to the rescue of the heavy brigades but later merely sat on its horses behind the wreck of the Household Brigade. They looked so shaky that when Lord Edward Somerset was ordered to withdraw the Householders to ground less exposed to fire he declined to obey, saying that 'should he move, the Dutch cavalry, who were in support, would move off immediately.'

Although few of the Netherlands cavalry crossed sabres with the enemy more than 11 % of them were missing at the end of the day compared to the heavily-engaged British who had only 7 % missing The most that can be said for them is that they behaved better than the Duke of Cumberland's regiment of Hanoverian Hussars who could not be induced to advance from a covered position in rear of the ridge, their colonel pleading that 'he had no confidence in his men, that they were volunteers and the horses their own property.'

The Netherlands cavalry regiments were numbered consecutively, irrespective of designation, and were distinguished as shown in the table opposite.

Plate 90. Brunswick Cavalry. See under Plates 127 & 128.

Plates 91-95. **British Artillery.**

Nothing illustrates the organizational chaos which had developed in the British army over the centuries better than the position of the Royal Artillery. They did not belong to the army, (nor did the Royal Engineers) They owed no allegiance to the commander in chief. Neither the Secretary for War nor the Secretary at War had control over them. They had their own system of supply, of medical care, of promotion. Even their chaplains were employed on a different basis and on a different scale of pay. Their political chief was the Master General of the Ordnance who sat in the Cabinet and, although he had no responsibility for the infantry or the cavalry, was the government's chief military adviser. On active service artillery units were attached to commanders in the field but the senior gunner officers had the duty as well as the right to report over the general's head to their own chiefs at Woolwich. Further to complicate the situation, the men who were responsible for moving the guns from place to place in the Foot Artillery (but not in the Horse Artillery) belonged to a separate corps, the Royal Artillery Drivers.

Royal Horse Artillery. Plates 91-94. Figure 20.

Horse Artillery, originally known as flying artillery, is essentially artillery intended to accompany cavalry and move at a cavalry pace. It was first introduced into the Austrian army as early as 1759. France (and Sweden) did not follow this example until 1792 and the British horsed branch was launched with two troops raised in January, 1793. From the start it was an *élite* corps and within five years it was granted precedence on parade over all other regiments of the army, a distinction it retained until 1869 when it was laid down that the Household Cavalry should take the right of the line when the Sovereign was present*.

Since the rocket was an eminently mobile form of artillery, the rocket troops were attached to RHA when they were

* This precedence for the RHA was a matter of hasting dispute and, although usually to them, is not admitted in the 'General Regulations and Orders for the Army' of 1811 which were in force in 1815.

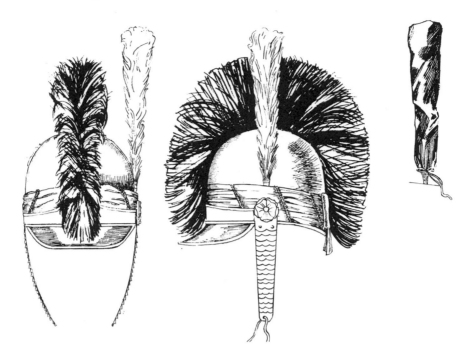

Fig. 20 Royal Horse Artillery. Helmet.

formed. 2nd Rocket Troop, RHA, which was at Waterloo had the battle honour, unique among British units, of 'Leipsic' having been present at that battle in 1813. Their performance there so impressed the Czar that he decorated with his own badge of the Order of St Anne the lieutenant in charge of them, Thomas Fox Strangways, who was wounded at Waterloo.

Horse Artillery wore the braided dolmans of hussars and the elegant helmet which Wellington had been anxious to retain for the light dragoons. Unlike the Foot Artillery they had their own drivers who wore a rather simpler jacket with three vertical lines outlined in piping compared to the horizontal lacing of the gun numbers. Members of the rocket troop wore a shoulder belt and carried a lance-like appendage which was, in fact, a bundle of sticks for the 6 pounder

rockets. The blue and white pennant on the rocket sticks was worn at Leipsic but not at Waterloo. It had been added 'by the captain and was discontinued'.

Royal Artillery. Plate 95.
The Royal Regiment of Artillery dated from 1716 and, together with the horsed branch and the Royal Engineers, was the only part of the army which went to the trouble of training all its officers before they were commissioned. While the vast majority of infantry and cavalry officers* learned their drill from the adjutants of their battalions and their tactics as they went along, all artillery and engineer

* The Royal Military College had been established in 1802 but during the time of the Peninsular war it supplied the infantry and cavalry with only 3.9% of their officers. More than that (5.4%) were promoted from the ranks (or 9.3% if Volunteers are included).

officers had to pass through the Royal Military Academy at Woolwich. This gave them a professionalism lacking in many other parts of the army although it made gunner officers (and still more engineer officers) clannish and pedantic.

The Foot Artillery uniform was the same as that of a royal regiment of infantry with the colours reversed, a blue jacket with red facings. The gunners carried a flintlock, which they refered to as a carbine but was in fact a musket with a 33″ barrel and bayonet. Sergeants, like those of heavy infantry, carried a pike and a shortsword. Officers were supposed to wear the infantry officer's regulation sword but since one gunner refers to it as 'good neither for cut or thrust and a perfect encumbrance,' it is reasonable to assume that many of them carried a more work-manlike weapon in battle.

The Foot Artillery or, as it was officially known, the Marching Battalions of Artillery, depended for the movement of their guns on the Corps of Artillery Drivers. Their dress was a combination of that of the Horse and Foot Artillery. They wore the jacket of the foot branch and the helmet and overalls of the Horse. The Drivers Corps had been founded in 1794 to replace the previous arrangements where the guns had been driven by hired civilians. Apart from the inconvenience of having gunners and drivers under separate control, the Drivers were a most unsatisfactory body. One gunner officer described them as 'a nest of infamy'. This was due almost wholly to the inadequacy of their officers who did not hold military rank but received their appointments as Lieutenants or Captains Commissary from the Treasury.

Plate 96. Brunswick Artillery. See under Plates 127 & 128.

Plates 97-122. **British Infantry**.

A few weeks before Waterloo Wellington, while walking in the park in Brussels, was asked how he thought the imminent campaign would go. 'Seeing a private soldier of one of our infantry regiments gaping about at the statues and images, he said, "There, it all depends on that article there whether we can do the business or not. Give me enough of it and I am sure."' He was not given enough of it. He had asked for '40,000 good British infantry'. When the campaign opened he had less than 25,000 British and German Legion infantry, many of them very young soldiers. This small contingent excelled themselves and, after the battle, the Duke paid them the highest compliment he knew: 'I never saw the British infantry behave so well.' A French officer who had faced them echoed the Duke's opinion. 'The British infantry is the finest in the world. Fortunately there are not many of them.'

The organization of the British army began, and almost ended, with the regiment. Apart from the three regiments of Foot Guards, there were 104 regiments of infantry. Each of these had from one to four battalions*, but it was very rare for two or more battalions to serve together since it was an organizational rather than a tactical grouping. Nevertheless, each regiment embodied a very real conception. In a day when a man who joined the ranks became a social outcast (even if he had not been one in civil life), the regiment stood in place of his family. The officers, in a very real sense, were *in loco parentis*

* Exceptionally the 60th (Royal Americans), a regiment largely composed of German mercenaries, had had eight battalions in 1814. Apart from the 5th (Rifle) battalion, the 60th was intended to garrison the West Indies where British soldiers were reluctant to serve.

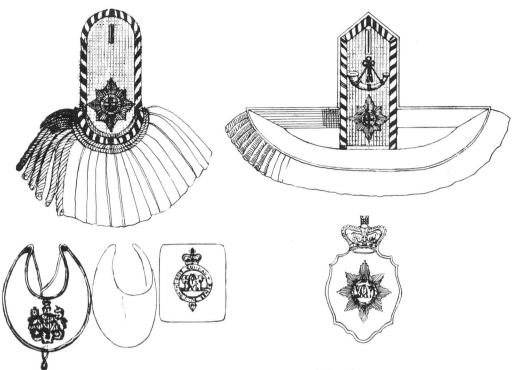

Fig. 21 Foot Guards. Gorget and Epaulettes.

to their men. Like natural families, some were better than others. Officers, like parents, ranged from the excellent to the deplorable. Many of the men in the ranks were, by any standards, very unsatisfactory but the regiment engulfed them and, in a way that is all but incomprehensible today, gave them a passionate loyalty to their comrades, to their officers and, above all, to their colours. Even in badly officered regiments, the spirit of pride in the regiment was sufficient to keep the men in their ranks under the hottest of fire. The performance of the British battalions, which were of very varied quality, was the ultimate proof of the old military dictum that 'There are no bad troops, only bad officers.'

The Regiment was an abstract idea but it was expressed outwardly in a multitude of small distinctions in the dress of each. These differences were made more varied by variations in role and nationality. It is, therefore, convenient to examine them under various heads: Guards, 'heavy' infantry, light infantry, Highlanders and Riflemen.

Foot Guards. Plates 97 & 98. Figure 21. The Brigade of Foot Guards which, like regiments of the line, was not a brigade for tactical purposes, consisted of three regiments. In the First Guards there were three battalions, in the Second and Third Guards two. The First and Second Guards dated from the Restoration of 1660 when the First was formed from those who had been the *Garde du Corps* of Charles II while in exile. The Second had been the rebel regiment of General Monk who played a key part in bringing back the monarchy. Immediately before the Restoration, Monk's regiment had been stationed at Coldstream in Berwickshire and this name has stuck to them ever since. The origins of the Third Guards are lost in obscurity. They are descended from the Guards of the Scottish kings but it is far from clear how they survived the Commonwealth. They were reformed in 1662 and first came south of the Tweed in 1687. At that time they were known as the Scots Guards but the national title lapsed in the eighteenth century and was not revived until the reign of William IV when they became the Scots Fusilier Guards*.

Like all British 'heavy' infantry the Guards battalions were organized in ten companies. Eight of these were 'battalion' companies, numbered from one to eight. As in the French army the flank companies were known as the Grenadiers and the Light infantry. Both flank companies wore the elaborate form of epaulette, worn to this day by bandsmen, known as 'wings'. While battalion companies wore a plume of white over red, grenadier companies had a white plume and the light companies green. For ceremonial duties inside the United Kingdom the grenadier companies of all three regiments wore the bearskin cap. Officers of the light companies wore a sash with cords and tassels tied in front of the right hip but all other officers had their sashes tied in a flat bow in front of the left hip. Companies were also distinguished by the badge on the rosette holding the plume in the shako. In the battalion companies this was a regimental button, in the grenadiers, a grenade and, in the light infantry, a bugle horn.

All companies were armed alike except that the officers of the light companies carried the curved light infantry sword and wore it on 'slings', straps hanging from the waist belt, while the officers of other companies wore straight swords in frogs attached to their shoulder belts.

Sergeants in light companies carried muskets like those in the ranks. Sergeants in other companies had seven-foot pikes and short swords.

These distinctions between companies were common to all heavy infantry. So too were the officer's badges of rank (see Plates 121 & 122). Guards officers, however, wore their army rather than their regimental rank since, by a curious anomaly, every lieutenant in the Guards ranked in the army as a captain and every captain as a lieutenant-colonel*.

The uniforms of the Guards (although usually better cut) were almost the same as the rest of the infantry. The officers had no elaboration to their buttonholes but had gold braid of regimental pattern to edge the lapels, collar, cuffs, false pockets (on the tails) and turnbacks. The other ranks had a similar trimming in white and, uniquely in the army, had a blue background to their counter-epaulettes. All ranks had a white lining to the jacket. For evening wear, the officers wore their jackets turned back, showing the whole of the lapel but on active service the jacket was buttoned across so that only the top of the blue lapels showed.

Regimental badges based on the star of the Order of the Bath (Order of the Thistle for the Third Guards) were worn in the shako but the easiest way of distinguishing between the three regiments was by the grouping of the buttons (and, for the other ranks, the white lace attached to the buttonholes). As now, the buttons of the First Guards were arranged evenly, those of the Second were in pairs, of the Third Guards in threes.

* The name Scots Guards was readopted in 1877.

* In recognition of the part played by the four battalions of Guards at Waterloo every Guards ensign subsequently ranked as a lieutenant in the army.

155

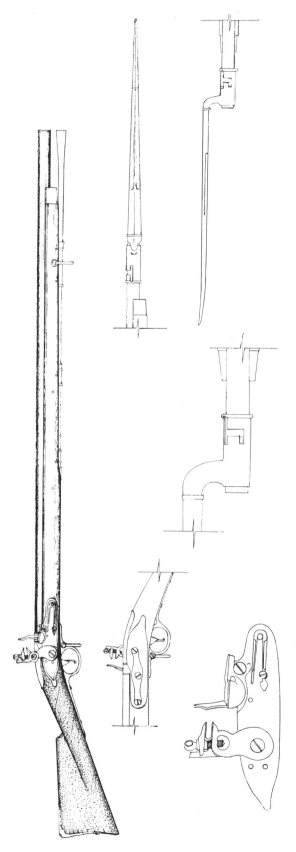

'*Heavy*' *Infantry*. Plates 99-106. Figures 22 & 23.

Apart from the braiding round the edge of the Guards' jackets, there was little difference between their uniform and that of the infantry of the line, the company distinctions being identical. There were, however, a multitude of minor distinctions between the various regiments depending, apart from the shako and cross-belt plates and occasional unauthorized modifications, on the regimental facing colours and the arrangement and colour of the lace. The braiding on the buttonholes on the front of the jacket of the other ranks, could be arranged either singly or in pairs. The ends of the braiding could be shaped in three possible ways: – square, pointed or in a spearhead shape known as 'bastion'.

The 'heavy' infantry regiments at Waterloo were differentiated as shown in the table opposite.

All the Line battalions of the King's German Legion wore eight square-ended lines of lace across the front of the jacket. The lace had a blue thread through the centre. Facings were blue and the officers' lace was gold. The battalions could only be distinguished by the numbers on the shako and cross-belt plates.

Of the native British regiments above, one, the Twenty-Third, had no grenadier company since it was a Fusilier regiment which, being by definition an *élite* regiment, had no place for a special *élite* company. In full dress and when on a home station (or at Gibraltar) all companies of Fusilier regiments wore a bearskin cap somewhat shorter than that of grenadiers. Another characteristic of Fusiliers was that their junior commissioned rank was that of Second Lieutenant rather than ensign.★

★ In the Seventh (Royal) Fusiliers the junior commissioned rank was lieutenant.

Fig. 22 Infantry. Tower Musket (Brown Bess).

Number & Territorial Designation	Facing Colour	Arrangement of OR's Buttonhole Lace & Type of End	Officers' Lace
1st Royal Scots	Blue	Pairs, Square	Gold
4th King's Own	Blue	Single, Bastion	Gold
14th Buckinghamshire	Buff	Pairs, Bastion	Silver
23rd Royal Welsh Fuzileers	Blue	Single, Bastion	Gold
27th Inniskilling	Buff	Single, Square	Gold
28th North Gloucestershire	Yellow	Pairs, Square	Silver
30th Cambridgeshire	Pale Yellow	Single, Square	Gold
32nd Cornwall	White	Pairs, Square	Gold
33rd 1st Yorkshire West Riding	Red	Pairs, Bastion	Silver
40th 2nd Somersetshire	Buff	Pairs, Square	Gold
44th East Essex	Yellow	Single, Square	Silver
69th South Lincolnshire	Green	Pairs, Square	Gold

Fig. 23 'Heavy' Infantry. Swords. Officers and Sergeants.

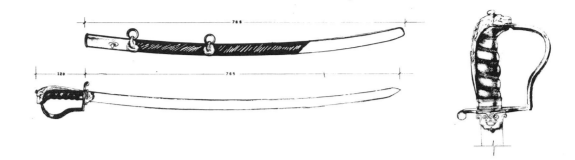

Fig. 24 Light Infantry. Officer's sword.

Light Infantry. Plates 107-110. Figure 24. Britain had raised her first regular light infantry regiment, 90th (Perthshire Volunteers), in 1794 but this soon reverted to being 'heavy' infantry and it was not until 1803, under the influence of Sir John Moore, that the first two continuing light infantry regiments were created by the conversion of the Forty-Third and Fifty-Second. In the next six years four more regiments became light infantry, giving a total of nine light battalions.

There was little difference between the dress of light infantry regiments and that of the light companies of the rest of the line. There were no grenadier companies and all ranks wore wings and the bugle horn ornaments of light companies. Officers all wore the tasselled sash and carried the curved sword suspended from slings. Sergeants carried muskets rather than pikes and wore a short sword. The weapon carried by sergeants and lower ranks was the New Land Service Musket, a better built weapon than either the Tower Musket (Brown Bess) or the East India pattern used by the rest of the infantry. It was three inches shorter (39″) than the former (which was carried by the battalions of 'heavy' infantry which had

Number & Territorial Designation	Facing Colour	Arrangement of OR's Buttonhole Lace & Type of End	Officers' Lace
51st 2nd Yorkshire, West Riding	Grass Green	Pairs, Pointed	Gold
52nd Oxfordshire	Buff	Pairs, Square	Silver
71st Highland	Buff	Single, Square	Silver

been sent to the Netherlands straight from England) and the same length as the East India model (which was the type used in the Peninsula and in America).

The easiest way to distinguish a member of a light infantry regiment from a flank company man was by his headwear. The light battalions had retained the tall tapering shako which the rest of the army had abandoned some years earlier. In it they wore their green plumes at the front, the rest of the infantry wearing theirs at the side.

One of the three light regiments at Waterloo was Scottish, the 71st. Their shakos were dark blue instead of black, and over them was shrunk a woollen band diced in red, green and white.

The distinctions of the three regiments were as in the table opposite.

Highlanders. Plates 111-117. Figure 25. Although there had been Scottish regiments in the British army since the Restoration and the Royal Scots was the senior regiment of the line, they had all been raised in the lowlands. It was not until 1739 that a regiment was raised in the north of Scotland and its original purpose was to police the highlands. So satisfactory was this body that it was taken into the line as the Forty-Second (Royal Highland) Regiment. Several more highland units were raised for the Seven Years War but they were all disbanded at its end. Another batch were raised for the American War of Independence and of these two survived, one of them becoming the Seventy-First, referred to above under light infantry. The outbreak of the French war in 1793 brought a great upsurge of highland recruiting and by the peace of 1814 there were twelve Highland regiments making up twenty-one battalions.

Apart from the Highland Light Infantry, four Highland regiments fought at

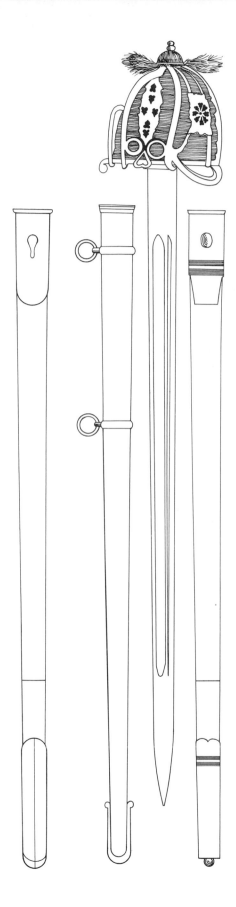

159

Fig. 25 Highlanders. Broadsword.

Waterloo. One of these was the Forty-Second, better known from the dark colours of its kilt as the Black Watch. Another was the Seventy-Third, which had been formed from the second battalion of the Black Watch in the seventeen-eighties and did not wear the kilt. The other two were battalions of the Seventy-Ninth (Cameron) and Ninety-Second (Gordon) Highlanders. Both had been raised as patriotic gestures by Scottish landowners, the Camerons by Alan Cameron of Erracht, the Gordons by the Marquess of Huntly, later 5th Duke of Gordon. The Duchess of Richmond was Huntly's sister and it was thus arranged that men of the Gordons should give a display of highland dancing at her ball on 15 June. The Camerons were very much a family affair. Alan Cameron was colonel of the regiment from its raising until his death in 1828 and, apart from a short period following the death of Phillips Cameron at Fuentes de Oñoro, at least one of the lieutenant-colonels was of the clan. At Waterloo the Cameron battalion had eight officers and the quartermaster with the surname of Cameron, six of them being wounded.

The Highland regiments wore the same jacket as the rest of the infantry but, apart from the Seventy-Third who wore the usual grey-blue trousers and the shako, were very recognisable from their kilts, their hose and their headress. The Black Watch wore a special tartan unconnected with any clan although their drum-major wore the Royal Stuart kilt. The Camerons wore the tartan of their clan and the Gordons wore the Black Watch tartan with a yellow stripe. Sporrans were not worn on active service. Below the kilt they wore hose in red and white 'cath-dath' dicing with a black seam at the back and held up with garters of red tape. The bonnet consisted of a cloth-covered wire

frame, surrounded by a turban diced in red, white and green. From the left side ostrich feathers cascaded over to the right. Also on the left side was a rosette of regimental pattern holding a plume in the same company colours as other infantry except in the Black Watch where all companies wore the red hackle (plume) to commemorate their gallantry at Gelder-malsen in 1795.* The bonnet had a detachable leather peak, held in place by black ribbons which fell down the back of the neck. Officers did not wear this peak.

Highland officers had several special distinctions. They wore their crimson sash over the left shoulder rather than round the waist and held it in place with a counter-epaulette. In the flank companies, the officers wore the thistle instead of either the grenade or the bugle horn on their wings. Since any officer was liable to have to ride in active service, the regulations laid down that they should wear trousers instead of the kilt but it is probable that this was widely disregarded. Similarly the regulation forbade the wearing of the plaid in action. Officers of all companies, regulations notwithstanding, carried the broadsword.

The regimental distinctions were as shown in the table opposite.

Rifles. Plate 118. Figure 26.
The introduction of the rifle into the British army has been referred to in Part II, Chapter 1. The first British manned rifle unit was raised in 1800 as Colonel Coote Manningham's Experimental Corps of Riflemen and established in the Army List as the Ninety-Fifth Regiment (Riflemen) three years later. It was the only corps in the army which had no difficulty in recruiting and by 1809

160

* The officer's hackle was of vulture's feathers.

Number & Designation	Facing Colour	Arrangement of OR's Buttonhole Lace & Type of End	Officers' Lace
42nd Royal Highland (Black Watch)	Blue	Single, Bastion	Gold
73rd Highland	Dark Green	Single, Bastion	Gold
79th Cameron Highlanders	Dark Green	Pairs, Square	Gold
92nd Gordon Highlanders	Yellow	Pairs, Square	Silver

had grown to a strength of three battalions. Companies from all these battalions fought at Waterloo.

The Rifles were dressed from head to foot in green so dark that it appeared black at a distance. The braid on the buttonholes and the officers' lace were both black and the Rifleman's accoutrements were all in black. All ranks wore a shoulder belt, that of the officers and sergeants being ornamented with a silver lion's head, chain and whistle in silver. Rather surprisingly buttons were of white metal and, for the other ranks, there was white piping at the collar and cuffs.

The officers wore the tasseled crimson sash of light infantry but the rest of their uniform had been modelled on that of light cavalry. * Their original headdress had been the old light dragoon helmet and, although this had given way to the tapered shako, they still carried the curved light dragoon sabre (a useless weapon for dismounted fighting) suspended from slings. They also carried the sabretache and, in full dress, wore the pelisse. None of these items can have assisted a skirmisher pushing his way through brushwood. As Rifle battalions had no Colours, their junior officers were Second Lieutenants rather than Ensigns.

Sergeants and Riflemen carried the Baker Rifle and the long (25″) brass-hilted sword bayonet. They also carried a powder horn containing fine powder for priming the Baker.

The two Light Battalions of the King's German Legion were also predominantly armed with the rifle. Their uniform closely resembled that of the Ninety-Fifth except that both battalions wore grey trousers, those of the 2nd battalion seeming to have been darker than those of the 1st. The differentiation between the battalions lay in the arrangements of the buttons, the 1st having a single row of 12 down the centre of the front while the 2nd had three rows. Officers of the 1st battalion wore silver wings. All ranks of the 2nd battalion wore a tall, peakless, tapering headdress known as a *Flügelmütze* round which the officers wore a

* There is a tendency to dress newly raised corps as light cavalry. The full dress of the Royal Air Force up to 1939 had several hussar features.

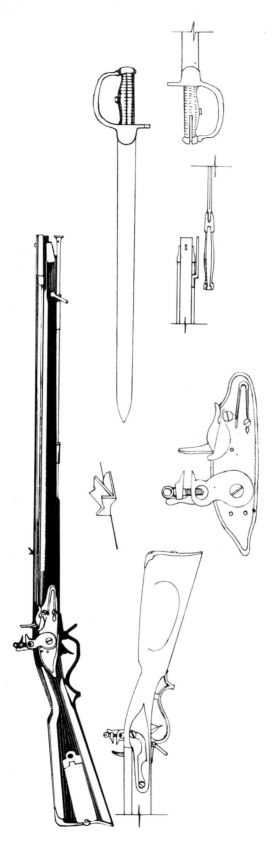

spiral of gold cord, the tassel of which was secured to the right breast.

Plate 123. **Hanoverian Infantry** (See also Plate 106(c)).

The kingdom of Hanover being a possession of the British king and the armies of the two states having operated together (except when the French occupied Hanover) since Marlborough's campaigns, it was natural that the Hanoverian troops should be dressed in British uniforms with only minor modifications such as the shako plate bearing the White Horse of Hanover. The most obvious difference was that the knapsacks of the regular (field) battalions, although British, were painted yellow.

The militia *(landwehr)* regiments should have been dressed in the same way but in fact were dressed in whatever was forthcoming from British clothing stores, usually items discarded in earlier clothing reforms of the British army. The Luneburg and Verden battalions had green coats, the latter wearing them with dark blue trousers.

Plates 124-126. **Netherlands Infantry.**

The Kingdom of the Netherlands had only existed for a few months at the time of Waterloo and it is scarcely surprising that the uniform of the new state's army was in a state of transition. The kingdom was composed of the old United Provinces (better but misleadingly known as Holland) and the former Austrian Netherlands, corresponding roughly to modern Belgium. At the time the two constituent territories were known as the North and

Fig. 26 Rifles. The Baker Rifle.

South Netherlands but it is convenient to refer to them as Holland and Belgium.

The Austrians had re-occupied Belgium in 1814 but they did not intend to retain it and appointed the Prince of Orange* Governor-General until the new kingdom should be established. They did, however, set about re-equipping the army and gave the infantry the type of false-fronted shako in use in their own army, which had served as a model for the British shako of 1812. The similarity to the British shako was heightened when the Netherlands authorities added a brass shako plate bearing a 'W' (for William) and, at the side an orange cockade carrying a plume, white for battalion companies and red for both flank companies. In silhouette, therefore, Belgian soldiers were indistinguishable from British. The Dutch troops, meanwhile, continued to wear the French shako fitted with a peak at the back as well as the front. On it was fitted a white metal plate in the form of a sunburst around a 'W'. The plume, held in an orange cockade, was white over red for all companies. Flank companies wore padded wings in the colour of the jacket but marked with white lines.

Officers had jackets cut longer in the tail than their men and wore an orange sash round the waist. Dutch officers wore silver epaulettes of rank and Belgian officers gold. Similarly Dutch soldiers wore white metal buttons and Belgians brass. The bandsmen wore a Germanic form of wings, known as 'swallows' nests', marked with chevrons and inverted chevrons in gold or silver lace according to nationality.

The facings of the Netherlands Line battalions at Waterloo were: –

2nd (Dutch)	Yellow
3rd (Belgian)	White
7th (Belgian)	Light Blue
12th (Dutch)	Red
13th (Dutch)	Crimson

Three battalions of Netherlands light infantry, known according to nationality as *Jägers* or *Chasseurs*, fought in the battle. Their uniform was green with yellow piping and padded wings. Irrespective of nationality they wore the Dutch bell-topped shako with a brass bugle horn in front.

The six militia regiments present were dressed similarly to the regular troops but with orange facings and the tapering shako worn by British light infantry bearing the white metal sunburst of the Dutch infantry of the line.

Since the reigning families of the Netherlands and Nassau were closely linked, five Nassau battalions formed a brigade of the Netherlands army under Prince Bernard of Saxe-Weimar. Both at Quatre Bras and on the extreme left wing at Waterloo these battalions contributed more to the French defeat than any other of the infantry allied to the British. Most of them were old soldiers who had fought under Napoleon. The uniforms they wore had been issued to them while Nassau was part of Napoleon's empire. Although they were green instead of blue they were indistinguishable from those of the French at any distance. The silhouettes were identical. It was unfortunate but thoroughly understandable that the Prussians, who expected to see their allies in scarlet, mistook Prince Bernard's brigade for Frenchmen and drove them from the position they had held so gallantly at Papelotte. An independent brigade of Nassauers in the centre of the line did not distinguish themselves.

* Later King William I of the Netherlands who should be distinguished from his son, the Hereditary Prince of Orange, who commanded one of Wellington's corps and became William II in 1840.

163

Plates 90, 96, 127 & 128. **Brunswick Troops.**

Since the Duke of Brunswick, Wolfen-büttel-Oels was brother-in-law to the Prince Regent of England, his troops were put under Wellington's command, unlike the other contingents of German troops which were (except for the Hanoverians) allocated either to the Austrians or the Prussians. A battalion of Brunswick light infantry had fought under Wellington in Spain and he had not regarded them highly. In 1811 he wrote, 'The men are either very old or very young; and they are very sickly. They are very irregular in their discipline and habits, and they desert to the enemy terribly. The officers are Germans who have no experience of service, (the lieutenant colonel, who is dead, may have had) but who have all the vanity of a good deal. I am not very fastidious about troops; I have them of all sorts, sizes and nations; but Germans in our army in the Peninsula pass for Englishmen: and it is really not creditable to be a soldier of the same nation as one of these people.'

The Brunswick contingent at Waterloo consisted of a small division of all arms. At their head was their Duke, 'Brunswick's fated chieftain' in Byron's poem. Reaching Quatre Bras among the earlier reinforcements the Duke led his hussars against Kellermann's Cuirassiers. He was killed and his horsemen driven back but, unlike their Netherlands allies, they had charged home. They were badly shaken by their repulse and the loss of their Duke.

The Brunswick infantry had a hard time at Waterloo. During the French cavalry attacks Captain Mercer saw them 'standing like logs and... every moment feared they would flee,' but they stood their ground and later, when they were brought across to the centre, Wellington

eventually managed to rally them when they broke and they took part in the final victorious advance. That they did their part can be seen by the fact that for every man missing twelve were killed or wounded.

The predominant colour in the Brunswick uniform was black, said to be in mourning for the Duke's father who was killed in action against the French at Auerstädt in 1806. Fanny Burney, who saw them march out of Brussels on 16 June, wrote that 'This gloomy hue gave an air so mournful to the procession that I contemplated it with an aching heart.' A British soldier who saw them a few hours later described them as looking 'as proud as a Spaniard on sentry or a turkey cock in a farm yard, dressed in a dark uniform, something like a horse's tail in their helmets, with the shape of a scalped face and a man's shin bone.' In fact the Death's Head badge was worn only by the hussars and the Guard battalion. The line troops had the white horse of Brunswick in their shakos and the light infantry the usual bugle horn.

The Guard had blue facings and those of the line battalions were red (1st), green (2nd) and white (3rd). The light battalions had light blue (1st bn), yellow (2nd) and orange (3rd). The foot artillery were dressed as infantry of the line with gold facings and a grenade badge in the shako.

THE PRUSSIAN ARMY

Prussia was a country poor in natural resources and and made poorer by the ravages of a long war and the presence for six years of a French army of occupation. In consequence, when she re-organized her army after the shattering defeats of Jena and Auerstädt in 1806, the uniforms adopted were (except of course in the

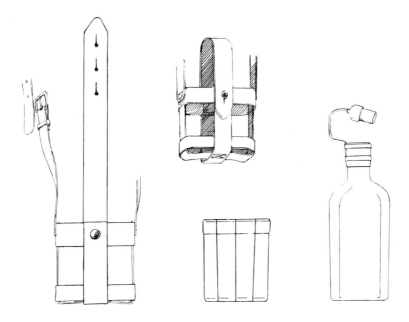

Fig. 27 All Arms. Flasks and water bottles.

hussars) plainer and more standard throughout the army than any other major army in western Europe. Two basic styles were adopted, a jacket and shako simplified from the French model worn with trousers very like those of the British, and a plainer style based on the *litewka*, a long tunic-like jacket of Lithuanian origin, which reached almost to the knees. Somewhat shortened, this second type became the standard dress of the German army until 1918 and is the ancestor of the 'service dress' of the British and other armies in the twentieth century. With it went a design of forage cap which continued almost unchanged until after the First World War. Pipeclay, the hall-mark of the victorious armies of Frederick the Great was largely abolished and accoutrements were made of black leather. This was the first attempt to design a functional uniform and, since it survived in all essentials for more than a century, it must be considered to have been very successful. It was admired at the time and a British surgeon, seeing the Prussians soon after Waterloo, wrote, 'The Prussian soldiers are exceedingly neatly dressed. The uniform of the officers is particularly well made, and I think they must frequently wear stays.'

Plates 129-30, 132. **Staff and Officers.**

Even though general officers wore the gold lace at collar and cuffs which were the marks of senior officers throughout Europe, the whole effect of the uniform of a Prussian general is markedly simpler than that of their opposite numbers in the French and British services. In particular, the saddlecloth in black fur with its two silver badges contrasts strikingly with the gorgeous shabraque of a French general (Plate 2) or with the royal blue cloth trimmed with a double line of gold braid and ornamented with the crowned royal cypher that covered the back of a British general's horse.

Distinctions of the dragoon regiments in the Waterloo campaign:

Number & Territorial Designation	Facing Colour	Lace & Buttons
1st (Queen's)	Crimson	Silver
2nd (1st W. Prussia)	White	Silver
5th (Brandenburg)	Black	Gold
6th (Neumark)	Pink	Silver
7th (Rhineland)	Yellow	Silver

Distinctions of the Uhlan regiments: –

1st (1st W. Prussia)	White	Gold
2nd (Silesia)	Red	Gold
3rd (Brandenburg)	Yellow	Gold
5th (1st Westphalia)	White	Silver
6th (2nd W. Prussia)	Red	Silver
7th (1st Rhineland)	Yellow	Silver
8th (2nd Rhineland)	Light Blue	Silver

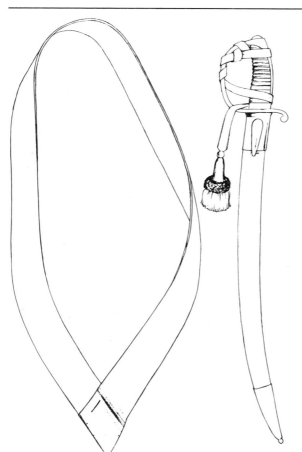

Fig. 28 Infantry of the Line. Shoulder belt and sword.

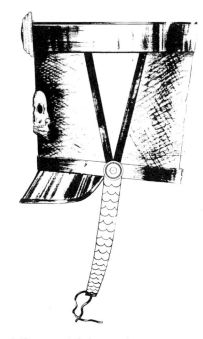

Fig. 29 Hussars. Shakos. Officers and Other ranks.

Perhaps to compensate for this simplicity, Prussian generals tended to wear more decorations. French generals at Waterloo would not have worn more than the cross of the Legion of Honour*. British generals may have worn the star of the Bath† and, in most cases, the Peninsular Gold Cross but the Prussians were inclined to wear not only the many decorations of their own sovereign but those of his allies. Thus the general in Plate 129 wears the '*Pour le Mérite*', the Iron Cross (which had been instituted in 1813), the Order of the Black Eagle, the Höhenlohe Order of the Phoenix, the Austrian Order of Maria Theresa and the Russian Order of St Anne.

---

* Up to 1814 they would also have worn the badge of the Order of the Iron Crown of Lombardy, symbolising Napoleon's Italian kingdom.
† Wellington had the Order of the Garter but, characteristically, wore it only on formal occasions. As riffle battalions had no colours, their junior officers were Second Lieutenants rather than Ensigns.

Plates 131, 133 & 140
Figures 29-31

Cavalry

Apart from their weapons and waist sashes, there was little to distinguish between the dragoons, uhlans and the regular infantry of the Prussian army except for variations in colour. Dragoons retained the pipeclayed belts of pre-Jena days and wore jackets of a lighter blue than the uhlans and the infantry. Uhlans tended to unofficial modifications to their plain uniform. Some adopted the lance-cap and some took to wearing the pelisse and woven sash of hussars.

Uhlans had pennants of black over white in the senior squadron of each regiment, and white over black in the other squadrons.

No amount of economy or functionalism could restrain the Prussian hussars from being splendidly dressed although at least every regiment wore the same dark grey

167

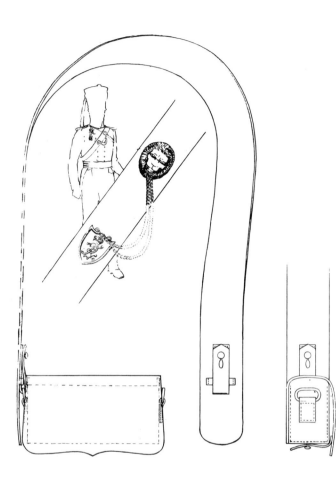

Fig. 30 Hussars. Shoulder Belt and Pouch.

overalls rather than fancy breeches. The two senior regiments were designated *liebhusaren* (bodyguard hussars) although there also existed a regiment of Hussars of the Guard. *Liebhusaren* were mounted on lighter horses than other regiments and only they wore the Death's Head in their shakos. On campaign they wore this badge painted on their canvas cap-covers. Other hussar regiments wore a black and white cockade similar to that of the other cavalry regiments.

The status of the *landwehr* will be referred to below when dealing with the infantry. Infantry and cavalry alike wore the *litewka* in dark blue faced with the colour of the province in which they were raised. These were:

Elbe	White
Kurmark & Neumark	Red
Pomerania	White
Silesia	Yellow
Westphalia	Green

Landwehr cavalry wore tall cylindrical shakos of a design of which stocks survived from before the reforms following Jena. They were armed with lances, light cavalry sabres and carbines.

Distinctions of the hussar regiments in the campaign:

Number & Territorial Designation	Jacket & Pelisse	Facing Colour	Lace
3rd (Brandenburg)	Dark Blue	Red	Silver
4th (1st Silesia)	Dark Blue	Dark Blue	Gold
5th (Pomerania)	Brown	Yellow	Gold
6th (2nd Silesia)	Green	Red	Gold
8th (1st Westphalia)	Dark Blue	Light Blue	Silver
9th (Rhineland)	Light Blue	Light Blue	Gold
10th (1st Magdeburg)	Green	Light Blue	Gold
11th (2nd Westphalia)	Green	Red	Silver

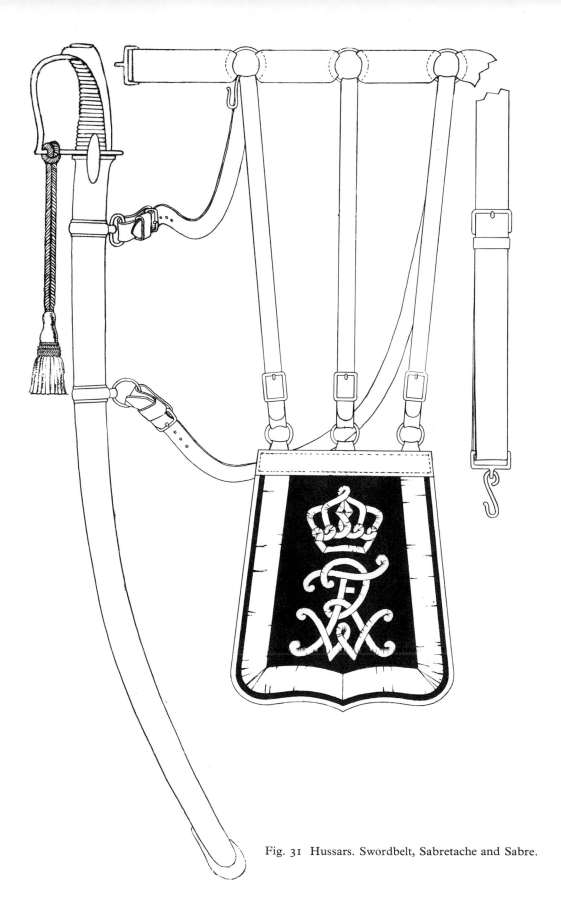

Fig. 31 Hussars. Swordbelt, Sabretache and Sabre.

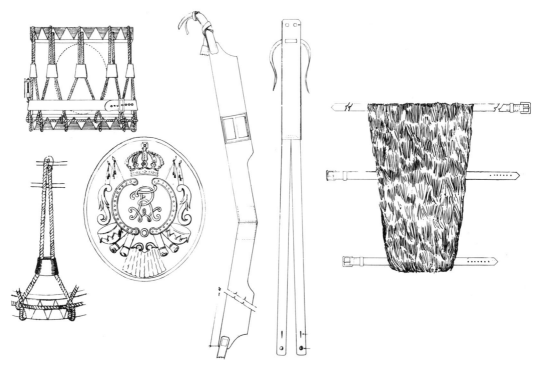

Fig. 32 Infantry of the Line. Drum.

Plates 141-145
Figure 28 & 32.

Infantry

The Prussian infantry was re-organized after Jena on the basis of four battalion regiments of which one was a grenadier battalion, two were 'line' battalions, and one consisted of light infantry. Grenadiers wore the grenade badge although the light infantry did not have the bugle horn. Membership of the various battalions could only be distinguished from the background of the officers' epaulettes and counter-epaulettes. This, for the 1st (grenadier) battalion was white, for the 2nd & 3rd battalions red and yellow, and for the 4th (light) battalion light blue. In addition there were battalions of riflemen (*jagers*) and sharpshooters (*schützen*). Equipment was black for other ranks except bandsmen who, like the officers,

wore white. Bandsmen also wore 'swallow's nest' wings like those in the Netherlands army but decorated with white bars on a background of the facing colour. These were allocated by provinces of origin, although they did not invariably agree with the colours used in the *landwehr*, being: —

Brandenburg	Scarlet
Magdeburg	Light Blue
Pomerania	White
Rhine	Madder
Silesia	Lemon Yellow
Westphalia	Pink
West Prussia	Carmine

The *landwehr* in its 1815 form dated, like so much else in Blücher's army, from the reforms that followed Jena. In the peace which Napoleon imposed on Prussia in 1807 a limitation was placed on the size of her army. With their usual ingenuity the Prussian high command devised

170

a system whereby men stayed in the regular forces only for a year and then reverted to the reserve. This reserve, the *landwehr*, could be called out in times of emergency. Thus although in 1813 the Prussian army was theoretically limited to 75,000 men, she was able to raise 300,000 trained soldiers.

The losses of 1813-14 and the dislocation of training caused by the short peace meant that the *landwehr* had insufficient trained men to fill the ranks when war broke out again in 1815. To make up the numbers a high proportion of recruits were drafted to the battalions and the quotas were filled with enthusiastic but untrained volunteers.

The *landwehr* were supposed to be dressed in the *litewka* and forage cap over grey trousers with knee-length black canvas gaiters. Their headdress was the forage cap *(feldmütze)*. In practice uniform was in very short supply and many men wore whatever could be found in the depots made up with civilian clothing. Some men of the *landwehr* are said to have marched to Waterloo wearing clogs. The supply of arms was no better than that of clothing. In some regiments muskets of three different calibres were being carried and some men were armed only with pikes and pitchforks. Sergeants, in any case, carried the pike like their British equivalents.

Glossary

Aiguilettes. Ornamental cords worn round, and sometimes over, the shoulder.

Austrian (or **Hungarian**) **Knot.** Arrangement of cord usually worn on the cuff or thigh. The usual pattern is of two rings at either side of the base of a more elongated shape.

Bastion. The ending of a strip of **Lace** in the shape of a spearhead (as distinct from a square or pointed end). So called from the similarity to a bastion (a projecting, five sided-work) in fortification.

Brassard. Originally the piece of armour which covered the arm, a brassard had become a distinguishing armband worn above the elbow.

Brandenburgs. Strips of **Lace** sewn horizontally across the breast of a jacket and terminating in **Austrian Knots.** A characteristic feature of hussar dress.

Bullion. Cord made from gold or silver thread and forming the fringe hanging from an epaulette. The thinner cord used for junior officer's epaulettes was known as 'fringe'.

Busbybag. The coloured flap (which was actually a flattened bag) hanging down the side of a **Kolbak.**

Carabineers. Originally a cavalryman armed with a **Carbine.** In the French army its use had been narrowed down to two regiments of cavalry or to the **Grenadier Companies** of battalions of light infantry. In the British army the word was used only to denote the 6th Dragoon Guards. In the army of the Netherlands it was, used for all three regiments of heavy cavalry.

Carbine. A short musket for use on horseback.

Chasseurs. Originally huntsmen (cf. Jäger), *Chasseur* had come to mean light troops, either mounted (*Chasseurs à Cheval*) or on foot (*Chasseurs à Pied*). Mounted *chasseurs* were all-purpose light cavalry. In the infantry, *Chasseurs* were the centre companies (see under **Flank Companies**) of light infantry battalions. The *Chasseurs à Pied* of the Imperial

Guard were only light troops in the sense that they were not quite as heavy as the Grenadiers of the Guard.

Chenille see **Crest.**

Cockade. A rosette worn in the headdress, usually concealing a plumeholder. French cockades were (from the outside) red, white and blue. The British wore black cockades, the Netherlands orange and the Prussians white outside black.

Colpack see **Kolbak.**

Counter-Epaulette see under **Epaulette.**

Crest. The fur or worsted worn along the comb of dragoon helmets. The French called it a *chenille*, a caterpillar.

Cross Belt see **Shoulder Belt.**

Cuirass. Body armour consisting, at Waterloo, of breast and back plates. So-called because it was originally made of leather.

Czapka (or **Czapska**). A Polish headdress also known as a lance-cap. It consisted of a leather skull cap surmounted by an oval base which swelled out into a square imperial (or top) which was cloth covered. Worn with a sunburst frontal plate in metal.

Dolman. Tight fitting, waist-length hussar jacket, ornamented with **Brandenburgs.** Should be distinguished from the similarly ornamented **Pelisse** which was worn over it.

Dragoon. A cavalryman who was supposed to be able to dismount to fight. The name derived from a type of **Carbine** known as a dragon because it breathed fire. In practice dragoons were medium-heavy cavalry.

Epaulette. A detachable shoulder-strap widening at the outer end and carrying a fringe of **Bullion** or 'fringe'. When worn without a fringe it was called a counter-epaulette, which was little more than an shoulder strap.

Facings. The collar, cuffs and turned-back lapels which carry a distinguishing colour.

Flank Companies. The companies, composed of picked men who formed on the flanks of an infantry battalion drawn up in line. On the right would be the **Grenadier** (or **Carabineer**) company. On the left would be the **Light** (or **Voltigeurs**). Between them would be, in the British army, the battalion companies; in the French infantry the centre companies were known as **Fusiliers** or **Chasseurs**.

Flugelmutze see **Mirliton**.

Fringe see **Bullion**.

Frog. An attachment to the **Shoulder Belt** for holding a sword or bayonet. Unlike slings, frogs did not allow the sword to drag on the ground and were thus worn by most infantry officers (except British light infantry and Rifles)

or

A small toggle used to fasten the **Pelisse** at the neck when both sleeves were not used.

Fusiliers. In the early seventeenth century, the infantry weapon was the matchlock, which was fired by the mechanical application of a slow burning match to the powder in the priming pan. The introduction of the flintlock (or snap-haunce) was effected only by degrees. The early military model, known as the fuzil (from the Italian *fucile*, a flint), was first issued to the troops guarding the army's supply of gunpowder, a task in which the presence of several hundred burning matches might prove a severe embarrassment. Such regiments were known as Fusiliers, a word spelled in several ways and which appeared in the Army List of 1815 as Fuzileers. Fuzils were also issued to **Grenadiers**, who already had enough trouble with slow burning matches on their **Grenades**. At the beginning of the eighteenth century, when flintlocks were issued to all the British infantry, the Fusiliers lost their special role but succeeded in slipping into that of **Grenadier** battalions. The three regiments, 7th (Royal), 21st (Royal North British) and 23rd (Royal Welch), succeeded in establishing themselves as *élite* regiments, wearing the grenadier cap although without its grenade badge and, in its fur version, rather shorter than that worn by grenadiers. Fusilier battalions had only one flank company, the light, since, in their own estimation, they were all grenadiers.

In the French army the centre companies (see **Flank Companies**) of the infantry of the line were, quite logically, known as Fusiliers.

Gorget. Vestigial throat armour, worn in a stylized form by officers as a badge of rank (see Plate 31).

Grenade. A hand-thrown bomb which was considered obsolete in the Napoleonic wars. It was commemorated in companies and regiments of **Grenadiers** and in the grenade badge, worn by grenadiers and others, which represented a flaming grenade.

Grenadiers. Picked troops, chosen for their strength and stature. Originally selected as being the men who would be able to throw a grenade furthest, they had survived the eclipse of their weapon and were formed into special units and sub-units for use as assault troops.

Hessian (or **Hussar**) **Boots.** Boots of soft leather coming to just below the knee with a V or heart shaped notch in the front. Usually ornamented with **lace** round the top and a gold or silver tassel at the front. This was the design of boot favoured by the Duke of Wellington for his own wear until varicose veins forced him to design a boot lower in the calf which became known as the Wellington boot.

Kolbak (or **Colpack**). A short round fur cap or busby of Hungarian origin which was worn by hussars.

Lace. Braid trimming applied to collars, cuffs, buttonholes or, in extreme cases, to almost any other part of the uniform. Usually in gold or silver for officers (although Rifle officers had black braid) Other ranks wore white, yellow or black braid.

Lance Cap see **Czapka**.

Light Companies. The left-hand **Flank Company** composed of the most agile and intelligent men in a battalion whose main role was skirmishing. An *élite* company of brain rather than, as in the Grenadier company, of brawn.

Mirliton (or **Flugelmutze**). A tall, tapering fur hat with a flying wing of cloth instead of the **Kolbak**'s **Busbybag**. An early form of hussar headdress which was retained by the 2nd Hussars and 2nd Light Battalion, King's German Legion.

Musket. A smooth bore firearm needing both hands to fire (as distinct from a pistol which could be fired with one hand). At this time all military muskets were fired by a flintlock.

Overalls. Long baggy trousers worn over breeches and gaiters or boots. In the cavalry overalls were usually reinforced with leather on the inside of the leg. Almost always secured at the ankle with a gaiter, strap or piece of string. According to OED, the first use of overalls to indicate a garment worn over all ordinary clothing is dated 1815.

Pelisse. A fur-edged jacket decorated with **Brandenburgs** worn, usually slung over one shoulder, by hussars. It derives from the rough wolfskin cloaks worn by Hungarian shepherds but had been formalized into a garment of largely decorative functions although, in the British army, it was the only item of cold weather clothing issued to hussar troopers.

Piping. Narrow tubular strips of cloth, usually in a distinguishing colour, sewn on to edges and seams.

Plastron. A broad, coloured front to a jacket, tapering from the shoulders to the waist.

Rifle. A musket with spiral grooves in the barrel which impart spin to the bullet thus increasing accuracy and range. The earliest rifles had been made about 1520 but they were not successfully mass-produced for military use until 1800.

Sabre-Briquet. A short sword carried, in addition to the bayonet, by grenadiers and light infantry in the French army. Seldom used for fighting, it was valuable for clearing brushwood and various tasks about the bivouac. The French word *briquet* means tinder box. Thus a **Sabre-Briquet** was a sword for lighting fires.

Sabretache. A satchel carried on slings from the left side of the belt. The unornamented reverse side could be used as a portable writing desk.

Shabraque. An ornamented cloth worn under the saddle.

Shako. A peaked and rigid cap in the shape of a cylinder or truncated cone. The word derives from the Magyar *Csako süveg*, a peaked cap.

Shoulder Belt. A belt worn over one shoulder and hanging down on the other side, frequently supporting a **Frog** and sword or bayonet or some other piece of equipment. When two shoulder belts are worn they are known as **Cross Belts.**

Surtout. A single breasted jacket without lapels.

Swallow's Nests. Padded and ornamented **Wings** worn by bandsmen in the Prussian and Netherlands armies.

Tirailleurs. Light infantry, in particular the Young Guard regiments which were the apprentice battalions for the Grenadiers of the senior Guards. At a later date the French army used the word to denote Riflemen but there were none of these in Napoleon's army at Waterloo.

Turban. A strip of cloth or fur wound round the base of a helmet.

Turnback. The edges of the tails of a coat where the coloured lining is turned and buttoned back.

Uhlan. A lancer in the armies of Germany and Austria where the word was taken over from the Polish *utan*.

Vélite. Light infantry, originally the light infantry of the classical Roman army. Napoleon used the term to denote special training battalions for the Guard.

Voltigeurs. Light infantry. In particular, the light companies of French battalions of the line and the Young Guard regiments which were the apprentice units for the Chasseurs of the Guard.

Wings. Epaulettes or counter-epaulettes which, in plan, were crescent shaped. They were worn in the British army by grenadiers, light infantrymen and bandsmen.